Greek Athletics
and the Olympics

Alan Beale

CAMBRIDGE
UNIVERSITY PRESS

CAMBRIDGE UNIVERSITY PRESS

Cambridge, New York, Melbourne, Madrid, Cape Town,
Singapore, São Paulo, Delhi, Tokyo, Mexico City

Cambridge University Press
The Edinburgh Building, Cambridge CB2 8RU, UK

www.cambridge.org
Information on this title: www.cambridge.org/9780521138208

First published 2011

Printed in India by Replika Press PVT. LTD

A catalogue record for this publication is available from the British Library

ISBN 978-0-521-13820-8 Paperback

ACKNOWLEDGEMENTS

Cover, pp. 10, 81, 90*t*, 94, 105*t*, 105*b*, 118, 123, 161 Ace Stock Limited/Alamy; p. 11 drawing of Hagi Triada
rhyton with restorations by Ruben Santos from Miller, *Ancient Greek Athletics* (2004), by permission of
Yale University Press; p. 14 tripod cauldron 8th cent. B.C. from Olympia, Olympia Museum, bronze,
2ft 1½ (65cm) © 2011 Marie Mauzy/Scala, Florence; pp. 15*t*, 69 akg-images/Nimatallah; p. 15*b* akg-
images/De Agostini Picture Library; pp. 24, 172 akg-images/John Hios; pp. 40, 54, 93 provided by
Alan Beale; p. 42 Hervé Champollion/akg-images; pp. 65, 89, 104*t*, 168 akg-images/Erich Lessing;
pp. 66, 90*b*, 119, 174 © The Trustees of the British Museum; p. 77 Discobolus, copy of a Greek original
(plaster) by Myron (fl.c.450 BC) (after), Museo Nazionale Romano, Rome, Italy/The Bridgeman Art
Library; p. 82 The J. Paul Getty Museum, Villa Collection, Malibu, California for Attic red-figure kylix
attributed to Carpenter Painter, 510–500 BC, terracotta, H. 11 x W. (with handles) 38 x Diam. (rim)
33.5 cm; p. 91 terracotta Panathenaic prize amphora, ca. 530 BC, attributed to Euphiletos Painter, New
York Metropolitan Museum of Art, copyright The Metropolitan Museum of Art/Art Resource/ Scala,
Florence; pp. 97, 100 Stéphane Compoint © stephanecompoint.com; p. 104*b* Wine cooler (psykter)
depicting pentathletes (detail), Phintias, Museum of Fine Arts, Boston, Henry Lillie Pierce Fund,
01.8018, photograph © 2011 Museum of Fine Arts, Boston; pp. 137, 152 Staatlich Antikensammlungen
und Glyptothek München; p. 178 Peter Erik Forsberg/Alamy; p. 179 drawing of the Atarbos relief from
Greek Athletics Sports and Festivals, E. Norman Gardiner, Macmillan, p. 240, 1910

Maps throughout by Peter Simmonett

Contents

Introduction

Where did the idea of celebrating Olympic Games every four years come from? The short answer is ancient Greece. The very name Olympic announces the origin of the competition: not Mount Olympus in northern Greece (the Greeks had no winter Olympics), but the great sanctuary of Zeus in southern Greece at Olympia. However, as with most of our classical heritage, it is easy for the superficial similarities to conceal major cultural differences. For example, it would seem very strange for a modern audience to be entertained by a mixture of boxing, dancing and singing, which the *Homeric Hymn to Apollo* mentions the Ionians enjoying while celebrating on Apollo's sacred island of Delos. There would be few advocates now for the Olympics to be held in honour of Zeus at a shrine in southern Greece where only athletes of Greek nationality competed naked for a crown of wild olive. Of course, there are similarities between ancient and modern sport that rely on natural instinct rather than cultural influence. The four-horse chariot race has not had a profound influence on Formula One racing, but the importance of choosing the right line for taking the corners is crucial for drivers and charioteers alike. Boxing and wrestling, like all combat sports, depend upon similar skills wherever they are practised in the world. However, as Thomas Scanlon observed, 'while the physical actions may resemble one another, the meanings of those actions are very much the unique construction of the society in which they occur' (p. 7).

The modern Olympic movement, however different from the ancient festival, owes its genesis to and still draws inspiration from the original games. David Young in his *A Brief History of the Olympic Games* made a strong claim for continuity when he wrote that 'our Olympic Games are not so much a revival of the ancient Greek games as a genuine continuation of them … they have the same spirit, the same dedication to the pursuit of excellence, and the same goal of bringing out the best in people' (p. 140). Young may be right to see a similar spirit and a similar pursuit of excellence, but ancient institutions such as the Olympic Games are never re-created; they only have new forms created in their name. Greek athletics and their contexts are substantially different from anything in the modern world, despite the many similarities.

It is inevitable that the principal focus on athletics in this book will be on the biggest competitions: the Olympic Games and the other **'crown' games** at Delphi, Isthmia and Nemea (see p. 171). But the celebration of athletic competitions was not always associated with the big festivals. Sometimes there were circumstances which might surprise us, as in a rite of atonement recorded by the historian Herodotus: around 535 BC, some Greek prisoners of war fell into the hands of the Etruscans of Agylla (later called Caere, not far from Rome). After they were stoned to death outside the town, any animal or human from Agylla who passed the site of the massacre was afflicted with crippling disability. The Agyllans sought advice from the oracle at Delphi and were told to sacrifice to the dead and establish athletic and equestrian games (**gymnikos agōn** and **hippikos agōn**).

> The following description of an athletic competition with a different context reveals some of the problems of interpretation that are commonly presented by the sources.
>
> Xenophon's *Anabasis* describes the attempt of Cyrus to overthrow his brother Artaxerxes, king of Persia, in 401 BC. When Cyrus was killed in battle, the Greek mercenary army he had recruited marched from the heart of the Persian empire to the Black Sea, where they were hospitably received by the people of an isolated Greek colony at Trapezus. The following extract describes an athletic competition (*Anabasis* 4.8.25–8).

0.1 After this they began to prepare the sacrifice which they had vowed. Enough cattle had arrived for them to make the offerings due to Zeus for their safe passage, to Herakles for guidance and to the other gods for what they had asked for in their prayers. They also held an athletic competition on the mountain where they were encamped. They appointed a Spartan called Drakontios to search for a race track and organize the games. He had gone into exile when he was a boy after accidentally killing another boy with a blow from a dagger. After the sacrifice was completed, they handed the **animal hides** to Drakontios and told him to take them to where he had made the race track. He pointed to the place where they happened to be standing and said, 'This hill is excellent for running, wherever one wants.' 'Yes,' they replied, 'but how will they be able to wrestle on ground so hard and overgrown?' **He said**, 'It will be rather more painful for the one who is thrown.' The majority of the **boys** competing in the sprint (*stadion*) were from the prisoners, more than sixty Cretans competed in the long-distance race (*dolichos*), and there were contests in wrestling, boxing and the *pankration*. It was a fine spectacle with many entries and considerable rivalry because their comrades were watching. There were horse races too. They had to ride the horses down a steep slope, turn them round in the sea and bring them back to the altar. On the way down there were many falls and on the way up the horses hardly managed to walk against the extremely steep slope. All this generated considerable shouting, laughter and cheering.

---

animal hides presumably to be given as prizes to the winners.

He said Drakontios, in typical Spartan fashion, gives a pithy and uncompromising reply.

boys there would not be many Greek boys accompanying a mercenary army.

Even though this is an ad hoc celebration with some unusual elements, it still manages to incorporate many of the typical features of Greek athletic contests. The first thing to notice is the religious context of a thank-offering to the gods: these games are conducted in association with the sacrifices performed immediately prior to the competition and the prizes are hides from the sacrificial animals. The prizes are valuable and a recognition of achievement, which was important to the Greek mind. There is rivalry here to spur on the participants to do their best and not lose face before the watching crowd, whose enthusiastic response shows their engagement with the spectacle. The games embrace both athletic events (*gymnikos agon*) and equestrian events (*hippikos agon*), although on this occasion the impossibly difficult race track for the horses is unusual and provokes laughter. Some events which formed part of the regular programme by Xenophon's time are missing from these games: the combat sports, which the Greeks termed 'heavy' events, are all represented, but there is no mention of the pentathlon (see Chapter 5) and while the sprint and distance races are included, there is no equivalent of the 400 metres among the track events (**diaulos**, see p. 92). Chariot races were clearly not an option in these particular circumstances. Although the competitors at Olympia had to be of Greek nationality, the boys competing here are from among the prisoners and therefore unlikely to have been Greek. The large number of Cretans in the distance race is also puzzling.

Xenophon might be taken as an author who offers us reliable evidence. After all, the *Anabasis* is an eyewitness account of the expedition of Cyrus and it would therefore seem to be as objective as an ancient source can be. But Xenophon, like any author, selected some details and suppressed others to make his narrative appealing to his audience: the usual elements of an athletic competition might evoke less interest than the unusual. Besides, how easy is it for a modern reader to detect overtones? Was Xenophon mocking the Spartan Drakontios for his ill-considered selection of sites, or suggesting that he deliberately sought to generate a therapeutic laughter after their long march? His laconic wit is apparent in his response over wrestling, and the fact that Xenophon chose to put this exchange in direct speech (whether remembered or invented) gives prominence to Spartan dry humour and indifference to hardship.

All ancient literature has limitations for use as evidence and presents problems of interpretation. Stephen Glass, in a brutally stark assessment of many of our sources, described them as 'disconnected, late, uncritical, relentlessly anecdotal, or usually all four at once' (in Raschke, p. 155). But for all that, we do have to rely on whatever evidence there is in order to gain any understanding of the past. For ancient athletic practices our information comes from a variety of sources and times: from the early wall paintings of Thera to the Byzantine encyclopaedias there is a span of over 3,500 years (see Timeline, pp. 5–8). Yet in all that time, there is no account of athletics or the Olympics such as a modern historian of sport would write; hence the need to piece together a picture from the fragmentary epigraphic, archaeological and literary evidence. The purpose of this book is to provide an introduction to Greek athletics and their most important competition at Olympia through a selection of the sources. Its scope is restricted by constraints of size: its principal focus is on the period from the Bronze Age to classical Greece, but because many of the sources are much later, there are inevitably some references to athletics in later times. The sources selected are predominantly literary, partly because of the challenges they offer and partly because of the amount of detail they include. The evidence from art and archaeology has received less attention than it warrants, but limitations of space and the focus of the series on texts have restricted its use here. A selection of the vast quantity of modern scholarship on the subject is introduced in the section on further reading.

For familiar Greek names such as Thucydides or Aeschylus the usual Latin spelling has been retained, with the exception of Herakles, who is thus distinguished from the Latin Hercules. For lesser known Greeks such as Kleomedes or Archemoros the spelling is closer to the Greek, although *ch* has been preferred to *kh*. The variability over the spelling of Greek names is regrettable, but unavoidable. Greek words are printed in italics and are explained on first appearance and also in the glossary (indicated by bold type). Macra (long marks) are included the first time a Greek word appears and also in the glossary. Primary sources are numbered by chapter (**1.1, 1.2** etc.) for ease of cross-referencing. Where longer passages of verse are translated, the line numbers of the original texts are provided.

Acknowledgements

I would like to thank the editors of the series, James Morwood and Eric Dugdale, who have been very generous in their support, making many suggestions to improve the book and giving help and encouragement at every stage. Any mistakes and deficiencies are my own. The librarians at the Literary and Philosophical Society in Newcastle upon Tyne responded to my constant requests for obscure texts with patience and good humour. My wife and family supported me at every stage. I am also grateful to the staff at Cambridge University Press for their help and guidance.

Timeline: selected dates, events and principal authors

The following table lists selected events and the approximate dates at which they occurred, alongside the names of the principal authors translated in this book.

Approximate date	Events	Authors
The Bronze Age		
c. 1600–1200 BC	Minoan and Mycenean period; evidence of athletics in visual arts	
1184	Traditional date for the fall of Troy	
The Dark Age		
776 BC	Traditional date for the first games at Olympia	
c. 750–700		Homer's *Iliad* and *Odyssey* composed in their present form
The Archaic Period		
7th century BC		Tyrtaeus, elegiac poet
676	Pisa takes over the Olympic Games (Strabo)	
c. 594/3	Solon, Athenian law-giver, **archōn**	
582	Pythian Games at Delphi founded	
581	Isthmian Games founded	
c. 580	Reorganization of the Heraia at Olympia	
c. 580	Elis regains control of Olympia from Pisa	
573	Nemean Games founded	
c. 570–c. 478		Xenophanes, poet and philosopher
566	Traditional date for the first Greater Panathenaic Games at Athens	
c. 556–468		Simonides, lyric poet

518 –c. 438		Pindar, lyric poet
c. 510–c. 450		Bacchylides, lyric poet
c. 508/7	Founding of Athenian democracy	
c. 496–406/5		Sophocles, tragedian
490–479	Persian Wars	
490	Battle of Marathon	
480	Battle of Salamis	
479	Battle of Plataea	

The Classical Period

480s–420s BC		Herodotus, historian
480s–406		Euripides, tragedian
c. 480–411		Antiphon, orator
c. 455–400		Thucydides, historian
456	Temple of Zeus at Olympia finished	
c. 450–c. 380		Lysias, orator
c. 450–c. 385		Aristophanes, comic poet
436–338		Isocrates, orator
431–404	Peloponnesian War	
c. 430–354		Xenophon, historian and writer
c. 428–347		Plato, philosopher
420	Eleans fine and ban Sparta from the Olympics; Spartan Lichas flogged at Olympics	
c. 402–400	Sparta invades and defeats Elis	
399	Death of Socrates	

388	First recorded case of bribery at Olympia	
c. 384–322		Demosthenes, orator
384–322		Aristotle, philosopher
c. 380		Panathenaic prize list inscription
c. 370–285		Theophrastus, philosopher
365–4	Arcadian invasion of Elis; battle in the Altis	
c. 340–330	Echo Colonnade built at Olympia	
338	Battle of Chaironeia	
323	Death of Alexander the Great	

The Hellenistic Period

3rd century BC		Apollonius of Rhodes, epic poet
c. 300–c. 260		Theocritus, poet
c. 200–118		Polybius, historian
146	Greece becomes a Roman province	
106–43		Cicero, orator and philosopher
1st century BC		Diodorus Siculus, historian
1st century BC		Vitruvius, Roman architect
Later 1st century BC		Dionysius of Halicarnassus, historian
64 BC–c. AD 24		Strabo, Greek geographer

Roman Empire

31 BC–AD 14	Reign of the emperor Augustus	
1st century BC–1st century AD		Chariton, Greek novelist

c. 15 BC–AD 50		Phaedrus, Latin poet
c. AD 35–c. 96		Quintilian, Latin writer
c. 40–112		Dio Chrysostom, orator and philosopher
c. 45–96		Statius, Latin poet
c. 50–120s		Plutarch, Greek writer and biographer
c. 55–135		Epictetus, Stoic philosopher
c. 90–c. 160		Arrian, Greek writer, author of *Discourses of Epictetus*
c. 120–80s		Lucian, Greek writer
121–80		Marcus Aurelius, philosopher and Roman emperor AD 161–80
c. 125–c. 180		Aulus Gellius, Roman writer
2nd century AD		Pausanias, Greek travel writer
160–70	Pausanias visits Greece	
c. 170–c. 235		Aelian, Roman writer (in Greek)
2nd–3rd century		Athenaeus, Greek writer
3rd century		Philostratus, Greek writer
		Diogenes Laertius, Greek writer
393	Edict of Theodosius I banning pagan cults	

After antiquity

c. 560–636		Isidore of Seville, author of a Latin encyclopaedia
c. 900		*Greek Anthology* assembled
11th century		***Tabula Heroniana***
12th century		Eustathius, Byzantine scholar

1 Athletics in early Greece and in myth

There are two distinct sources of evidence for athletics in early Greece: artistic representations and literary texts. Each offers tantalizing glimpses of athletic events, but each comes with its own limitations. Our earliest evidence comes from the fragments of Minoan and Mycenean art unearthed on the islands of Crete and Thera (in the southern Aegean) in particular. These seem to show that there were traditions of familiar sports such as boxing and wrestling as well as the famous bull-leaping, for which no evidence has been discovered in later Greek culture. That, along with the unusual features of the other sports depicted, suggests that later Greeks did not directly inherit their athletic practices from their Minoan and Mycenean predecessors. Nevertheless, this early evidence makes a fascinating prelude to the long tradition of Greek athletics.

Minoan and Mycenean athletics

The best-known depiction of combat sport in this period comes from Thera. It is a fresco painted some time before the Santorini eruption (*c.* 1500 BC) which depicts two boys who seem to be boxing (**1.1**). The fresco is fragmentary and is put together rather like a jigsaw missing most of its pieces. If it has been correctly assembled, it looks as if the boys are wearing a single glove on the right hand and some form of covering on their heads from which long braids of hair emerge, but are otherwise naked except for a belt (or perhaps loincloth). Each aims a blow at the other's head, one with the gloved right hand, the other with his bare left.

Fragment from a fresco from Thera, possibly c. *1625 BC.*

> 1 How has the artist arranged the figures to show the profile of the boxers to the best advantage?
> 2 How violent does this combat appear to be?

On a rhyton (drinking horn) from Hagia Triada in Crete (*c.* 1550 BC) (**1.2**) several sports seem to be illustrated in bands, although the fragmentary and worn vessel is hard to interpret. On the top band two men look as if they are boxing, although there is no indication of gloves. Separated from them by a column are three other figures. Two, with arms raised like boxers, face a figure whose lower legs partially survive in a pose suggesting that he is crouching with his back to the others.

Below this is a second band depicting bull-leapers, and on the third band the four figures have also been interpreted as boxers. All wear helmets with cheekpieces and seem to have gloves. Two stand upright in a pose which might represent them delivering a left hook while the right arm is bent back to deliver the next blow. Their legs are spread apart and firmly set in the classic stance for unleashing powerful blows. The other two figures are on the ground, one leaning on his right elbow, the other slumped forward on his knees and hands, his head close to the ground as if he were struggling up from a prone position. The lowest band has parts of three figures standing in a very similar pose to those in the third. Two figures on the ground survive in part, with one or two legs in the air as if they have been thrown in wrestling. Other interpretations would have the lower bands representing armed combat, the standing figures holding short knives in their right hands drawn back to thrust at an opponent.

1.2

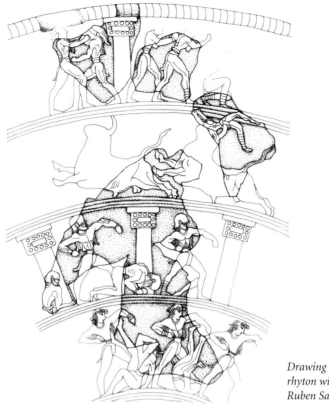

Drawing of the Hagia Triada rhyton with restorations by Ruben Santos, c. 1500 BC.

1 Does the illustration of bull-leaping in the second band help to provide a context for the other bands?

2 Is it possible to be certain which, if any, sports are depicted?

3 What purpose might training in sports such as these have served?

There are problems about the relationship of these combat sports (if this is what they are) to later Greek practices. First, there is no sign of a judge, a figure constantly present in later Greek competitions. On the Hagia Triada rhyton almost all individual combat is subsumed under largely repetitive patterns. The boxing gloves bear little resemblance to the thongs that later served as gloves and the wearing of helmets would rule out any suggestion of boxing to later Greeks who fought bare-headed. While there are images of chariots from the period, even when they appear to speed one behind another it is impossible to be certain that a race is indicated without corroborating evidence. Although it is always rash to judge from the absence of evidence (one never knows what archaeology may turn up), the fact that most of the events which are so regularly depicted later are not represented in this early period also points to the conclusion that any direct influence of Minoan and Mycenean sports on the athletic tradition of the later Greeks remains tantalizingly elusive.

These visual images are extremely difficult to interpret, not only because of their poor condition and heavy restoration, but principally because we have no context for them except that which archaeology can provide, and without written evidence we have to rely heavily on conjecture to interpret physical remains. In the next section we are faced with the opposite problem. Homeric epic offers some detailed descriptions of both the context for athletic competition and the events themselves. However, it is hard to determine just how closely the heroic society depicted by Homer is related to the Bronze Age or Dark Age societies whose physical remains nevertheless often seem to reflect Homeric description.

It is clear from the characteristics of the verse that the *Iliad* and *Odyssey* were composed by one or more poets in an oral tradition. At some point, probably around 750 BC, they were given their current form (and it is then that Homer, traditionally held to be their author, may have lived), although their transfer onto the written page may have been somewhat later. They describe mythical events of an earlier period traditionally dated to the Bronze Age, around 1200 BC.

There are two contexts in these passages in which competitive sports take place. The funeral games in honour of Achilles' close friend Patroclus are held immediately after the cremation of the body. Eight events are contested, two of which, armed combat and archery, do not feature in later Greek sports, and it is not entirely clear whether throwing the iron weight is meant to represent the discus. The fact that throwing the discus is mentioned twice in the narrative of the chariot race (*Iliad* 23.287–533) suggests that it was familiar at least to Homer's audience of the eighth century BC if not earlier. The association of armed combat with funeral games inevitably invites comparison with the origins of gladiatorial combat in Rome, but in this Homeric context it is major heroes who take up weapons (*Iliad* 23.798–825) and the contest is brought to an end before serious damage is done.

In fact, all the events in the *Iliad* are contested by the major heroes of the epic with the exception of boxing (*Iliad* 23.651–99), where Epeios' claim to pre-eminence is the first hint of a contestant specializing in a particular discipline. In this epic world the social order is dominated by heroes whose prowess extends from the battlefield to athletics, even including the chariot race which in later times brought honour not so much to the charioteer as to the owner of the victorious team of horses (see p. 58). Galen (second century AD) remarked that there was no name for 'athletics' or 'trainer' in Homer's time. He thought the change to specialization exemplified by Epeios began shortly before Plato (fourth century BC). The practice of awarding prizes to all the contestants (except for throwing the iron weight, *Iliad* 23.826–49) also contrasts markedly with the later award of first prize only (but see **9.2**) and the absence of especially valuable prizes from the 'crown' games. But the ethos of 'all must have prizes' suits the heroic world of the *Iliad* in which only heroes compete for prizes and in which leaving empty-handed would be an affront to their honour; and prizes could be hotly disputed (as they were at the end of the chariot race in *Iliad* 23). Indeed, Achilles had withdrawn from the fighting in

Iliad 1 precisely because of the slight to his honour by Agamemnon taking away the woman who was allotted to him in the division of war booty. With the funeral games, Achilles is reintegrated into the company of heroes by his generous distribution of prizes.

The context for athletics in the *Odyssey* is very different from the funeral games in the *Iliad*. Odysseus is being entertained on the fantasy island of Phaeacia and his hosts indulge in some athletic sports as an after-dinner entertainment. Here there are no prizes, and only the winners are mentioned. Yet the ethos is still that of the heroic world, as is sharply revealed when Euryalos insults Odysseus, a hero of royal status, by comparing him to a merchant (**1.9**, lines 159–64), the implication being that only the leisured aristocracy have the time and resources to practise athletics seriously. Prowess in this field is therefore a mark of social class. There is a story in Herodotus (*Histories* 6.126–9) which describes similar elite behaviour in the sixth century BC. Cleisthenes, tyrant of Sicyon *c.* 600–570 BC, looking for a suitable son-in-law, issued an invitation at the Olympic Games to any eligible young men to demonstrate their qualities for a year at Sicyon. As part of his assessment he observed them in the **gymnasium**, but of crucial importance was their behaviour when dining in public. This is not far from the world of Phaeacia.

Missing from Homer is the context we find for later athletic competitions, held on occasions to honour the gods and in particular religious festivals. However, there were many ways in which the Greeks traced the origins of festivals back to the heroic age, or even further, as the foundation myths at Olympia reveal (see Chapter 2). The myth at Nemea attributed the foundation of the games to funeral games for the infant Opheltes.

The funeral games of Patroclus: Homer, *Iliad* 23.257–70 and 287–895

In the following extract from *Iliad* 23 (lines 257–70), Achilles announces the funeral games in honour of his dead friend Patroclus and brings out the prizes.

1.3   Achilles stopped the crowd leaving and made the broad assembly sit down. From his ships he brought prizes: cauldrons, tripods, horses, mules, several head of   260 strong oxen, **well-girdled** women and grey iron.

---

well-girdled compound epithets (adjectives describing a characteristic) are a regular feature of epic diction and often, along with other adjectives, are attached to nouns to form regular metrical units to aid oral composition (see also 'broad assembly' in the first line).

First he offered glittering prizes for the swiftest charioteers to take away: for the winner, a woman skilled in fine crafts and a tripod with handles holding **22 measures**; for the second, a six-year-old mare, not broken in and pregnant 265 with a mule foal; for the third a lovely cauldron holding four measures and not yet put on the fire, but still shining and new; for the fourth **two talents of gold**; for the fifth an unused two-handled cooking bowl. 270

Cauldrons like **1.4** were valuable items and from the ninth century BC were frequently offered as dedications to the gods. In Homer's *Iliad* (11.698–701) Nestor refers to Neleus sending four horses to Elis to race 'for a tripod', and tripods feature among the prizes in **1.3** (line 264) and **1.7** (line 702). However, it is not clear whether the dedications found at Olympia were actual prizes. Many have handles like those represented here and in **1.5**.

1.4

A tripod cauldron found at Olympia.

In this scene of a chariot race from the François Vase (**1.5**), a tripod with handles is visible under the first team of horses and a dinos (mixing bowl) under the second. They are probably meant to indicate prizes. Racing towards Achilles with a tripod at the finishing line (not shown) are three chariots with Automedon in the lead, Diomedes second and Damasippos third, their names clearly visible in front of their chariots.

22 measures we don't know what a 'measure' amounted to, but this must have been a very big tripod bowl as it is five and a half times the size of the cauldron for third prize.

two talents of gold in Homer a talent was a weight used only for gold; we do not know its value.

1.5

A chariot race from the François Vase, c. 575 BC.

This fragment of a bowl (**1.6**) shows the crowd at Patroclus' funeral games. They are sitting on tiers of seats as in a modern **stadium**, a unique image of the crowds which gathered to watch athletic competitions. The bowl is signed by Sophilos and names both Patroclus' games and Achilles.

1.6

Fragment of a bowl by Sophilos, c. 600–575 BC.

1 How has the painter indicated audience reaction?
2 How many horses are depicted?

After the chariot race (*Iliad* 23.271–533) and the boxing (*Iliad* 23.651–99), Homer describes the wrestling.

Wrestling: *Iliad* 23.700–39

1.7 The son of Peleus at once put out on display to the Greeks the third set of prizes for 700 painful wrestling. For the winner there was a large tripod to go over the fire, which the Greeks among themselves reckoned worth twelve oxen. For the loser he put on display a woman with skill in many tasks and they thought she was worth four 705 oxen. He stood up and addressed the Greeks, 'Two men come forward to take part in this contest.'

So he spoke and then great Ajax, son of Telamon, got up and cunning Odysseus with his knowledge of tricks was up on his feet. Wearing loincloths, they both strode into 710 the centre of the crowd and grasped each other by the arms with their strong hands, **like interlocking rafters** which a renowned builder has fitted in a high building to resist the force of the wind. Their backs creaked from the firm pressure of their strong arms. Sweat began to pour down them in streams, and clusters of bruises 715 red with blood swelled up over their ribs and shoulders. Their desire for victory and for the well-made tripod never wavered. Neither could Odysseus **bring his opponent to the ground** with a trip, nor could Ajax as Odysseus' strength held 720 firm. But when they began to make the well-greaved Greeks anxious, great Ajax son of Telamon said to Odysseus, 'Son of Laertes, Odysseus of divine descent and full of wiles, either lift me, or I'll lift you. Then everything will be up to Zeus.'

With that he lifted him up, but Odysseus did not forget his cunning and caught Ajax 725 in the hollow of the knee with a blow from behind, making his leg give way. Ajax fell backwards and Odysseus landed on his chest. The crowd watched in amazement. Much-enduring, godlike Odysseus made the second lift. He did actually get him a little way off the ground, but he failed to complete the lift. Then he hooked his leg 730 behind Ajax's knee and they both fell to the ground side by side and were soiled with dust. And now they would have leapt up again and begun to wrestle for a third time if Achilles himself had not stood up and stopped them. 'Don't get yourselves 735 set again and wear yourselves out in the struggle. Victory goes to you both. **Take equal prizes** and make way for other Greeks to compete too.'

---

like interlocking rafters   the opening stance as the wrestlers lean towards one another. See **7.3**.

bring his opponent to the ground   this sentence contrasts the technique of Odysseus with the strength of Ajax as they try to throw each other. This type of wrestling was later decided by three throws, but this contest ends prematurely and does not reveal what was required to win.

Take equal prizes   not an easy task when one is worth twelve oxen and the other four.

So he spoke and they did as he said, wiping off the dust and putting on their tunics.

> 1 'Victory goes to you both': do you think it was an equal contest or did one of the competitors seem to have the edge?
>
> 2 What indications are there of what motivates the heroes to compete with each other?
>
> 3 Is there any indication of how the use of cunning in sport is viewed?

The foot race: *Iliad* 23.740–97

1.8 At once the son of Peleus laid out other prizes for the sprint. There was a **mixing** 740 **bowl made of silver** which held six measures, and in its beauty it was by far the greatest in all the world, since Sidonian craftsmen had made it with skill. The Phoenicians who transported it over the misty sea had given it as a gift to Thoas when they moored in the harbour. Euenos son of Jason gave it to the hero 745 Patroclus in payment for Priam's son Lykaon. Now Achilles set it up to honour his companion as a prize for whoever proved the fastest in the sprint. For the runner-up he brought out a huge ox rich in fat and for the last prize he set down 750 half a talent of gold. Then he stood up and addressed the Greeks: 'Competitors for this event stand up.' So he spoke and instantly swift Ajax son of Oileus got up, followed by cunning Odysseus, then Nestor's son Antilochus as he was the fastest 755 runner of all the younger men. They stood in line and Achilles pointed out the **finishing post**. From the start they set a fast pace and the son of Oileus quickly established a lead, but godlike Odysseus was in very close pursuit. As close as a 760 **heddle-rod** is to the breast of a girdled woman when with her hands she pulls it

---

mixing bowl made of silver this prize is given a fuller description than any other in the games. The fact that it belonged to Patroclus makes it particularly appropriate for games in his honour. By recounting its history Homer gives it a significant value. Made in Phoenicia at Sidon (a coastal city in modern Lebanon), it is brought to Lemnos by Phoenician merchants who give it to Thoas, the king of the island. Jason married Thoas' daughter Hypsipyle and their son Euenos gave it to Patroclus as ransom for Lykaon, a son of Priam captured and enslaved by Achilles. After being ransomed, Lykaon met Achilles a second time and was killed. His story is told at length in *Iliad* 21.

finishing post it is hard to tell whether this race conforms to the later *stadion* (one length of the track, approximately 200 metres) or *diaulos* (a double leg, approximately 400 metres). The finishing post might equally well be the turning post, and 'the final part of the course' the return leg.

heddle-rod this simile essentially says that Odysseus is as close to Ajax as a woman weaving is to the part of the loom she pulls towards her. As is typical in Homeric similes, this one also contains a more detailed comparison, with the woman's effort and skill implying the same qualities in Odysseus.

firmly and holds it close to her breast as she draws the shuttle along through the **warp**, so close was Odysseus running, only behind him, with his feet falling in Ajax's tracks before the dust settled. Godlike Odysseus kept running fast all the 765 time and was breathing down on his head. All the Greeks were cheering his will to win and shouting advice as he made every effort. But as they were completing the final part of the course, at that moment Odysseus prayed to grey-eyed Athene in his head, 'Hear me goddess, and come with kind aid for my feet.' So he spoke 770 in prayer and Pallas Athene heard him. She made his limbs light, his feet and, above them, his hands. Just when they were about to make a dash for the prize, Ajax slipped as he ran – it was Athene who did the damage – where dung was scattered from the bellowing oxen that **swift-footed** Achilles had slaughtered in 775 honour of Patroclus. His mouth and nose were filled with cow dung. But it was patient, godlike Odysseus who picked up the mixing bowl as he had come first, and famous Ajax took the ox. There he stood holding in his hands the horn of 780 the ox of the fields as he spat out dung and he addressed the Greeks, 'Damn it all! It must have been the goddess who tripped me, the one who has always stood beside Odysseus like a mother and helped him.' So he spoke and everyone laughed cheerfully at him. With a smile Antilochus took the last prize and spoke 785 to the Greeks, 'My friends, you all know, but I'll say it. Even now the gods still honour the older men. For Ajax is only a little older than me, but **this one** belongs to an older generation, one of our senior men. They say he's on the threshold 790 of old age. It is hard for the Greeks to compete with him in running, with the exception of Achilles.' So he spoke, honouring the swift-footed son of Peleus. In reply Achilles said to him, 'Antilochus, your praise will not be spoken in vain, but 795 I shall give you an extra half talent of gold.' With these words he handed it over and Antilochus received it with pleasure.

---

1 How might a modern athlete invoke divine aid?
2 What humorous elements can you find in the description of this event?
3 How much attention does Homer devote to proceedings after the race? How similar is that to the coverage of modern athletics and other sports?

---

warp   vertical threads on the loom. Familiarity with the loom is assumed, but nowadays this is no longer a household item as it used to be. Briefly, alternate vertical (warp) threads are tied with a leash to the heddle-rod. The shuttle passes the horizontal threads under and over alternate warp threads. Then the heddle-rod is pulled towards the weaver, allowing the shuttle to pass under and over the opposite warp threads.

swift-footed   the regular epithet for Achilles. His prowess as a runner features prominently in this section, especially in Antilochus' praise.

this one   Odysseus.

After describing competitions for armed combat, throwing the iron weight and archery, Homer brings the funeral games to an end with javelin throwing (*Iliad* 23.884–97).

Games at Phaeacia: Homer, *Odyssey* 8.96–233

Phaeacia is the last stop on Odysseus' voyage home from Troy. Before this extract he has been washed up naked on the shore after his raft was destroyed by Poseidon. Exhausted by his ordeal at sea, he slept until woken by the princess Nausicaa and her companions. They clothed him and took him to the court of King Alcinoos, where he was entertained with a feast. The singer Demodocos brought tears to Odysseus' eyes with his song about the quarrel between Odysseus and Achilles. Alcinoos, the only one to notice the tears, now suggests going outside for these games.

1.9   'Listen, leaders and counsellors of the Phaeacians, now that our appetites are satisfied by the feast we've shared and the music of the lyre, the proper accompaniment for a rich feast, let us go outside and try our luck in all the athletic   100
competitions so that when our guest returns home he can tell his friends how far we surpass others in boxing, wrestling, jumping and running.'

With these words he led the way and they went with him. An attendant hung up **Demodocos'** clear-toned lyre on a peg, and led him by the hand out of the hall,   105
taking him along the same route as the others, those best of the Phaeacians, to admire the events.

They made their way to their place of assembly and with them went a great crowd in huge numbers. There, up stood many a fine young man: **Acroneos,**   110
Ocyalos, Elatreus, Nauteus, Prymneus, Anchialos, Eretmeus, Ponteus, Proreus, Thoön, Anabesineos, Amphialos son of Polyneus and grandson of Tecton, and then Euryalos too, that equal of man-slaying Ares, the son of Naubolos who in   115
looks and physique was the best of all the Phaeacians after faultless Laodamas. And three sons of faultless Alcinoos also got up, Laodamas, Halios and god-like Klytoneos.

Demodocos   a blind singer who entertains the company: Greek tradition thought Homer too was a blind bard.

Acroneos, Ocyalos   these and the other names in the list have associations with the sea, as befits 'famous sailors' as they are called in line 191 below. Note how the sons of King Alcinoos form the climax of the list at the end.

First of all they tried their luck at running. From the start it was a race in which 120
they stretched themselves and they all went flying quickly, raising dust from the
flat track. By far the best of them at running was faultless Klytoneos. The rest were
left behind as he outstripped them on reaching the spectators, by the **distance
two mules plough** in a fallow field. 125

When they turned their attention to painful wrestling, at this Euryalos beat all
the leading contenders. At the long jump Amphialos was by far the best of the
field, at the discus it was Elatreus and when it came to boxing it was Laodamas, 130
Alcinoos' noble son.

When they had all enjoyed themselves at the games, Alcinoos' son Laodamas
addressed them. 'Come now, my friends, let us ask our guest if there is an event
in which he has acquired expertise. He's not badly built with those thighs and 135
legs, and in his upper body, his two arms and stout neck. Yet despite their great
strength and no shortage of youthful vigour, he is broken down by his **many
hardships**. For, I tell you, there's nothing worse than the sea for sapping a man's
stamina, however strong he may be.'

In answer to him Euryalos said, 'Laodamas, what you have said is perfectly 140
appropriate. Now go and challenge him yourself and tell him what you have to
say.' When Alcinoos' noble son heard this, he went and stood in front of everyone
and said to Odysseus, 'You too, our respected guest, come over here and try 145
your luck in the sports, if you have acquired skill in any. It seems likely you are
practised in athletics. For as long as a man lives, he has no greater fame than
what he achieves with his hands and feet. But come, have a try and dismiss cares
from your heart since it will not be very long now until you sail: a ship is already 150
launched and your crew is ready.'

In reply cunning Odysseus said, 'Laodamas, why are **you men** provoking me with
this challenge? I have got my own problems on my mind rather than sporting
competitions. I have suffered many tribulations in the past and I've been through 155
many struggles. Now I'm just sitting in your assembled company with my heart
set on returning home and with an appeal before the king and all your people.'

---

distance two mules plough   probably signifying the standard width of the plot.

many hardships   Homer regularly uses the epithet 'much-enduring' to describe one of
Odysseus' main characteristics.

you men   Odysseus uses the plural to include Euryalos, or, more likely, all the young
men. By doing so he tactfully avoids confrontation with Laodamas, whom he also treats
as his host (as Alcinoos' oldest son) in lines 207–9.

Euryalos replied, abusing him to his face, 'Stranger, I don't think you resemble someone with experience of athletic contests, such as are commonly found among men, but you look like a man who makes regular voyages in an oared ship, captain of a crew of traders, his mind on his cargo, his eye on the goods in his greed for profits. You don't look like an athlete.' Cunning Odysseus gave him a black look and said, 'That, my friend, was not well said. You seem like an arrogant man. So it is that the gods don't give all men equally the graceful gifts of build, brains or eloquence. For one man may be less well endowed with looks, but a god puts a crown of charm on his words and people look at him with pleasure. He speaks without faltering and with winning modesty, standing out in an assembly, and when he goes through the town, they look on him as a god. Another man is like the immortals in appearance but his words are not garlanded with grace. So in your case, physically you are most distinguished – a god would not have made you any different – but mentally you are simply vacuous. You provoked anger in my heart with your inappropriate words. I am not without experience of athletics as you say, but I think I was among the best while I could rely on my youthful vigour and strength of arm. But as it is, I am in the grip of distress and sufferings since I have had much to endure in getting through men's wars and the painful waves. But despite the many hardships I've been through, I will try my luck in your competitions. Your words cut me to the quick and you provoke me by saying them.'

With these words he leapt up and, still wearing his cloak, he picked up a bigger, bulky **discus**, considerably more substantial than the sort the Phaeacians were competing with against each other. Then, swinging it round, he let it fly from his strong hand and the stone made a booming sound. The Phaeacians, famous sailors, rowers with long oars, ducked down to the ground at the flight of the stone. It flew past the markers of all the others in the speed of its flight from his hand. Athene, adopting the physical appearance of a man, marked the limit of his throw and called out, 'Stranger, even a blind man could distinguish your marker by feeling around, since it is not among the group at all, but is first by a long way. You can feel confident about this event. None of the Phaeacians is going to come near this or throw beyond it.'

These were her words and much-enduring, godlike Odysseus was delighted, glad to see a supporter on his side in the crowd. Then he addressed the Phaeacians less severely: 'Get near this, young men and perhaps later I will throw another, either as far, I suspect, or still further. As for the others, since you made me very angry, if any of you feels impelled or spirited enough, come over here and let him try at boxing, wrestling or even running – I have no objections – any one of you Phaeacians except Laodamas himself, since he is my host – and who would fight with a benefactor? Foolish indeed and of no worth is the man who would engage

---

discus   note the variation in size. See pp. 75–6.

in athletic rivalry with someone who receives him hospitably in a foreign land. 210
He cuts off everything that serves his interests. As for the others, there is none I
turn my back on or consider unworthy, but I am willing to get to know him and
test myself against him face to face. In all the competitive sports among men I
am not bad, I know how to **handle the polished bow** well. I would be first to 215
hit a man when shooting the enemy in the throng of battle even if very many of
my comrades were standing beside me and targeting men. Only Philoctetes was
better than me with the bow in the land of Troy, whenever we Greeks were firing. 220
I can claim that I am much better than all others who eat food, every mortal now
on earth. But I will not compare myself with men of earlier generations, such as
Herakles or Eurytos of Oechalia who used to compete with the gods in archery. 225
Actually, this was the reason for Eurytos' sudden death and old age not overtaking
him in his palace. He made Apollo angry by challenging him in bowmanship and
Apollo killed him. With the javelin my throw goes further than any other man's
shot with an arrow. It is only in running that I fear one of the Phaeacians might 230
beat me. For on my long voyage I was reduced to such a shameful condition
because there were not enough provisions on board and that is why I have lost the
strength in my legs.' At these words of his, everyone was hushed in silence.

1 Is there any indication of the distance the athletes run in the foot race?
2 What emphasis is given to the spectators? Was watching an important aspect
   of early sport?
3 In lines 190–1, emphasis is given to the fact that the Phaeacians are sailors. Is
   there an element of humour here?
4 'No greater fame than what he achieves with his hands and feet.' What does
   this reveal about the value Greeks attached to sporting competition?
5 Why does Odysseus say, 'Your words cut me to the quick'?
6 How tactful is Odysseus throughout this passage?
7 Why do you think Odysseus chose the discus as the event in which to
   compete?

• From what you have read, how would you describe the function of athletic
   competition in Homeric society?
• Who were the athletes and why did they compete?
• Why do you think it was appropriate to hold athletic competitions at
   Patroclus' funeral?

handle the polished bow   when Odysseus takes his revenge on the suitors at the end
of the Odyssey, his bow is the most significant weapon. Odysseus' claims here are not
reflected in the *Iliad*, although heroes such as Odysseus are portrayed as outstanding for
both their physical strength and range of skills.

2 Olympia: from myth to history

Athletic competition in the heroic age of the Homeric epics may have had different contexts from the religious festivals at which the later Greek athletes competed, but the Greeks were keenly aware of their past and had a mythology rich in aetiological stories about causes (*aitiai*). At Olympia there was more than one foundation myth to explain the origins of the Olympic Games, as the following passages show. None, however, is consistent with the historical development from 776 BC recorded by the Greek travel writer Pausanias, who lived in the second century AD (**2.4**). In Pausanias' mythological sequence of founders, the first is a Herakles, who was one of the Idaean Daktyls or Curetes (Cretan divinities who kept the infant Zeus hidden from his father Cronos before Zeus supplanted him as king of the gods), a myth referred to briefly by Strabo (**2.2**). This Herakles, as Pausanias tells the tale, brought wild olive to Olympia from the Hyperboreans (who lived beyond the North Wind) and used it to crown the winner of a foot race between his four brothers. Pausanias also records a myth which credits Zeus himself with the foundation of the games (see **5.19**).

A key figure of myth connected with Olympia is Pelops, who gave his name to the whole region of the Peloponnese. The hero shrine of Pelops is a prominent feature in the **Altis**, the sacred area of the site, and the funeral games for Patroclus might hint at a similar way of honouring Pelops, although archaeology has revealed no link between the later shrine and the Bronze Age. Pelops also makes an impressive appearance on the east pediment of the great Temple of Zeus (mid-fifth century BC). In myth he comes to be associated with the area through his marriage to Hippodameia, daughter of Oenomaus, king of Pisa. Pelops was the son of Tantalus whose punishment in Hades is the source of the verb 'tantalize' in English. As Homer tells the story in *Odyssey* 11.582–92, Tantalus stands in water which recedes when he tries to drink, and the fruit hanging above him is blown out of reach when he tries to pick it. Tantalus was punished for testing the omniscience of the gods by killing his son Pelops and then serving up his flesh to the gods at a feast. Only Demeter (distracted by grief for Persephone) fell for the deception and ate part of a shoulder. When the gods restored Pelops to life, he received a new shoulder of ivory. Pausanias reports a story of a shoulder-blade of Pelops being kept in the sanctuary, although it had disappeared by his time.

When Pelops arrived as a suitor for the hand of Hippodameia, he had to win his bride by defeating her father in a deadly chariot race. The odds were stacked against the challenger because Oenomaus had divine horses and in previous races he had killed a number of suitors, whose heads were nailed on the palace doors.

According to the poet Pindar, Poseidon gave Pelops some indefatigable winged horses to secure victory, but in the best-known version Pelops bribed Oenomaus' charioteer Myrtilos to sabotage his chariot and Oenomaus was killed in the resulting crash. Pelops reneged on his promise that Myrtilos could spend the night with Hippodameia and threw him into the sea. As Myrtilos fell to his death, he delivered the famous curse which led to generations of conflict through Atreus and Thyestes, Agamemnon and Aegisthus to the murder of Clytemnestra by Orestes and Electra. Among the origins that Pausanias gives for the mound of Taraxippos in the **hippodrome** (**4.2**) there is a story that Pelops made an empty burial mound for Myrtilos, where he sacrificed to propitiate him, calling it Taraxippos because Myrtilos' sabotage had frightened Oenomaus' horses.

Despite the prominence of Pelops, and Pausanias' statement that no other hero was given greater honour at Olympia, Herakles (son of Zeus) too has a strong connection with the site. His 12 labours are the subject for the sculptures on the **metopes** of the temple of Zeus, above the porches at the west and east entrances to the temple. The cleansing of the Augean stables was a labour closely related to Olympia. Augeas, king of Elis (about 37 miles from Olympia: see map on p. 31), had agreed to pay Herakles a handsome reward if he could clear away in one day the vast amount of dung his huge herds had produced, a task which Herakles performed by diverting rivers. When Augeas refused to pay up, Herakles invaded with an army and after suffering an initial defeat (**2.1**), conquered Elis and celebrated his victory with games at Olympia. Pausanias says that his charioteer Iolaos won the

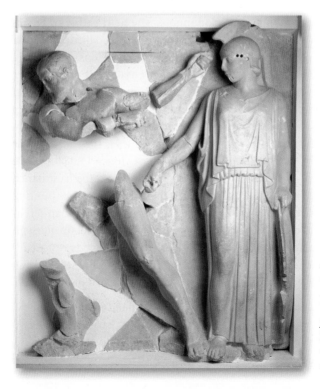

*A metope from the temple of Zeus, Olympia, showing Herakles, helped by Athena, 'cleansing the land of dung for the Eleans' (Pausanias, Description of Greece 6.10.9). See **2.1** for further details about the myth.*

chariot race with the mares of Herakles and observed that 'it was a long established custom to race with another's horses', citing the games celebrated for Patroclus as an example. Castor won the foot race, Polydeukes (**7.16, 7.17**) the boxing, while Herakles himself carried off the prizes for wrestling and the ***pankration***. Such a version of the myth is given an aura of authority by its Homeric parallel and a spurious historicity by its victor list.

The first Olympics

Pindar has the following version of Herakles' activities at Olympia in *Olympian* 10 (lines 24–77), written on commission to celebrate and immortalize Hagesidamus' victory in the boys' boxing in 476 BC.

2.1   The laws of Zeus have provided the impetus to sing of the special games which Herakles founded with **six altars** beside the ancient tomb of Pelops. It was when 25 he had killed the noble **Kteatos**, son of Poseidon, **and Eurytos** in order to exact payment for his willing service from an unwilling and arrogant Augeas. Herakles lay in wait for them among the bushes below **Kleonai** and killed them on the road 30 because on an earlier occasion the arrogant **Moliones** had destroyed his army from **Tiryns** when it was encamped deep in the land of Elis. And indeed, not long after, the **king of the Epeians** who had cheated his guest saw his wealthy land, his 35 own city, sinking into a deep pit of ruin under the cruel grip of fire and blows of

---

six altars   Pausanias mentions far more than six in his list (*Description of Greece* 5.14–15). Olympia was a busy religious sanctuary.

Kteatos... and Eurytos   sons of Poseidon and Molione, hence their name Moliones or Molionides. They were twins joined as one with two heads and four legs and arms. When Herakles led an army from Tiryns to punish Augeas, king of Elis, for failing to pay him the reward for cleaning the Augean stables, Augeas put them in charge of his army and they helped inflict a defeat on Herakles' force. Later Herakles ambushed and killed them near Kleonai when they were on their way to the Isthmian Games near Corinth. He then captured Elis and founded the Olympic Games.

Kleonai   to the north of Argos and south of Corinth, close to where Herakles killed the Nemean lion.

Moliones   see note on Kteatos, above.

Tiryns   a settlement with an impressive citadel in the Bronze Age, but later falling under the influence of, and finally destroyed by Argos *c.* 470 BC.

king of the Epeians   Augeas. According to Pausanias, the Epeians were named after Epeios, son of Endymion, king of Elis. He made his three sons compete for the throne by a race at Olympia, won by Epeios. After Epeios, his brother Aitolos became king and he was succeeded by Eleios, a grandson of Endymion, and the people thereafter took their name from him. Epeians and Eleans are therefore two names for the people of Elis.

---

iron. It is difficult to avoid a dispute with those of greater power. As a result of his 40
ill-advised behaviour Augeas was finally captured and did not escape the oblivion
of death.

The mighty son of Zeus gathered his entire army and all the plunder at Pisa and
measured out a sacred precinct for his almighty father. He put a boundary around 45
the Altis, setting it apart in an open space, while the area around it he designated
as the place for feasting, honouring the stream of the Alpheios along with the
twelve mighty gods. He named the hill of Cronos, previously unnamed when 50
Oenomaus ruled, and saturated with many falls of snow.

At this first performance of the rite, standing nearby were the Fates and the only
one who discovers the real truth, Time. As Time went on, he declared the plain 55
truth, how Herakles divided the spoils, the gift of war and performed a sacrifice,
and how he established the four-yearly festival with the first Olympiad and its
victories.

Who actually won one of the first crowns with hands and feet, or chariot, hoping 60
for success in the contest and achieving it in action? For running the straight
stretch of the *stadion*, victory went to **Oiōnos**, son of Lykymnios. He had come 65
from Midea with his army. In wrestling, **Echemos** won glory for Tegea, and
Doryklos who lived in the city of Tiryns won the prize for boxing. And in the
four-horse chariot race it was **Sāmos**, son of **Halirhothios**, from Mantinea. With 70
the javelin, **Phrastor** hit the mark. **Nikeus**, with a whirling sweep of his hand,
achieved a distance with the stone he threw beyond all the others, and the allied
troops raised a great roar of approval. Meanwhile, the lovely light of the **fair-faced** 75
moon lit up the evening and in joyful feasting the whole sanctuary resounded
with song, all by way of praise.

---

stadion see pp. 91–2 and glossary.

Oiōnos a cousin of Herakles from Midea in Argolis.

Echemos king of Tegea, later famous for killing Hyllos, a son of Herakles, in single
combat.

Doryklos, Sāmos known only by their names.

Halirhothios a son of Poseidon, god of horses, providing a suitable lineage for a
charioteer.

Phrastor, Nikeus known only by their names.

fair-faced moon the Olympic Games took place at the second full moon after the
summer solstice.

1 Compare this account of the founding of the games with Pausanias' history of their development (**2.4**). Which account of the games' genesis or development seems more likely to be true?

2 Are there elements of this account that are similar to the games in Homer?

3 Are there any details in this passage which suggest later practice?

4 Strabo (**2.2**) said that one should listen to old stories with some scepticism. Would you agree?

Among the founders, King Iphitos of Elis, who Pausanias tells us was a contemporary of the Spartan Lykourgos (probably eighth century BC), is said to have restored the games and Olympic truce (see **10.1**) on the advice of the Delphic oracle after they had been discontinued. Plutarch (*Lykourgos* 2.3) says Lykourgos helped Iphitos put the festival on a more secure footing. When Pausanias reaches 776 BC in his historical survey (**2.4**), he says there was a gradual recollection of the tradition, which was revived little by little, thus making a neat transition from the mythical past to recorded history, however insecure those records might be. Elsewhere Pausanias mentions the discus of Iphitos on which the Olympic truce was written (**10.1**). Whatever political or military conflicts for the control of the north-west Peloponnese may be concealed in these myths, the myths which see the foundation of athletic competitions at a religious shrine to celebrate success introduce a context very different from those of the games in Homer.

The steady expansion of the programme in Pausanias' account (**2.4**) may seem a likely scenario, but it is not without objection: the initial games, consisting of one brief sprint lasting a few seconds, seem unlikely to have played a major part in the festival. And if games are to be established, why do they not have a range of events after the pattern in Pindar and Homer? Even the traditional starting date for the games of 776 BC, often regarded as a certainty, has been called into question. Nevertheless it does provide a starting point for a **Panhellenic** system of dating by **Olympiads**, and as such it is highly convenient. In favour of the gradual development, one might look at the way pop festivals have expanded from small beginnings. In 40 years the audience at the Glastonbury Festival in England has grown from 1,500 in 1970 to 137,500 in 2009. The growth of the modern Olympics is similarly spectacular: there were 245 participants from 14 nations in 1896 and by 1996 10,310 athletes came from 197 nations (216 countries are expected in 2012). While the speed of growth in Pausanias' list is somewhat slower (it takes half a century for a second event to be added), there is some possible archaeological evidence for growing numbers of spectators from the discovery of an increase in the provision of wells at Olympia around 700 BC. At about the same time the stream of the Kladeos was redirected to make more room in the western part of the site and a retaining wall was built to keep it in its channel. The number of dedications, particularly animal figurines and tripods (see **1.4**), show that the site was already attracting visitors in significant numbers by the ninth and eighth centuries, before the games were established (if we can trust the traditional date). The scanty records of victors in the early games show that they were dominated by local athletes, but increasingly participants came from the whole Peloponnese and central Greece, and by the sixth century athletes were coming from the wider Greek world, with a notable contingent from Greek cities in southern Italy and Sicily who had relatively easy access by sea and whose participation in a Panhellenic festival would have been an affirmation of their Greek identity. See **8.16** for a list of victors and their cities in the early fifth century.

Strabo's account (**2.2**) gives a brief outline of the competition between Elis and Pisa for the control of Olympia, with the Eleans organizing the festival until 676 BC when Pisa assumed control (for perhaps a hundred years) before Elis regained the upper hand (*c.* 580 BC) and eventually absorbed Pisa and Triphylia. Elis thereafter ran the festival with little interruption apart from a Spartan invasion in 400 BC (**3.27**) and an Arcadian invasion in 364 (**5.3**), both of which resulted in military action in the Altis itself.

Strabo and Pausanias on Elis, Pisa and the Olympic festival

Strabo wrote his *Geography* in the age of Augustus (31 BC–AD 14). In Book 8 he begins his description of Greece and at this point he turns his attention to Olympia in the north-west Peloponnese (8.3.30).

2.2 It remains for me to talk about Olympia and the transfer of everything to the Eleans. The temple is in **Pisatis**, less than three hundred **stades** from Elis. In front of it there stands a grove of wild olive trees where the stadium is. The Alpheios flows past on its way to the **Triphylian Sea** in the south-west. Originally it owed its fame to the **oracle of Olympian Zeus**, but when that ceased to function, the fame of the temple remained undiminished and achieved the considerable increase that we know, both because of the festival crowds, and because of the Olympic Games which have a crown for a prize and were considered sacred beyond all others.

Pisatis or Pisa, the district around Olympia. See map on p. 31. The town of Pisa has not been located and some doubt whether a town ever existed there.

stades a stade was approximately 200 metres; the total distance is therefore 60 km or about 37 miles.

Triphylian Sea the Ionian Sea to the west of the Peloponnese. Triphylia is that part of Elis south of the Alpheios river. See map on p. 31.

oracle of Olympian Zeus according to Pindar (*Olympian* 6) Iamos was given the power of prophecy at the hill of Cronos by Apollo, his father, and, when Herakles established the games, the place of prophecy became the summit of Zeus' great altar. There are few other references to the oracle at Olympia, but Sinn (chapter 3) links it with warfare and prophecy by seers connected to the priestly families of Olympia, where the prevalence of victory monuments as thank-offerings attests the military significance of the oracle. See **5.4** for Tisamenes, a member of the priestly family of the Iamidae.

It was embellished with a great number of offerings which were dedicated from all over Greece. They included a Zeus of beaten gold dedicated by **Kypselos**, tyrant of Corinth, but the greatest of them was the **statue of Zeus which Pheidias of Athens, son of Charmides, made out of ivory**. So big was it that even though the temple was very large, the artist appears to have got the proportions wrong by making it seated but almost touching the roof with its head so that it gives the impression that if it stood up, it would take the roof off the temple. Some recorded the measurement of the statue and Callimachus described it in an iambic poem. His nephew and collaborator Panainos the painter shared much of the work with Pheidias on the decoration of the statue when it came to colours and particularly the drapery. There are also many admirable paintings by him on show around the temple.

There is a story about Pheidias that when Panainos asked him what model he was going to use for the statue of Zeus he said that it was a Homeric model characterized by the words, 'He spoke and the son of Cronos gave a nod of assent with his dark brow, and his ambrosial hair fell in waves from the head of the immortal king as he made great Olympus tremble.' [*Iliad* 1.528]

[*Strabo praises Homer's depiction of gods*]

The Eleans are credited with particular responsibility for the magnificence of the temple at Olympia and the honour it enjoys. At the time of the **Trojan war** and even before that, they didn't enjoy prosperity since they had been brought low by the people of Pylos and later by Herakles when their king Augeas was overthrown. There is some evidence for this because they made the expedition to Troy with forty ships while Nestor and the Pylians had ninety. Later, after the **return of the Heraklids**, the opposite happened. The Aetolians returned with the Heraklids under the guidance of **Oxylos**, and formed a joint community with the Epeians in accordance with their ancient blood ties. They expanded hollow Elis, appropriated

---

Kypselos   first tyrant of Corinth, seventh century BC.

statue of Zeus which Pheidias of Athens, son of Charmides, made out of ivory   one of the seven wonders of the ancient world, actually of ivory and gold on a wooden frame. Pheidias' workshop, later converted into a church, has been found just outside the sacred area. Some fragments of ivory and moulds for the gold drapery were discovered there, as well as a cup inscribed 'I belong to Pheidias'.

Trojan war   *Iliad* 2.615–24 lists the contingent of four commanders with ten ships each from Elis (and lines 591–602 Nestor's contingent from Pylos, south of Elis).

return of the Heraklids   after the death of Herakles, Eurystheus, who had imposed the twelve labours on Herakles, continued to persecute his children, who took refuge in Athens. When Eurystheus attacked Athens, he was killed and the Heraklids then tried to re-establish themselves in the Peloponnese. Their first invasion was thwarted by a plague, but three generations later, their descendants successfully returned and took control of Argos, Sparta and Messenia.

Oxylos   he acted as guide for the Heraklids and helped them conquer the Peloponnese. In return he asked to be made king of Elis.

a large area of Pisatis and took control of Olympia. The Olympic competition is actually their invention and they celebrated the first Olympic Games. We should ignore the old accounts of the founding of the temple and the establishment of the games. Some say that **Herakles, one of the Idaean Daktyls**, was the founder, others that it was Herakles, son of Zeus and Alkmene, who was first to compete and win.

Such stories have many variations and not much credibility. More reliable is the account that from the first Olympiad, in which Coroebus of Elis won the *stadion*, up to the **26th**, the Eleans had control of the temple and the games. At the time of the Trojan war either there was no crown competition or it had no fame, and nor had any of the others which are famous nowadays. For **Homer makes no mention** of these, but does mention some different **funeral games**. Yet some people think he does mention the Olympics when he says that Augeas refused to hand over our victorious horses which had come in quest of prizes. They say that the people of Pisa took no part in the Trojan war because they were regarded as Zeus' sacred people. But only Elis and not Pisatis (where Olympia is) was ruled by Augeas at the time and the Olympic Games were not once celebrated in Elis, but always at Olympia; yet the games now in question appear to have happened in Elis where the debt was owed: 'for a great debt was owed him in divine Elis, four victorious horses.' [*Iliad* 11.698] Besides, this was not a crown competition (they were going to run for a tripod), but the Olympic competition was.

After the 26th Olympiad the people of Pisa recovered their territory and put on the games themselves, seeing that the games were becoming famous. At a later date Pisatis returned to Elean control and the organization of the Olympic games reverted to them too.

After the **final dissolution of Messenia**, the Spartans acted in alliance with the Eleans (the opposite of Nestor's descendants and the Arcadians who fought alongside the Messenians). So successful was their joint action that the whole country as far as Messenia was called Eleia and has remained so to this day, whereas the names of Pisatae, Triphylis and **Caucones** have disappeared.

Herakles, one of the Idaean Daktyls   these magic-working smiths are often considered to be the same as the Curetes who guarded the infant Zeus on Mount Ida in Crete. Their number and home vary in different accounts.

26th   676 BC. See glossary for the meanings of Olympiad.

Homer makes no mention   in *Iliad* 11 Nestor delivers a long speech about the conflict between Elis and Pylos (lines 670–761) in which he mentions his father sending a four-horse chariot to compete for a tripod in the games at Elis, but King Augeas kept the team and sent back the charioteer with an insult.

funeral games   for Patroclus (**1.3–8**).

final dissolution of Messenia   the Spartans had conquered Messenia by the late eighth or seventh century BC.

Caucones   a people who had once settled in the area of Triphylia.

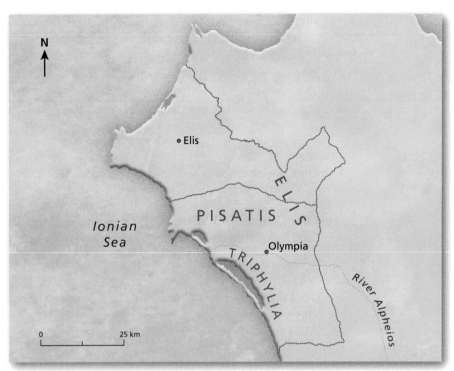

Elis, Pisatis and Triphylia.

When Pausanias visited the site of Pisa, he wrote, 'Of the wall or any other building there is no longer any trace, but vines were planted across the whole area where Pisa used to stand' (*Description of Greece* 6.22.1). He continues with a brief history of the relations between Elis and Pisa (6.22.2–4).

2.3   The people of Pisa brought disaster on themselves because of their hostility towards the Eleans and their eagerness to run the Olympic festival instead of the Eleans. At the **8th Olympiad** they brought in **Pheidon of Argos**, the most arrogant of tyrants in Greece, and they organized the games together with Pheidon. At the 34th Olympiad [644 BC] the people of Pisa and their king Pantaleon, son of Omphaleon, assembled an army from the local area and conducted the Olympic festival instead of the Eleans. These Olympiads and in addition the 104th [364 BC] which was run by the Arcadians are called 'anolympiads' by the Eleans and they do not record them in their list of Olympiads.

8th Olympiad   748 BC, probably a mistake for the 28th (668).

Pheidon of Argos   tyrant of Argos perhaps around 680–560 BC. Herodotus (*Histories* 6.127) says Pheidon removed the Elean organizers and conducted the festival himself. He also refers to Pheidon as most arrogant, but makes no mention of Pisa.

At the 48th Olympiad [588 BC] Damophon, son of Pantaleon, made the Eleans suspect that he was plotting against them. When they invaded Pisa with an army, he persuaded them by appeals and oaths to return home without taking action. When Pyrrhos, son of Pantaleon, became king after his brother Damophon, the people of Pisa on their own initiative entered upon a war with the Eleans … As it turned out Pisa and all her allies were laid waste by the Eleans.

1 Is there any agreement about the relations between Elis and Pisa in these two accounts?

2 Is there any indication of evaluation of the evidence in these accounts?

Pausanias (*Description of Greece* 5.8.6–5.9.1) gives the date at which each event was introduced into the festival programme (here in table form).

Square brackets indicate information supplied from elsewhere. Philostratus, who was writing a treatise on athletic training in the third century AD, includes a very similar list (*Gymnasticus* 12), omitting the equestrian events but otherwise, with a few exceptions, agreeing with Pausanias. Philostratus does add a few touches of colour by recording the big feet of Lygdamis (33rd Olympiad) or the boy runner who was fast enough to catch hares (46th Olympiad, when he has the first boys' *stadion*).

2.4

Date	Olympiad	Event	Winner
776 BC	1	foot race (*stadion*)	Koroebos of Elis
724	14	double *stadion* (*diaulos*)	Hypenos of Pisa
720	15	distance race (**dolichos**)	Akanthos of Sparta
708	18	pentathlon and wrestling	Lampis and Eurybatos, Spartans
688	23	boxing	Onomastos of Smyrna
680	25	four-horse chariot race (**tethrippon**)	Pagondas of Thebes
648	33	*pankration* for men and horse race (**kelēs**)	Lygdamis of Syracuse and Krauxidas of Krannon
632	37	boys' *stadion* and wrestling	Polyneikes of Elis and Hipposthenes of Sparta

… the translation omits Pausanias' list of the local allies of Pisa.

628	38	boys' pentathlon, immediately discontinued	Eutelidas of Sparta
616	41	boys' boxing	Philytas of Sybaris
520	65	race for men in armour (**hoplitodromos**)	Damaretos of Heraia
500	70	race for mule-cart (**apēnē**)	Thersios of Thessaly
496	71	race for mares (**kalpē**)	Pataikos of Dyme
444	84	*apene* and *kalpe* discontinued	
408	93	two-horse chariot race (**synoris**)	Evagoras of Elis
[396	96	heralds and trumpeters]	
384	99	chariots drawn by foals	Sybariades of Sparta
268	128	chariots and pairs of foals	Belistiche, a woman from Macedonia
256	131	single foals with rider	Tlepolemos of Lycia
200	145	boys' *pankration*	Phaidimos, an Aeolian from Troas

The order of events

Pausanias concludes his list of events with this observation about the order in which they took place (*Description of Greece* 5.9.3).

2.5 **In our day**, the order of events in the games, so that the sacrifices to the god are later than the pentathlon and the equestrian events […] contests, is the order established for them at the **77th Olympiad**. Before this they held the competition for men and horses alike on the same day. **On that occasion** the *pankration* was prolonged into the night because they weren't called to compete on time. This was caused by the horse racing and even more so by the competition in the pentathlon. Kallias of Athens was victorious in the *pankration*. From that time on, however, the pentathlon and the horse races were not going to impede the *pankration*.

In our day   second century AD.

…   some have assumed there is a gap in the text here, partly on grammatical grounds and partly to interpret the meaning of the Greek. This sentence has caused much debate, and there are possible alternative translations to the one given here which assumes that the main sacrifice to Zeus is meant (rather than individual sacrifices by athletes) and that the pentathlon and equestrian events preceded it.

77th Olympiad, On that occasion   472 BC.

- This passage in Pausanias is perhaps our most important evidence for the order of events at the festival from 468 BC, but its meaning has been subject to various interpretations. What conclusions can you draw from the translation offered here?

In Plutarch's *Moralia* 639a there is a discussion of events in the Pythian Games at Delphi, but with some comparison with Olympia.

2.6 And so which of the events would one say was the first? Was it the *stadion* as at Olympia? [...] Here, with us, they bring in the competitors in the order of each discipline, after the boy wrestlers, the adult wrestlers, the boxers after the boxers and likewise the pankratiasts. But there, they summon the men only when the boys have completed their competitions.

1 Which order of events indicated in this passage would seem more logical, the one at the Pythian or the Olympic Games? Why?
2 Could the order of events have changed by Plutarch's day?

Trumpeters and heralds

Trumpeters and heralds were important for the organization of the games. We are told that trumpeters summoned the athletes and indicated the last lap in horse racing, while heralds proclaimed silence (essential for religious rites) and announced the contestants. They probably made a whole variety of announcements and would have been essential for conveying information to the large crowd in the absence of a public address system (e.g. **6.14**). Their competition was not included in the programme of events until 396 BC. They are mentioned by Pausanias (*Description of Greece* 5.22.1).

... there is a gap of uncertain length in the text at this point.

2.7 In the Altis near the entrance that leads into the stadium is an altar on which the Eleans sacrifice to none of the gods, but it is the custom for the trumpeters and heralds to stand on it while competing.

The festival programme

The following timetable is perhaps how the festival was organized around the middle of the fifth century BC. The order of events is by no means certain. For the preliminaries in Elis, see **3.20**.

Day 1

Taking of the oath (**3.18**) in the council chamber (**Bouleuterion**).
Competition for heralds and trumpeters (introduced in 396 BC).
Vetting the athletes?

Day 2: Equestrian events and pentathlon

Equestrian events probably began soon after sunrise (**4.6**, **4.12**) and would have required several hours for all the competitions to be completed.
The duration of the pentathlon is difficult to estimate without a clear idea of the number of competitors or method of deciding the winner (see p. 72).

Day 3: Rites for Pelops

Great Sacrifice: the high point of the festival, followed by feasting on the meat from the sacrifice.
Boys' contests?

Day 4

Track events.
'Heavy' events.
Hoplitodromos.
The track events were probably held in the order *dolichos* (**6.4–6**), *stadion* (**6.1**) and *diaulos* (**6.3**), as suggested by Polites' achievement (**6.11**).

Day 5

Awards ceremony and banquet for the victorious athletes (**8.11**).

3 Olympia: the site and the festival

> There are many things to see in Greece, and amazing things to hear, but it is particularly the rites at Eleusis and the games at Olympia that receive divine care.
>
> Pausanias, *Description of Greece* 5.9.6

The site

Olympia is situated in the north-west Peloponnese, about ten miles or so from the sea (see map, p. 31). It lies at the foot of a conical hill called the hill of Cronos on the northern edge of the flood plain of the 'large and very attractive' (Pausanias) River Alpheios and close to the confluence with its tributary, the Kladeos. Its geographical position is not the most convenient for access, but there were overland routes from other parts of Greece, and it was relatively easy to approach from the sea. The site, however, was at risk from flooding and seismic activity. The Kladeos swept away part of the gymnasium in late antiquity and the major buildings suffered total collapse after severe earthquakes in AD 522 and 551. After that, the site was abandoned, gradually buried under silt and not rediscovered until the eighteenth century.

The sanctuary evolved from simple beginnings into a massive complex with many amenities and spectacularly impressive architecture and art works, especially Pheidias' great statue of Zeus (**2.2**). As a religious centre, Olympia would have been visited at other times as well as during the five-day period of the games held once every four years. Pausanias mentions a large number of altars dedicated to numerous deities, all of which had their own rites to be observed, but his statement that daily offerings were made at the altar of Zeus is the clearest indication that there was constant activity on the site. At the time of the games, the sanctuary must have been very busy. The large number of spectators, camping at or near the site, must have attracted numerous tradesmen who took the opportunity to sell their wares. Dio Chrysostom (see **8.25**) mentions them at the Ismian Games, along with sophists and their bickering students, historians, poets, jugglers, fortune-tellers and lawyers. There appears to be a separation of the religious and athletic sections of the site, although there are indications that strict segregation of functions was not observed (**5.3**).

The Altis

The sacred area of the sanctuary was called the Altis, a term which Pausanias tells us was a local variant of *alsos*, the Greek for a sacred grove or precinct. In

Pausanias' guide to the site, the great temple of Zeus by the local architect Libon (finished in 456 BC) is the first building he describes. Impressed by its size, he records its dimensions as 20 metres high, 28 metres broad and 70 metres long, but it is the sculpture of the pediments and metopes, and the great cult statue by Pheidias (added two decades later) which attract most of his attention. Pausanias also mentions Pheidias' workshop, which has been identified just outside the Altis.

Just to the north of the temple of Zeus was the **Pelopion**, a precinct sacred to Pelops containing statues and a grove of trees within an enclosing wall. Here Pausanias reports that yearly sacrifices of a black ram were still being made to the hero in the second century AD. Attempts to link the hero shrine to the foundation myth have not been supported by the archaeology, which has not only failed to yield any evidence for a cult going back to Mycenean times, but has located a dark area of ash across the northern Altis that extends beneath part of the Pelopion and is dated to the seventh century BC, suggesting that the Pelopion postdates this level. North of Pelops' shrine was the temple of Hera, the oldest on the site and originally with wooden columns, one of which still survived in the back porch in Pausanias' day. The contents of the temple mentioned by Pausanias include a table which held the crowns for the winners, and the discus of Iphitos (**10.1**).

The great altar of Zeus stood just to the east of the Pelopion and temple of Hera. It was constructed from the ashes of thighs of sacrificial animals and with ash from the **Prytaneion** (the administrative hall), mixed with water from the Alpheios. According to Pausanias it was 6 metres high. In the early days of the sanctuary, it seems from Philostratus that there was a close link with the race track which came right up to the altar (**3.2**). Pausanias briefly mentions two other buildings, the Metroon or temple to Rhea, the mother of Zeus, and the Philippeion, built by Philip II of Macedonia to celebrate his victory over the Greeks at Chaironeia in 338 BC. There were many other dedicatory offerings, most conspicuously in the form of statues, and on a terrace at the foot of the hill of Cronos various cities built treasuries, small temple-shaped buildings to house offerings; one was used to store three discuses in Pausanias' day (**5.10**).

Several colonnades, welcome providers of shade, were constructed in the fourth century BC. The so-called Echo Colonnade (*c.* 340–330) at the eastern edge of the Altis separated the sacred area from the stadium. Unfortunately, it is difficult to tell from the archaeological traces what relationship existed between the first stadium and the altar of Zeus, but it did reach into the area of the Altis. How significant the changes were for the relationship of games and cult remains a matter for debate. The 70 or so different cults mentioned by Pausanias had little to do with either the games or Zeus. In the stadium itself there was an altar of Demeter (**3.3**).

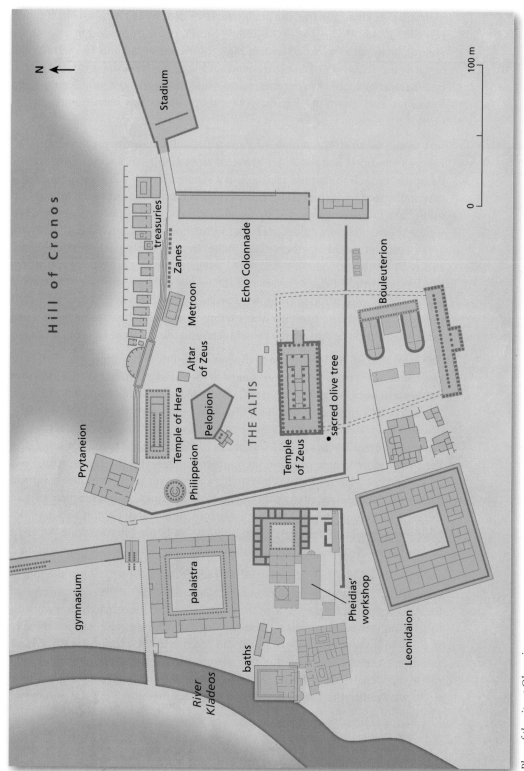

Plan of the site at Olympia.

Hill of Cronos

N

Stadium

treasuries

Zanes

Metroon

Echo Colonnade

Bouleuterion

Altar
of Zeus

Temple of Hera

Pelopion

THE ALTIS

Prytaneion

Philippeion

Temple
of Zeus

sacred olive tree

Pheidias'
workshop

Leonidaion

palaistra

gymnasium

baths

River
Kladeos

100 m

0

Administrative and other buildings

The Prytaneion is actually inside the Altis, in the north-west corner, next to the entrance opposite the gymnasium. Here the celebratory banquet for victorious athletes (**8.11**) was held, and one room was occupied by the hearth of the sanctuary with its sacred fire (**10.11**).

The Bouleuterion or council chamber lay just outside the southern entrance to the Altis (see the plan of the site on p. 38). The Olympic Council (**Boulē**), mentioned as fining **Hellānodikai** (**3.16**), probably met here, and the Olympic oath was sworn here (**3.18**), probably in the central square room. The apsidal wings may have held records. Pausanias mentions a priest's house, but it is unclear whether it had any further function. Where the *Hellanodikai* were housed during the festival is unknown.

Pausanias tells us that the Leonidaion was opposite the processional entrance to the Altis. It takes its name from its donor Leonidas, said by Pausanias to be a local, but known from an inscription to be from the Aegean island of Naxos. The building was a splendid structure with a central courtyard or garden surrounded by four wings. Pausanias records that in his day it was used as accommodation for the Roman governors of Greece. It certainly must have offered a more comfortable experience for the privileged visitor to the site than that enjoyed by the crowds (**3.5–8**). **Stoas** (colonnades) were a common feature of Greek civic architecture, providing covered walkways where shelter could be sought from sun or rain. A stoa at the south of the site provided a place for spectators to watch competitors make their way to the hippodrome, where there was another, the stoa of Agnaptus (named after the architect).

There were other improvements related to the games. Baths for the athletes were available from the fifth century BC, a facility improved and developed over the years. A *palaistra* (third century BC) and gymnasium (second century BC) were built to the west of the Altis. These were probably reserved for the competitors to practise in during the games, but they offered a permanent amenity for athletes, spectators and visitors (**3.1**). The hippodrome is described on pp. 56–8. The most important structure was the stadium, built in its present position perhaps in the mid-fifth century BC (at any rate, earlier than the mid-fourth-century Echo Colonnade).

The gymnasium and *palaistra*

Pausanias makes brief references to the gymnasium and *palaistra* in *Description of Greece* 5.15.8 and 6.21.2–3.

3.1   In this gymnasium are running tracks and wrestling grounds for the athletes. (5.15.8)

In the gymnasium at Olympia pentathletes and runners are accustomed to exercise. … There is another smaller enclosed space on the left of the entrance to the gymnasium where there are wrestling grounds (*palaistrai*) for the athletes. Next to the wall of the colonnade on the east side of the gymnasium are the lodgings for athletes, facing south-west. On the other side of the Kladeos, a mound of earth surrounded by a stone wall is the tomb of Oenomaus and beyond the memorial are the ruins of buildings where they say Oenomaus' mares had their stables. (6.21.2–3)

> 1 Does Pausanias make a clear distinction between the gymnasium and the *palaistra* and what they were used for?
> 2 Look at the layout of these buildings on the plan of Olympia. What events does each seem designed to accommodate?

The origin of the stadium

Philostratus prefaces his discussion of the origin of events by stating that he used the evidence supplied by the Eleans because it was the most accurate. The following extract is his account of the origin of the *stadion* (*Gymnasticus* 5). Archaeologists have discovered that the early stadium was located about 75 metres further west than the one we see. Traces of it were found beneath the later Echo Colonnade, but it did not reach the altar of Zeus.

3.2

The origin of the *stadion* is as follows. When the Eleans made their usual sacrifices, the offerings were placed upon the altar, but fire was not yet introduced among them. The runners were a stade distance from the altar in front of which stood a priest holding a torch and acting as judge. The winner set fire to the offerings and went away as Olympic victor.

The 'Hidden Entrance' to the stadium at Olympia, third century BC.

> • What does this section of Philostratus tell us about the original relationship between the stadium and the altar of Zeus?

Pausanias describes the stadium in *Description of Greece* 6.20.8.

3.3   At the end of **the statues**, which were made with the athletes' fines, is what they call the Hidden Entrance, through which the *Hellanodikai* and the competitors enter the stadium. The stadium is a bank of earth and a seat has been made on it for those presiding over the games. Directly opposite the *Hellanodikai* is an altar of white stone. On this altar sits a woman, the priestess of Demeter Chamyne, to watch the Olympic competitions. Different women are appointed to this office by the Eleans from time to time. They do not prevent **unmarried girls** from watching. Towards the end of the stadium, where the starting line for the *stadion* race has been made, is the tomb of **Endymion**, as the Eleans claim.

> • What problems can you think of that would make the attendance of unmarried girls at the Olympics unlikely?

In Chariton's first-century AD novel *Callirhoe* (6.2), Chaireas and Dionysios are going to trial to determine which should be husband of the outstandingly beautiful Callirhoe.

3.4   As at the Olympics it is possible to see the athletes arriving at the stadium with an escort, so it was with them. A crowd of most distinguished Persians escorted Dionysios and the ordinary people escorted Chaireas. There were countless prayers and cheers from the supporters on either side, shouting, 'You are the better man. You will win.' The prize was not wild olive wreath nor apples nor pine, but supreme beauty, for which even the gods might have justly competed.

> 1 How would the 'Hidden Entrance' contribute to the drama of the occasion?
> 2 Would entry into the stadium have been similar to any of the entrances made in modern sports?
> 3 What features described by Pausanias are visible in the photograph of the stadium (p. 42)?
> 4 Why are the rivals for Callirhoe's hand compared to Olympic athletes?

the statues   the *Zānes* (see **3.28**).

unmarried girls   Pausanias does not offer any explanation for this exception and it has been called into question.

Endymion   king of Elis, who set his sons a race for the throne which was won by Epeios (hence Eleans are also called Epeians). He was loved by Selene (the moon goddess), and they had 50 daughters according to Pausanias. Zeus allowed him to sleep for ever while retaining his youth.

The experience of spectators

Depictions of spectators are rare in Greek art, but there are some graphic descriptions of their responses. The description of the chariot race in Sophocles' *Electra* (**4.12**) mentions the audience's reaction to Orestes' supposed crash (lines 749–50), and the description of the argument among the spectators in Homer's *Iliad* (book **23**, lines 448–98) shows how heated spectators could become. In **1.8**, the crowd cheers Odysseus and shouts advice. In **5.5** Automedes is urged on by the roar of the crowd as he launches a javelin and in **7.34** the wild celebrations over Arrichion's victory are very like the emotional reactions of some modern spectators when the team they support achieves something special. See **1.6** for a unique representation of spectators on a vase-painting and **7.18** for a remarkable change of attitude.

In the second century AD Arrian wrote down the oral teachings (*Discourses*) of the Stoic philosopher Epictetus. In the following passage Epictetus is talking about the capacity for overcoming hardships. You go to Olympia, he says, to see the work of Pheidias (the gold and ivory statue of Zeus). The hardships he mentions at Olympia are probably only experienced at the Olympic Games (*Discourses of Epictetus* 1.6.26–8).

The stadium at Olympia. Halfway along the bank for spectators on the left is the altar for the priestess of Demeter Chamyne, and opposite this are the seats for the Hellanodikai. *The starting line across the track is visible in the foreground, and there is another at the far end.*

3.5   Some harsh and unpleasant things happen in life – and don't they happen at Olympia? Don't you suffer from the heat? Aren't you packed together in a crowd? Don't you find bathing a bad experience? Don't you get drenched every time it rains? Don't you get a bellyful of noise, shouting and other irritations? But I think you put up with and endure all these things when you set them against the remarkable nature of the spectacle.

> This anecdote told by Aelian in the early third century AD gives a similar picture of harsh conditions at Olympia (*Historical Miscellany* 14.18).

3.6   A man from Chios was angry with his slave and said, 'I will not put you on the mill, but I'll take you to Olympia.' Apparently he thought it was a much harsher punishment to be baked by the sun as a spectator at Olympia than to be handed over to the mill and grind corn.

> Diogenes Laertius has even worse to report about Thales, the sixth-century BC philosopher (*Lives and Opinions of Eminent Philosophers* 1.39).

3.7   The philosopher died while watching an athletic competition on account of the heat of the sun, thirst and weakness, since he was old by then.

> Just as flies can be a major source of irritation to campers in some regions today, this short extract from Pausanias (*Description of Greece* 5.14.1) reveals that they could be a menace at Olympia.

3.8   They say that when Herakles son of Alkmene was sacrificing at Olympia, the flies became really irritating. And so, either because he found out for himself or was informed by someone else, he sacrificed to Zeus the Averter of Flies and in this way the flies were diverted to the other side of the Alpheios. The Eleans are said to sacrifice in the same way to Zeus Averter of Flies, driving the flies away from Olympia.

> The following anecdote about Pythagoras incidentally reveals the presence of traders, and interestingly places the highest value on spectators (Diogenes Laertius, *Lives and Opinions of Eminent Philosophers* 8.8).

3.9   [Pythagoras is said] to have compared life to the crowd assembled at a festival: just as some go to a festival to compete, some to trade, but the best go as spectators, so in life some are servile by nature and pursue fame and personal profit, whereas philosophers pursue the truth.

> • Do you think that spectators at festivals make a good illustration of the superiority of a contemplative life?

Aelian (*Historical Miscellany* 4.9) tells a story about Plato sharing a tent at Olympia, but not revealing his true identity to the strangers he was sharing with. It was only when they later visited him in Athens that they discovered he was the famous Plato.

3.10   Plato, son of Ariston, shared a tent at Olympia with some men he didn't know and who didn't know him. He won them over and made them firm friends by his sociability, getting along with them simply and spending the days with them all. As a result, they were delighted to have met him. He never mentioned the Academy or Socrates, but the only thing he revealed to them was that his name was Plato.

Plutarch (*Life of Themistocles* 17) mentions the appearance of Themistocles at the Olympiad following the battle of Salamis in 480 BC when the Greeks had defeated the invading Persian fleet. Themistocles had played a significant part in the success of the Greek fleet.

3.11   During the subsequent Olympic festival when Themistocles entered the stadium, those present are said to have paid no attention to the competitors, but to have looked at him all day long, pointing him out to strangers with admiration and with rounds of applause. He was naturally delighted and admitted to his friends that he was receiving the fruits of his labours on behalf of Greece.

> 1   How similar are these conditions to those experienced at a modern pop festival?
> 2   Are there any other inconveniences not mentioned here which must have been part of the experience of spectators at Olympia?

In Lucian's *Anacharsis* 12, Solon gives a different perspective on the spectators' experience. Here he is trying to convince Anacharsis of the value of athletics.

3.12   Anacharsis, if it had been the right time for the Olympics, the Isthmian Games or the Panathenaia, what actually happens there would have taught you that we do not enthusiastically pursue these activities to no purpose. One cannot in conversation make you appreciate the pleasure in what happens there as much as if you were sitting in the midst of the spectators and seeing with your own eyes the excellent performances of the men, the beauty of their bodies, their amazing condition, formidable skill, unbeatable strength, daring, ambition to succeed, indomitable resolve and their indescribable will to win. I am certain that you would not have stopped expressing approval, shouting out and applauding.

> •   Does Lucian make Solon identify the essential ingredients of spectator sports?

Competition at Olympia was tough, and defeat was not a pleasant experience. Pindar describes a defeated athlete as 'bitten by disaster' as he 'scuttles down back-alleys away from his enemies' (*Pythian* 8.86–7). In this extract from Arrian's *Discourses of Epictetus* (*On Cynicism* 3.22.51–3), the philosopher uses the Olympic Games as an illustration of the importance of recognizing one's limitations.

3.13   Do you see how you are going to undertake such a thing? First take a mirror, look at your shoulders and observe well your lower torso and thighs. You are intending to enter the Olympic Games, my dear man, not some wretched, chilly little competition.

At the Olympic Games it isn't possible just to accept defeat and leave. But first, with the whole world watching (not just Athenians or Spartans or the people of Nikopolis), a man has to suffer disgrace. Then if he withdraws without good reason, he must even be flogged, and before the flogging he has to have endured the thirst, the scorching heat and mouthfuls of sand. Take more careful thought. **Know yourself!**

> 1 What particular event that one should not enter at the Olympics does Epictetus seem to have in mind?
> 2 Is Epictetus referring to the period athletes spent in Elis before the games?
> 3 What does this passage suggest about the actual competitors at Olympia?
> 4 What does it tell us about shame in Greek culture?

Officials and judges at Olympia

The *Hellanodikai* organized the Olympic Games and wore purple for their time in office, which made them easy to identify, as Lucian makes Anacharsis comment (**7.38**). They were assisted by various officials and possibly supervised by an Olympic Council (*Boule*) (**3.16**).

The impartiality and integrity of the judges

In this extract from Herodotus (*Histories* 2.160), the Egyptians question whether the judges from Elis can be impartial when there is a competitor also from Elis.

Know yourself   this famous maxim attributed to the Spartan sage Chilon was inscribed in the temple of Apollo at Delphi. Plato (*Charmides* 164d) says that it is equivalent to advising self-control, which here is manifested as recognition of one's limitations. For a Greek athlete, training the body and disciplining the mind through self-control were both part of their practice. The Greek *askēsis* (training) came later to be used for monks or hermits, from where we get the English word 'ascetic'.

3.14   In Egypt during the reign of **Psammis** messengers from Elis arrived boasting that of all men they had established the games at Olympia in the most equitable and fair way. They imagined that not even the Egyptians, the wisest of men, would have devised anything comparable. When the delegation from Elis reached Egypt and explained the reason for their arrival, this king called together those with the reputation of being the wisest of the Egyptians. In response to questions from the assembled Egyptians, the Eleans said that they were taking all the appropriate measures with regard to the games. When they had given a full account, they said that they had come to find out whether the Egyptians could come up with anything more equitable than these arrangements. After some deliberation, the Egyptians asked the Eleans if their own citizens took part in the games. When they declared that anyone of their own citizens or other Greeks who wished was equally entitled to take part, the Egyptians said that in making this rule, they had failed to be completely fair because there was no way they would not favour a competitor from their own city at the expense of a foreigner. But they told them that if they really wanted to establish a just institution and for that reason had come to Egypt, they should establish games for foreign competitors and not allow any Eleans to compete.

> In Plutarch's *Sayings of Kings and Generals* he records the following response by the Spartan king Agis (190c–d).

3.15   When the Eleans were praised for conducting the Olympic games fairly, he said, 'What is remarkable about what they do, if on one day in four years they make use of justice?' And when people persisted with their praises, he said, 'What is remarkable if they fairly make use of a fair thing, justice?'

> 1   Are there any modern Olympic sports where the impartiality of the judges has been called into question? How does the International Olympic Committee try to ensure impartiality?
>
> 2   Spartans were renowned for their pithy comments (hence the word 'laconic' from Laconia, the region where they lived). Does this anecdote tell us anything about the reputation of the ancient Olympics?

> Among the statues of successful athletes Pausanias describes at Olympia, that of Eupolemus is interesting for the light it sheds on judging and the authority of the *Boule* (*Description of Greece* 6.3.7).

Psammis   Psammetichus II ruled Egypt for six years, 595–589 BC.

3.16   Daedalus of Sicyon made the statue of Eupolemus of Elis. The inscription on it reveals that Eupolemus won a victory in the men's sprint (*stadion*) at Olympia, and he also had two crowns for the pentathlon in the **Pythian Games** and another at the Nemean Games. Also there is a story about Eupolemus that three judges (*Hellanodikai*) were standing on the track and while two of them gave victory to Eupolemus, the third gave it to Leon of **Ambracia**. Leon then got the Olympic Council (*Boule*) to impose a fine on each of the judges who judged Eupolemus the winner.

> • What information does this incident give us about the system of judging at Olympia?

In this extract, Pausanias comments on the statue of Troilus at Olympia (*Description of Greece* 6.1.4–5).

3.17   But at the same time that he was *Hellanodikēs*, it so happened that he won victories with horses in the two-horse chariot race (*synoris*) and with colts in the chariot race. His victories were in the 102nd Olympiad [372 BC], but after this occasion the Eleans made a law preventing any of the *Hellanodikai* from entering horses in future. Lysippus made the statue of Troilus.

3.18

The Olympic oath

In his catalogue of the statues representing Zeus at Olympia, Pausanias describes the particularly awesome statue of Zeus Horkios (God of Oaths) in the council chamber (Bouleuterion) (*Description of Greece* 5.24.9–11).

Of all the statues of Zeus, the one in the council chamber (Bouleuterion) is particularly designed to strike terror into cheats. His additional name is Horkios (God of Oaths) and he holds a thunderbolt in each hand. Next to this statue it is the custom for athletes, their fathers and brothers, and also their trainers to swear an oath on pieces cut from a sacrificed boar that they will engage in no malpractice to harm the Olympic competition. The athletes in the men's events also take this additional oath that over ten months in succession they have perfected themselves completely in their training. Oaths are also sworn by all those who judge the status of boys or foals (of the competing horses) that they will make a decision in fairness and without bribes, and that they will carefully keep secret everything about those who are approved or not. I forgot to ask what they are accustomed to do with the boar

---

Pythian Games   at Delphi.

Ambracia   a city in north-west Greece.

---

after the athletes have taken the oath since in earlier times at least it was the custom in relation to sacrificial victims that one on which an oath was taken was not for **human consumption**. *... There is a bronze plaque in front of the feet of Zeus Horkios with elegiac verses written on it, meant to instil fear in those who break their oath.*

The practice of swearing an oath was resurrected at the Olympic Games of 1920 in Antwerp, where the oath was sworn by a Belgian competitor on behalf of all. This was adapted in later years, and in 2000 a reference to doping was added. The oath now reads:

In the name of all the competitors I promise that we shall take part in these Olympic Games, respecting and abiding by the rules which govern them, committing ourselves to a sport without doping and without drugs, in the true spirit of sportsmanship, for the glory of sport and the honour of our teams.

The first officials' oath was introduced in 1972:

In the name of all the judges and officials, I promise that we shall officiate in these Olympic Games with complete impartiality, respecting and abiding by the rules which govern them in the true spirit of sportsmanship.

- Compare the modern oath with what Pausanias tells us of the ancient oath. What might make these oaths effective?
- What other steps were taken to curb cheating?
- Does anything surprise you about the oaths?

Changes to the number of officials

In his account of the development of the Olympic Games (*Description of Greece* 5.9.4–6) Pausanias catalogues the changes made to the panel of supervisors or judges. Because it is difficult to make precise distinctions between the names used for officials, they are transliterated rather than translated.

3.19 They think that the rules for the *agōnothetai* are not the same in our day as those which were established from the beginning. Iphitos himself organized the games on his own, and after Iphitos the descendants of Oxylos organized them in the same way.

---

human consumption Pausanias refers to a passage in Homer, *Iliad* 19.266–8 where a boar on which an oath was taken was thrown into the sea after the sacrifice.

agōnothetai literally, 'those who set out the competition'.

[580 BC] At the 50th Olympiad the organization of the games was entrusted to two men chosen by lot from among all the citizens of Elis and for a long time after that the number of *agonothetai* remained two.

[400 BC] At the 95th Olympiad they appointed nine *Hellanodikai*. Three of them were entrusted with the horse racing, three others with overseeing the pentathlon, while the remaining events were under the supervision of the rest.

[392 BC] In the second Olympiad after this a tenth ***athlothetēs*** was appointed in addition.

[368 BC] At the time of the 103rd Olympiad there were twelve tribes in Elis and one man from each tribe became a ***Hellānodikēs***. When they were at war with the Arcadians, they were put under pressure and lost part of their territory along with all the demes in the annexed area.

[364 BC] Consequently at the 104th Olympiad, with the tribes reduced to eight, the number of *Hellanodikai* chosen was equal to the number of tribes.

[348 BC] At the 108th Olympiad the number of men went back up to ten and from this time to our own day it has remained constant.

Hellanodikai in action

> In the following extract Pausanias describes the training of the *Hellanodikai* at Elis, their ten months in the *Hellanodikaion*, and their supervision of the athletes during the period of training (*Description of Greece* 6.23–4, with omissions).

3.20   One of the things worth mentioning in Elis is the old gymnasium. In this gymnasium the custom is for them to do everything they normally do with athletes before they go to Olympia. Tall plane trees grow between the race tracks inside a wall. The whole of this enclosed area is called *xystos* (scraped) because every day it was the practice of Herakles son of Amphitryo to scrape away the prickly plants growing there. There is a separate track for competitors in the foot races, called 'sacred' by the locals, and a different one where runners and pentathletes practise their running.

In the gymnasium is an area called *plethrion*. In it the *Hellanodikai* match the athletes according to their age and level of experience, and they arrange the bouts for wrestling.

[*Pausanias mentions altars of gods and Achilles' cenotaph.*]

There is another gymnasium with a smaller enclosed area which is next to the larger one and called 'square' because of its shape. Here places for wrestling practice (*palaistrai*) are created for the competitors and here too they pair off

---

athlothetēs   literally, 'one who sets out the prizes'.

athletes no longer wrestling for boxing with softer boxing straps (*himantes*). Also dedicated here is one of the two statues which were made for Zeus from the fine paid by Sōsander of Smyrna and Polyctor of Elis.

There is also a third gymnasium called *maltho* because of the softness of the ground and it is made available for **ephebes** for the entire duration of the festival.

[*Pausanias describes statues in the gymnasium and the place where speeches were made before he tells the story of the Street of Silence.*]

The other way from the gymnasium to the **agora** leads to a building called the *Hellanodikaion*. It is beyond the grave of Achilles. This is the route the *Hellanodikai* normally use to get to the gymnasium. They enter before sunrise to match the runners, at midday for the pentathlon and all the events called 'heavy'.

The agora of Elis is not like those in **Ionia** and all the Greek cities near Ionia. It is built in an older style with **stoas** set apart from each other and with streets between them. The name of the agora in our day is 'hippodrome' and it is where the locals train their horses. Of the stoas, the one to the south is constructed in **Doric style** and the columns divide it into **three sections**. The *Hellanodikai* spend most days here. Next to the columns in the open space of the agora they make themselves altars to Zeus, but there aren't a great many since they are easily dismantled, being of rough and ready construction. The Hellanodikaion is at the end of this stoa, on the left if you enter the agora by the stoa, and there is a street separating it from the agora. In this Hellanodikaion those who have been selected to serve as *Hellanodikai* live for ten consecutive months and are instructed by the *nomophylakes* in everything they need to do for the games.

At the end of Book 5 of Philostratus' *Life of Apollonius of Tyana* (5.43), as Apollonius is about to leave Egypt, he delivers this speech to his followers.

---

himantes   the thin leather straps boxers used to wind round their hands and wrists, called 'soft' to distinguish them from the 'sharp' gloves introduced in the fourth century BC. See **7.25, 26**.

maltho   Greek for soft is *malthakos* or *malakos*.

ephebes   youths mature enough for military training (at Athens, aged 18–20).

agora   the market place and focal point of the city.

heavy   i.e. combat sports, boxing, wrestling, *pankration*.

Ionia   an area settled by Greeks on the west coast of what is now Turkey.

stoas   colonnades.

Doric style   the architectural 'order' or style used for many Greek temples such as the Parthenon in Athens or the temples of Zeus and Hera at Olympia.

three sections   this stoa apparently had three rows of columns, two of which were internal, dividing the building into three long aisles.

nomophylakes   'guardians of the law', about whom nothing else is known.

3.21 Gentlemen, I must make an Olympic announcement to you. An announcement at Olympia would be like this. When the Olympic Games come round, the Eleans train the athletes for thirty days in Elis itself. At the Pythian or Isthmian Games when they have gathered them together, the Delphians and Corinthians say, 'Go to the stadium and become men capable of winning.' But when they go to Olympia, the Eleans address the athletes like this: 'If you have trained hard enough to be worthy of going to Olympia and there has been nothing slack or demeaning in your work, go with confidence. But those who have not practised like this, go where you like.'

> 1 What do these passages tell us about the preparations of athletes for the Olympic Games?
> 2 The 30-day training period is not attested earlier. Judging by **2.4**, when do you think it may have been introduced?
> 3 Why would a selection process be important at Olympia?

After mentioning the origin of wrestling and the *pankration* from their usefulness in war, Philostratus offers some insights into the practice of these events (*Gymnasticus* 11).

3.22 For while the competition at Olympia is terrible, the training seems even more gruelling. When it comes to the light events, the runner of the *dolichos* practises for perhaps eight or ten stades and the pentathlete practises one of the three and the runners practise either the *diaulos* or the *stadion*, or both. What terrible thing arises from such pursuits? None. For the method of training is the same whether the Eleans or others are conducting it.

The heavier athlete is trained by the Eleans at the time of year when the sun bakes the mud in the Arcadian valley, and he endures dust hotter than the sand of Ethiopia and bears it, starting at midday. And given that these things are so painful, the wrestling is the event of greatest endurance. For when it is time for the boxer to enter the stadium, he will stand toe to toe, suffering and inflicting injuries, but during training he will exhibit a shadow of the contest. The *pankratiast* will compete using all the techniques of the event, but he practises different techniques at different times, while wrestling is the same in the preliminaries and in the competition. Each bout provides experience of how much he knows and what he is capable of. It is correctly called 'stooped' since even the upright stance in wrestling is bent over (see **7.3**). This is the reason why the Eleans crown the most well trained and only from among those who trained.

dolichos see Chapter 6 for the different races.

Pausanias has described the temple of Hera in the Altis and the Heraia, or games in honour of Hera, conducted by 16 women (see **8.54**). At the end of his discussion of the origin of the 16, he adds this comment on purification (*Description of Greece* 5.16.8).

3.23 Whatever the appointed tasks for the Sixteen Women or the *Hellanodikai*, they perform none before they are purified with a pig suitable for purification and water. Their purification happens at the spring Piera. The way to reach the spring Piera is to take the road on the plain from Olympia to Elis.

This story from Herodotus, *Histories* 5.22.1–2 shows the *Hellanodikai* at work vetting the nationality of the athletes hoping to compete.

3.24 I personally happen to know that these **descendants of Perdiccas** are actually Greeks, as they themselves claim, and I will prove that they are Greeks in **a later account**. Besides, those who organize the games of the Greeks at Olympia recognized that this was the case. When Alexander decided to compete and came down to enter, the Greeks who were going to race against him prevented him by claiming that the games were not for foreign competitors, but Greeks. But when Alexander proved he was an **Argive**, he was judged to be Greek. He took part in the *stadion* and tied for first place.

Pausanias mentions two cases of the assessment of the age of athletes (*Description of Greece* 6.14.1–2).

3.25 Pherias of Aegina … was excluded from the competition at the 78th Olympiad [468 BC] because he was thought altogether young and was considered not yet qualified to wrestle. At the next Olympiad, when he was admitted into the boys' competition, he won the wrestling. Nikasylos of Rhodes had a different experience at Olympia, absolutely unlike that of Pherias. He was 18 years old and excluded from the boys' competition by the Eleans, but won the men's competition and was proclaimed victor.

Fines and punishments

The use of flogging seems to have been widespread in athletics. We hear of rod bearers (*rhabdouchoi*) who Thucydides says inflicted the punishment on Lichas (**3.27**), and whip-bearers (**mastigophoroi**) who are mentioned by Lucian in **7.2**. Indeed, vase-paintings regularly show either judge or trainer equipped with a

---

descendants of Perdiccas   i.e. Macedonians.

a later account   see Herodotus, *Histories* 8.137 for the full story.

Argive   Perdiccas was expelled from Argos with his two brothers, seven generations earlier.

(forked) rod to punish transgressions (**7.4**, **7.6**, **7.35**) and Herodotus (**6.7**) tells us that runners were flogged for a false start. Epictetus comments that if a competitor withdraws without good reason, he is flogged (**3.13**). Aelian even mentions a trainer called Hippomachus flogging a wrestler for lack of technique (**8.34**). A fragmentary bronze tablet found at Olympia which seems to contain a list of rules has a line forbidding punishment to the head, which presumably refers to flogging. A free citizen would not put up with being flogged under any other circumstances, since it was the punishment for slaves. Besides, athletes were naked and their flesh thus more exposed to lesions from the lash. Why were they willing to be subjected to such a form of discipline? Was it a test of their manhood, manifested through indifference to suffering?

> Philostratus, in criticizing the strict regime of training for athletes, makes a contrast with the practice of the *Hellanodikai* at Olympia, and the consequent penalties for not conforming to their rules (*Gymnasticus* 54).

3.26   The *Hellanodikai* do not train by a pre-ordained system, but everything is done impromptu to suit the moment and the whip threatens the trainer if he does anything contrary to their instructions. There is no appeal against their orders and they are prepared to exclude from the Olympics those who refuse to carry them out.

> The following incident from 420 BC is also recorded in Thucydides (*Histories* 5.49–50). Archesilaos and Lichas were Spartans. Pausanias is describing the statues at Olympia (*Description of Greece* 6.2.2).

3.27   Archesilaos had won two Olympic victories, but his son Lichas entered a chariot in the name of the people of Thebes because at that time the **Spartans were debarred** from the games. When his charioteer was victorious, he tied a **ribbon** on him with his own hands, and for this transgression the *Hellanodikai* whipped him. It was because of this Lichas that there was a Spartan expedition against Elis in the time of King Agis and a battle inside the Altis. After the war Lichas put up the statue here, but the Eleans' records of Olympic victors have the People of Thebes, not Lichas, as the winner.

---

1   Why do you think the punishment of Lichas could be treated as a pretext for war?

2   What does this incident tell us about the extent of the authority of the *Hellanodikai*?

Spartans were debarred   because they had refused to pay a fine to Elis for violating the Olympic truce.

ribbon   *tainia*, tied round the victor's head or limbs as a token of victory. See **8.13**.

Set up next to the Hidden Entrance to the stadium (**3.3**) were a series of statues of Zeus called *Zanes* in the local dialect. They functioned as a warning to athletes against the use of bribery. This is what Pausanias has to say about the first group of six (*Description of Greece* 5.21.2–4).

3.28 As you follow the path from the Metroon to the stadium, at the foot of the hill of Cronos on the left there is a stone terrace right beside the hill with some steps up through it. Next to the terrace are dedicated some bronze statues of Zeus from the money imposed as fines on athletes who showed contempt for the games. The locals call them *Zanes*. The first group of six were set up in the 98th Olympiad [388 BC]. Eupolos of Thessaly bribed those entering the boxing, Agetor of Arcadia and Prytanis of **Kyzikos** and with them Phormio of **Halicarnassus** who had been the winner at the previous Olympiad. They say that this was the first offence committed against the games by athletes, and that Eupolos and those who accepted his bribes were the first to be fined by the Eleans.

Two of the statues are the works of Kleon of **Sicyon**, but I don't know who made the next four. Apart from the third and fourth statues, the others have **elegiac**

Some of the bases for the Zanes arranged in a line before the Hidden Entrance to the stadium, with the terrace on the left.

Kyzikos   a Greek city on an island in the Propontis, north-west Turkey.

Halicarnassus   the capital of Caria, south-west Turkey, later famous for the Mausoleum.

Sicyon   a city west of Corinth.

elegiac   from c. 500 BC the elegiac couplet (consisting of a longer line and a shorter, both with a basically dactylic rhythm) became the standard poetic form for epigrams.

inscriptions on them. The first of the epigrams is intended to show that an Olympic victory is secured by speed of foot and strength of body, not by money. The epigram on the second says that the statue is set up in honour of the divinity, by the piety of the Eleans, and as a deterrent to athletes who break the rules. On the fifth the gist of the epigram is to praise the Eleans generally and specifically for fining the boxers, while on the sixth and last, the sense is that the statues are a message to all Greeks not to offer bribes for an Olympic victory.

---

1 Why are the *Zanes* set up in this particular place?
2 Why was a commemorative statue a more effective punishment than a simple fine?
3 How do modern forms of punishment for athletes compare with those in ancient Greece?

Among his descriptions of the *Zanes* and of those convicted of breaking the rules Pausanias mentions the following incident over a late arrival (*Description of Greece* 5.21.12–14).

3.29   Among those later fined by the Eleans was an Alexandrian boxer at the 218th Olympiad [AD 93]. His name was Apollonios … He was the first **Egyptian** convicted of wrongdoing by the Eleans. He wasn't convicted of giving or receiving bribes, but for this different type of offence against the games: he failed to arrive at the published time. The only option was for him to be excluded from the competition by the Eleans, if they obeyed the rules. His excuse was that he was held up by unfavourable winds in the **Cyclades islands,** but Herakleides (himself a native Alexandrian) showed it was a lie and that his late arrival was the result of picking up money from games in Ionia. So the Eleans excluded Apollonios – as they did with any other boxer who did not arrive at the appointed time – and allowed the crown to go to Herakleides without a fight (*akoniti*). At that point Apollonios equipped himself with 'gloves' (*himantes*) for a fight, rushed at Herakleides and attacked him when he was already crowned and had taken refuge with the *Hellanodikai*. His mindless behaviour was to be seriously detrimental to him.

---

1 What does this passage tell us about the importance of local festivals for athletes?
2 Is modern sport free from 'mindless behaviour' like Apollonios' assault?
3 Judging from the evidence presented in this chapter, is it possible for us to get a very clear idea of how the ancient Olympics were organized?

Egyptian   a Greek from Egypt.

Cyclades islands   in the southern Aegean.

himantes   see **3.20n** and glossary; by this date, the 'sharp' version (**7.25, 26**)

4 Equestrian events

The hippodrome at Olympia

Equestrian events took place in the hippodrome. At Olympia this lay between the stadium and the River Alpheios, but subsequent flooding of the plain has completely obscured it. Recent geophysical surveys by German archaeologists resulted in a claim to have identified the hippodrome in 2008 but although the results look positive – a round feature perhaps corresponding to the Taraxippos altar (see **4.2**) has been observed – confirmation will only come with excavation. The best evidence for the appearance of the hippodrome is still Pausanias' description of the second century AD (**4.2**), but this offers no measurements and omits other details such as the turning post (passing which was the crucial part of the race). As no other ancient Greek hippodrome has yet been discovered, there are no parallels for comparison.

Recent interpretation of an eleventh-century AD text on measurement (the *Tabula Heroniana*) by Joachim Ebert gives some exact measurements for the hippodrome at Olympia.

4.1   each of the long sides: 3 *stadia* and 1 **plethron** long,
width to the starting gates: 1 *stadion* and 4 *plethra*,
Total: 4,800 feet [1,463 metres].

> • How far can we rely on these measurements? Do they refer to the actual track or the area for spectators too?

Pausanias describes the hippodrome in his *Description of Greece* 6.20.10–16 and 6.20.19–6.21.1.

4.2   Going beyond the stadium by where the *Hellanodikai* sit is an area dedicated to horse racing and there is a starting place for horses, the shape of which looks like the prow of a ship with its ram turned towards the course. Where the prow is close to the **stoa of Agnaptos** it becomes wide, and right at the tip of the ram a bronze dolphin has been constructed on a pole. Each side of the starting place is

---

plethron   6 *plethra* = 1 *stadion* or stade (approximately 200 metres).

Total   roughly based on 8 stadia = 1,600 metres (1,750 yards).

stoa of Agnaptos   the precise location has not yet been found, but it must be at the west end of the hippodrome.

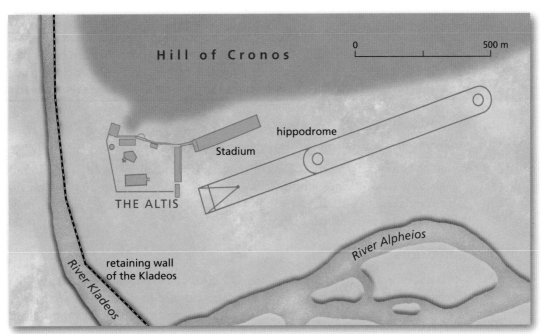

The location of the hippodrome according to the recent survey (2008). Note the position of the stadium in the top left of the plan.

more than 120 metres long and has stalls built into it. Those who enter the horse races have these stalls assigned by lot. In front of the chariots or race-horses is stretched a cord instead of a *hysplēx*. An altar of unbaked brick, plastered on the outside, is made at each Olympiad right in the middle of the prow and on the altar is set a bronze eagle with its wings fully outstretched.

The official appointed for the race sets in motion a mechanism in the altar. When it has been activated, the eagle is made to leap up so as to become visible to the spectators and the dolphin falls to the ground. The first starting gates (*hysplēges*) on either side (the ones towards the stoa of Agnaptos) are released and the horses standing by these gallop out first. As they run, they draw level with those who were allotted to stand in the second row and at that point the *hyspleges* on the second row are released. The same procedure is followed for all the horses until they are level with each other at the ram of the prow. After this it becomes a demonstration of the charioteers' skill and the horses' speed. Kleoitas was the original inventor of the starting mechanism and he seems to have taken pride in his invention, enough to have an epigram inscribed on a statue in Athens:

> I was made by the man who first invented starting gates for horses at Olympia, Kleoitas, son of Aristokles.

They say that after Kleoitas, Aristeides made a clever addition to the mechanism.

---

hysplēx, pl. *hysplēges*   the starting gate for athletes. See p. 97.

The race course has one of its sides longer than the other. The longer side is an embankment and on it, next to the passage through the bank, is **Taraxippos**, the terror of horses. Its shape is that of a round altar and as the horses run past it they are suddenly seized by a mighty fear for no apparent reason and from their panic arises confusion which generally results in the chariots crashing and the charioteers getting hurt. This is why charioteers offer sacrifices and pray that Taraxippos is kind to them.

[*Pausanias here relates various stories about the origin of Taraxippos.*]

At one turning post there is a bronze statue of **Hippodameia** holding a ribbon and about to crown **Pelops** for his victory. The other side of the race course is not an embankment of earth but a low hill at the end of which a sanctuary has been built for Demeter with the name Chamyne.

Competitors

It was expensive to pay for the upkeep of horses, and so equestrian events were the preserve of the wealthy, as is amusingly demonstrated by Aristophanes in *Clouds*. In the play Strepsiades, a farmer of moderate means, has married a woman from a comparatively wealthy family who has brought up their son Pheidippides with aristocratic tastes, and a particular love of horses. He has become completely besotted, like a modern youth with his fast car, but his extravagant expenditure threatens to ruin his father Strepsiades, who at the beginning of the play is worrying about his debts. One horse has cost him 1,200 drachmas (a small fortune – about four years' pay for a craftsman) and a chariot-board and a pair of wheels came to another 300 – although these sums are probably inflated for comic effect.

Strepsiades represents the type of Athenian who could not afford to keep horses and about whom we normally hear very little outside comedy; but the very rich who indulged in chariot and horse racing were celebrated, as we hear in Plato's *Lysis* (205c) where generations of a family are known by the whole city for both their wealth and their horses, along with their victories at Delphi, Isthmia and Nemea in chariot and horse races. The rich also left memorials to their success in the form of statues dedicated at the festival sites and in celebratory victory odes commissioned from leading poets (see **8.10**). Alcibiades of Athens and Hieron, tyrant of Syracuse, are conspicuous examples. Interest and involvement in horse racing was not, however, confined to the wealthy, since it was possible for a city to support horses and enter them in competitions, an example of which can be found in an Olympic victor list (**8.16**) which records victory for the people of Argos in the chariot race of 472 BC. Alcibiades bought a chariot owned by the city of Argos (**4.4**). The excitement generated among spectators can be detected in Sophilos' representation of the crowd on a fragment of a bowl (see p. **1.6**).

Taraxippos   the name means 'panicking horses'.

Hippodameia, Pelops   see pp. 23–4.

Alcibiades at the Olympics

The historian Thucydides, who was writing about contemporary events, tells us that the speeches in his history of the Peloponnesian War were composed with as careful attention as possible to the gist of what was actually said or likely to have been said.

In 415 BC, at a meeting five days after the Athenians had voted to send an expedition of 60 ships to Sicily, Nicias advised the Athenians to reconsider. In his speech he attacked Alcibiades, the most enthusiastic supporter of the expedition, for, among other things, wishing to be admired for his horses. In the following extract Thucydides makes Alcibiades justify his extravagance at the start of his reply (*Histories* 6.16.1–2).

4.3   Men of Athens, it is more appropriate for me to be in command than others – I must make this point at the beginning since Nicias has attacked me – and I think that I am worthy of it. The issues over which I have been subjected to hostile criticism both enhance the reputation of myself and my ancestors, and are actually beneficial to the state too. Previously the Greeks expected our city to be exhausted by war, but they even came to overestimate its power because of the magnificence of my contribution at the Olympic festival. I entered seven chariots, more than any other individual before, and I won, as well as coming second and fourth. Besides, I arranged everything else in a style worthy of my victory. Such achievements normally convey honour but successful action also suggests the presence of power.

Plutarch in his *Life of Alcibiades* 11–12 gives some more details of the attention attracted by Alcibiades at Olympia.

4.4   He was famous for keeping race-horses and for the number of his chariots, because nobody else, whether private citizen or king, entered seven at the Olympic Games, but he was the only one. His victory, his second place and fourth place (according to Thucydides, but third according to Euripides) surpasses in splendour and fame every aspiration in this field. This is what Euripides says in his **ode**:

> Son of **Cleinias**, I shall sing of you.
>
> Victory is a noble thing, but the most noble – which no other Greek has done –
>
> Is to race home first with your chariot – and second, and third
>
> And to come away without the physical effort, and be crowned with the olive of Zeus,
>
> giving the herald something to proclaim.

---

ode   i.e. an *epinikion*, or victory ode, like those of Pindar (see pp. 133–6, esp. **8.10**). Euripides was a tragedian and no other *epinikia* by him are known.

Cleinias   Alcibiades' father.

Nevertheless, this magnificent achievement was made more notable by cities competing in generosity. The Ephesians put up a magnificently adorned tent for him. The state of Chios provided him with fodder for his horses and with a large number of sacrificial animals. The Lesbians supplied wine and the other means for lavishly entertaining many guests. But then either a malicious accusation or actual malpractice arising over that rivalry made him even more talked about.

The story is that there was in Athens a certain Diomedes, not some disreputable character, but a friend of Alcibiades. He was keen to secure a victory at Olympia and when he heard about a publicly owned racing chariot at Argos, he persuaded Alcibiades, who he knew had considerable influence and many friends in Argos, to buy him the chariot. When Alcibiades bought it, he entered it as his own without a second thought for Diomedes, who was deeply hurt and called on gods and men to witness. Apparently even a lawsuit arose over this, and there is a speech, written by Isocrates for the son of Alcibiades, 'On the Team of Horses', in which it is Tisias, not Diomedes, who is the plaintiff.

> In this extract from the speech by Isocrates mentioned by Plutarch, Alcibiades the younger defends his father's lavish spending at the Olympic Games (Isocrates, *Team of Horses* 16.32–4).

4.5   At about the same time my father observed that the festival at Olympia was loved and admired by all mankind, that the Greeks made a display there of their wealth, strength, and training, and that the athletes were envied while the cities of winners became celebrated. Besides, it was his opinion that public services in Athens bring credit to the individual in the eyes of his fellow citizens, but expenditure for that festival brings credit to the state in the eyes of all Greeks.

Such were his thoughts, but despite having talents and physical strength second to none, he looked down on athletic contests because he knew that some of the athletes were of low birth or inhabitants of minor cities, or poorly educated. He turned his hand to keeping race-horses, a pursuit of the wealthiest and not something that a common man would engage in. Not only did he outdo his competitors, but he even surpassed every winner to date.

In the competition he entered a larger number of chariots than even the biggest cities, and they were of such excellent quality that he came first, second, and **third**. Apart from this, when it came to the sacrifices and the other costs related to the festival he was so extravagant and magnificent, it became apparent that the public expenditure of the **others** was less than his personal outlay. By the end of

---

third Thucydides says first, second and fourth. See Plutarch, **4.4**.

others   other official representatives at the festival (***theōroi***).

his embassy to the festival he had made the successes of his predecessors appear trivial compared with his own, he had stopped winners in his own day being envied, and he had left future race-horse owners no chance of surpassing him.

1 What do these extracts tell us about attitudes to athletics and the equestrian events?
2 What do they tell us about the importance of Olympia as a Panhellenic shrine?
3 How did Alcibiades' extravagance aid or harm him?

Hieron

Hieron, tyrant of Syracuse, belonged to the most prominent family in Greek Sicily in the early fifth century BC. He was clearly keen to make a name for himself in the wider Greek world through success in the equestrian competitions. His victories were considerable. He won the horse race (**kelēs**) at Delphi in 482 and 478 BC, and at Olympia in 476 and 472. He also won the chariot race at Delphi in 470 and at Olympia in 468 and a third victory (festival and date unknown).

We have six odes by Bacchylides and Pindar celebrating the equestrian victories of Hieron. As a sample of these, here are an extract from Bacchylides, *Odes* 5.37–49 and the whole of his short fourth ode, which has no mythological section – a regular feature of the longer odes. This short ode was composed immediately after the victory in the chariot race of 470 and performed at Delphi, as 'by the earth's navel … he is hymned' suggests.

4.6   Dawn of the golden arms saw the chestnut colt Pherenicos, swift as the wind, victorious beside Alpheios' wide stream, and at holy **Pytho**. Calling on earth to 40 witness, I proclaim that he has never yet been defiled by the dust of horses running in front of him in a race as he rushed towards the finish. Fast as the North Wind 45 blows and attentive to his jockey, he gallops, trying to win for hospitable Hieron a victory that brings fresh applause. (5.37–49)

Golden-haired Apollo still loves the city of Syracuse and honours its just ruler Hieron. For, by the **earth's navel** in the land of **high cliffs** he is hymned as victor 5 in the Pythian Games for the **third time** with his excellent swift-footed horses.

Pytho   Delphi.

earth's navel   Delphi was supposed to be the centre of the earth and this was represented by a stone navel (*omphalos*) at the shrine of Apollo.

high cliffs   the cliffs called the Phaedriades tower over the site at Delphi.

third time   previously in the horse race (*keles*) in 482 and 478 BC.

... The **sweet-voiced cockerel** of **Urania**, the queen of song ... but with a willing mind ... hurled songs.   10

... fourth time ... if someone ... held up the scales of Justice,
we would be honouring the **son of Deinomenes**.

We may crown him with garlands as the only one among mortals to achieve these 15
feats in the glens of **Crisa** beside the sea, and we may sing of his **two Olympic victories**. What is better than to be dear to the gods and to obtain a full share of 20
good things of every kind? (*Ode* 4)

> Among the many statues described by Pausanias in Book 6 are the following memorials of Hieron's Olympic victories (*Description of Greece* 6.12.1, 8.42.8–10).

4.7   Nearby is a bronze chariot with a man mounted in it. Next to the chariot are some race-horses, one standing on each side with boys sitting on them. They are memorials to the Olympic victories of Hieron, son of Deinomenes, tyrant of Syracuse after his brother Gelon. It wasn't Hieron who sent the offerings, but it was his son Deinomenes who gave them to the god. The chariot was the work of Onatas of Aegina while the horses on either side and the boys on them were made by Calamis.

4.8   **Hieron died** before he could dedicate to Olympian Zeus the offerings which he vowed for the victories of his horses. So his son Deinomenes fulfilled the vows on behalf of his father. These works too were by Onatas, and there are inscriptions at Olympia, one of which is about the dedication: 'After his victories in your holy games, Olympian Zeus, once with a four-horse chariot and twice with a single horse, Hieron gladly gave you these gifts. His son Deinomenes dedicated them as a memorial to his Syracusan father.' The other inscription reads: 'Onatas son of Mikon made me. The home where he lives is on the island of Aegina.'

... the text of these lines does not survive well enough to reconstruct.

sweet-voiced cockerel the adjective may seem odd, but the cock seems to stand for Bacchylides because he heralds victory as it heralds the dawn.

Urania one of the nine Muses who inspired poetry. Later, Urania becomes the Muse of astronomy, but in Bacchylides' time the Muses had not been apportioned specific spheres of influence.

son of Deinomenes Hieron.

Crisa the port close to Delphi. The hippodrome at Delphi was on the coastal plain.

two Olympic victories in the horse race (*keles*), 476 and 472 BC.

Hieron died 467 BC.

Because the winner of the equestrian events was the owner of the horses, jockeys and charioteers were not usually given the recognition received by their modern-day counterparts such as Formula One drivers. Indeed they may often have been slaves. Given the skill required, especially in chariot racing, and considering the significance of the event in the literary accounts by Homer (*Iliad* 23.271–533) and Sophocles (**4.12**) where the charioteers have heroic status, it is remarkable that the wealthy had the influence to take all the glory from what must have been the most exciting of the spectator events. Occasionally a charioteer is mentioned. Pindar names Phintis for victory with the mule-cart, or charioteers Nicomachus for winning at Olympia (*Isthmian* 2) and Karrhotos, who is even addressed in the poem (*Pythian* 5: see **4.13**). However, these are exceptional cases.

Kyniska

The precedence given to the owner allowed a woman to become an Olympic victor if she owned a successful team. The first and most celebrated woman to achieve this was Kyniska, sister of the Spartan king Agesilaos, probably in 396 BC. Of these three passages the first is a dedicatory epigram (Anon., *Greek Anthology* 13.16).

4.9

Spartan kings were my fathers and brothers.
  I, Kyniska, was victorious with a chariot team of swift-footed horses
  And set up this statue. I claim that I am the only woman
  From all of Greece to win this crown.

In Plutarch's biography of the Spartan king Agesilaos, an ulterior motive is given for Kyniska's entry at Olympia (*Agesilaos* 20.1).

When he saw that some of the **citizens** were becoming self important and arrogant as a result of breeding horses, he persuaded his sister Kyniska to enter a chariot in the competition at the Olympic Games, because he wished to show the Greeks that the victory was not the result of any outstanding quality, but of wealth and cash outlay.

In Pausanias' historical sketch of Spartan kings he mentions the anonymous epigram celebrating Kyniska's victory and gives her a different motive for competing (*Description of Greece* 3.8.1).

citizens   of Sparta.

Archidamus also had a daughter called Kyniska who was extremely ambitious to compete at Olympia. She was the first woman to keep horses and the first to win an Olympic victory. After Kyniska there were Olympic victories for other women, especially Spartans, none of whom became more famous than her for their victories.

1 What attitudes to horse racing are revealed in these passages about Kyniska?
2 How significant is the disparity in the way that Kyniska is presented in these sources?
3 Are equestrian events still the preserve of the rich?

Equestrian competitions

Pausanias recorded the inclusion of events (2.4), but did not feel the need to provide any details of these events for his Greek audience. The *Tabula Heroniana* (see 4.1) gives details of the length of each race (*stadion* = about 200 metres):

foals: 6 *stadia*

horses: 12 *stadia*

chariots with two foals: 3 circuits

chariots with two adult horses: 8 circuits

chariots with four foals: 8 circuits

chariots with four adult horses: 12 circuits.

This list includes all the equestrian events that remained part of the Olympic programme once they had been introduced, but omits the two which Pausanias tells us were abandoned in 444 BC.

1 Why might we question the reliability of this source?
2 How reasonable do the distances it gives seem to be?

Chariot racing

This charioteer (4.10) belongs to a four-horse chariot group of which some other fragments survive. The charioteer's upright stance and forward focus suggest he is depicted at the start of the race or perhaps in a victory parade. He holds reins in his right hand, but his left arm is missing. He wears a band round his head, tied at the back. His tunic is ankle-length and his feet are bare. His tunic has a belt and cords running under his armpits over his shoulders and across his back. These may be to keep his hair and tunic under control in the wind (see 4.11).

4.10

Bronze statue of a charioteer from Delphi; life-size (height 1.8 metres). The statue was probably dedicated to celebrate a victory by Polyzalos of Gela in 478 or 474 BC.

The charioteer on the following detail (**4.11**) of a Panathenaic **amphora** (see also p. 174) leans forward, holding the reins. In his right hand he also holds a rod used as a goad, but it is not deployed here as he manoeuvres his team into position to round the turning post (visible on the right, painted white). His long, white tunic billows out behind his right shoulder and his hair is windswept, as are the tops of the horses' manes and the one visible tail, all indicating the chariot's speed.

On this and other vase-paintings it is possible to see the type of chariot used for racing. It had a light, open superstructure with low, curved rails at the sides and a higher section in front of the charioteer. The wheels have four spokes. Other vases show the yoke pole attached to the bottom of the chariot and projecting forwards and upwards between the two central horses. The two inner horses are tied to the yoke but the outer trace horses are controlled only by the reins. Just behind the horses' necks a vertical peg in the yoke pole is often shown tied to the superstructure of the chariot by a long cord, probably to give it stability. Even on a smooth track, a light chariot with no suspension must have been hard to control.

4.11

*Detail of a Panathenaic
amphora showing a
four-horse chariot
(tethrippon).*

In Sophocles' play *Electra*, Orestes has returned in disguise to Argos to avenge the murder of his father Agamemnon by his mother Clytemnestra and her lover Aegisthus. He has arranged for his old *paidagōgos* (tutor) to give a fictitious account of his death in order to prepare the way for himself and his friend Pylades to be accepted into the palace when they arrive with an urn supposedly containing the ashes of Orestes. This is the account the tutor delivers (*Electra* 681–763).

4.12 He went to the famous festival, the showpiece of Greece, to take part in the Delphic games. When he heard the loud proclamation of the herald announcing the foot race, the first contest to be decided, he entered in a blaze of glory, a   685
marvel to everyone there. The outcome of the race matched his appearance and he came away with the prize for victory and all its honour. To summarize his many feats in a few words, I do not know of his like in achievements or strength. But there's one thing you have to know: he won the prize in absolutely every   690
contest announced by the judges and his success was acclaimed. Announcements said he was a man from Argos called Orestes, son of the Agamemnon who once   695
assembled the famous army of Greece.

That's how it was up to this point, but when one of the gods is intent on causing harm, not even a strong man can escape. On another day, when the fast chariots raced at sunrise, he entered among many charioteers. One was an **Achaean**, one   700
from Sparta, and there were two Libyans, masters of yoked chariots. Orestes with

---

Achaean Achaea in the classical period was on the south side of the Corinthian Gulf.
Libyans were noted for their association with horses, as were the Thessalians, whose land
was more suitable for keeping horses than most parts of Greece. The other places in the
catalogue are in northern Greece except for Athens and Boeotia, which are in central
Greece. Note the wide geographical spread of Greek states represented here.

Thessalian horses was the fifth among them. The sixth was from Aetolia with chestnut colts, and the seventh was a man from Magnesia. The eighth, an Aenian, had white horses. The ninth was from Athens, built by the gods. There was also a Boeotian, making up the tenth chariot. 705

They took their positions where the appointed judges had sorted them by lot and placed their chariots. At the sound of the bronze trumpet they shot off, all shouting to their horses and shaking the reins in their hands. The whole course was filled with the din of rattling chariots, and dust flew up. They were all bunched together and showing no restraint with the whip, each trying to overtake the wheel hubs and snorting horses of the others. The breath from the horses blew foam both over their backs and onto the revolving wheels. 710 715

Orestes, each time keeping tight to the very edge of the turning post, brought his wheel hub close in and gave rein to his right-hand trace horse while holding back the horse on the inside. So far all the chariots remained upright, but then the Aenian's colts disobeyed and bolted out of control, and wheeling right round as they finished the sixth lap and entered the seventh, they crashed headfirst into the chariot from Barca. From then, as a result of one disaster, they kept colliding and smashing into each other, and the whole plain of Crisa was filled with broken chariots like shipwrecks. When the skilful driver from Athens realized what was happening, he pulled away to the outside and held back, allowing the surge of horses seething in the middle to pass. 720 725 730

Orestes was driving last, keeping his horses at the back and trusting in his finish, but when he saw that the Athenian was the only one left, he made the ears of his swift colts ring with a piercing cry and set off in pursuit. They brought their teams level, driving their chariots forward, as first one and then the other took the lead by a head. 735 740

Orestes had successfully completed all the other laps safely and he, poor man, was safe, with his chariot intact. Then he slackened his left-hand rein as his horse was turning and accidentally struck the edge of the turning post. He shattered the axle box across the middle, and slipped over the chariot rail. He became entangled in the leather strips of the reins, and as he was falling to the ground, his horses rushed erratically into the middle of the track. 745

When the crowd saw him fallen from the chariot, they cried out in grief for the young man because of all he had achieved and because of the terrible fate he suffered, now being dashed to the ground, now with his legs shown to the sky until the charioteers with some difficulty managed to restrain his careering horses and free him, so covered with blood that none of his friends would have recognized him if they had seen that poor body. Men chosen from the Phocians burned him on a pyre without delay and are bringing in a small bronze urn his mighty body of pathetic ash for burial in his fatherland. That is the news I have for you, distressing enough to tell, but for those who saw it, as we did, it was the greatest disaster that I have ever seen. 750 755 760

Chariot racing was a dangerous sport. In this short extract (*Pythian* 5.46–53) Pindar addresses the charioteer Karrhotos driving the chariot of Arkesilas of Cyrene – the only charioteer to complete the course of 12 laps on this occasion in 462 BC.

4.13   You are blessed in having a memorial of the finest words after your great exertions. For in the midst of forty charioteers falling, you with your fearless spirit brought your chariot through undamaged. Now you have returned from the glorious competition to the plain of Libya and your home city.

The mule-cart race (*apene*) was discontinued at Olympia in 444 BC after being introduced in 500. In the *Iliad* the *apene* is described as a four-wheeled wagon drawn by mules, but depictions on Panathenaic vases show a two-wheeled chariot with a seated driver. Although this was a less glamorous event and less exciting because mules are slower than horses, Pindar wrote at least two odes celebrating the victors in this race (*Olympian* 5 and 6). Pausanias describes it in his *Description of Greece* 5.9.2.

4.14   The mule-cart race was not an ancient invention and was devoid of dignity. From long ago, even the birth of the animal in their country put the Eleans under a curse. For the cart had a pair of mules instead of horses.

Horse racing

In this bronze statue (**4.15**) the horse's front legs are foreshortened and the jockey is small for the size of the horse, but his legs are spread to fit on its back. The jockey is wearing a short tunic (***exōmis***) with a belt to stop it flapping, but it is still caught by the wind, as is the hair on his brow, indicating speed. He leans forward, gripping the reins in his left hand, and he also holds something in his right hand, probably a whip as seen in vase-paintings. Attached to the back of each foot is a spur, a short, sharp spike held in place by straps.

Bronze statue of a horse and jockey, mid-second century BC, from the same shipwreck off Cape Artemisium as the famous bronze statue of Zeus. The front part of the horse and the jockey were found together by archaeologists in 1928 and the rear of the horse was dragged up some distance away by fishermen in 1936.

1 How does the jockey control his horse?
2 What modern equipment do they lack and how would that affect the way they raced?
3 What conclusions about jockeys can you draw from this representation and **4.7**?

In the following anonymous epigram from the *Greek Anthology* (9.20) an old horse addresses those who stop to read his epitaph.

4.16   I who was once a winner of the crown by the Alpheios, who was once announced victor on two occasions beside the water of **Castalia**, I who was once proclaimed winner at Nemea, and once at Isthmia when still a colt, I who once ran as fast as the winged winds, now that I'm old – just look at me! – I am driven round and round, as I turn the rotating millstone, an insult to my crowns.

Castalia   the spring at Delphi.

1 Can we rely on an epigram like this as evidence for the treatment of race-horses?

2 What did this horse actually achieve?

3 How does repetition enhance or undermine the effectiveness of the epigram?

This extract from Pausanias' *Description of Greece* (6.13.9) tells how a riderless horse came first in a race.

4.17   The mare of Pheidolas the Corinthian was called Aura ('Breeze') according to the Corinthians. She happened to throw her rider while still at the beginning of a race, but nevertheless ran correctly, going round the turning post, and when she heard the trumpet, she put on a spurt, reached the *Hellanodikai* first and, realizing she had won, stopped running. The Eleans announced Pheidolas as the winner and gave him permission to erect a statue of this mare.

1 Would a horse without a rider be able to win a modern race?

2 Why was it acceptable in Greece for Pheidolas to be declared winner?

3 Does this brief extract give us any other information about the conduct of horse races?

Pausanias describes the race with mares (*kalpe*) in *Description of Greece* 5.9.2. This race was discontinued in 444 BC after being introduced in 496. It may have been practised elsewhere, but it remains quite obscure. The details that Pausanias gives here are not altogether clear, but it is usually assumed that the home-straight after the last turn is what 'the last stretch' refers to.

4.18   The *kalpe* was a race using mares. In the last stretch of the race they used to jump off the mares and run beside them, holding onto the bridles just as those called *anabatai* still do, even down to my day. The **signals** for the *anabatai* are different from the *kalpe* race and their horses are male.

1 How useful would this event be for military training?

2 Why do you think it was discontinued?

anabatai   presumably riders who dismount and run beside horses, as the *apobatai* did beside chariots (see p. 172).

signals   it is not clear what Pausanias refers to.

5 The pentathlon

The pentathlon consisted of five disciplines: discus, javelin, long jump, running (*stadion*) and wrestling, the first three of which were confined to this competition and are discussed in this chapter. Running and wrestling are covered in Chapters 6 and 7.

Physique and skills

In the following extract from *Erastai* (*Amatores* or Lovers), which is included among the works of Plato although its authenticity is disputed, Socrates is trying to get his interlocutor to define the sort of skill a philosopher has. This brief comparison with pentathletes occurs during the dialogue (135e1–136a4).

5.1   I said, 'Do I understand what sort of man you are saying a philosopher is? It looks to me as if you are saying they are like pentathletes competing with runners or with wrestlers, because pentathletes are inferior to the specialists in their particular disciplines, and while they come second against these, they are the best of the other athletes and beat them. Maybe you mean that philosophy has a similar sort of effect on those who practise this pursuit: they are inferior to the leading practitioners in understanding with regard to particular skills, but while they come second, they are better than the rest; and in this way a man who has studied philosophy becomes second best in everything. It looks to me as if you mean someone like that.'

Victory in the pentathlon depended on athletic versatility. Here Aristotle discusses the physique for the pentathlete (*Rhetoric* 1361b).

5.2   Every age has a different kind of beauty. So, a young man's beauty consists in having the type of physique fit for exertions, whether for running races or for employing strength, and fit for enjoyment by being appealing to the eye. This is why pentathletes are most endowed with beauty, because they are naturally built for strength and speed. When he is in his prime a man's beauty consists in having the sort of body that is fit for the exertions of war and can look appealing as well as inspiring fear. An old man's beauty consists in having the sort of body that is up to the essential tasks, but **causing no pain** because it doesn't suffer from the vexations of old age.

---

causing no pain   the Greek could mean not suffering pain or not causing it to others. The latter meaning would be in line with the comments on the attractiveness of the other ages.

Strength consists in the power to move another as one wishes, and it is necessary to move another either by pulling or pushing, lifting or crushing, or squeezing so that the strong man is strong in all or some of these. Excellence of physical size consists in being taller, broader and more thickset than most but not to such an extreme that movements are made slower.

Physical excellence for athletics requires a combination of size, strength and speed (the fast man is also strong). For the man with the ability to propel his legs in a certain way with rapid forward movement is a runner, one with the ability to squeeze and maintain a hold is a wrestler, one with the ability to thrust with his fist is a boxer. The man with ability in these last two is a pankratiast, and the one with ability in all is a pentathlete.

- Was the pentathlon an event for the all-rounder or did it require a greater focus on specialized skills?

The order of elements and deciding the winner

Since we have no detailed explanation of how the winner of the pentathlon was decided, we have to rely on passing references to attempt a reconstruction. Unfortunately no reliable picture emerges, despite valiant efforts by scholars to produce a credible scenario. One way of determining the winner could have been to allocate points for positions in each element, a simpler version of the system in the modern games for the decathlon, where contestants accumulate points for precise times, heights or distances achieved according to a set of tables. But this was not an option when accurate measurement – especially for timing races – was not available. Another system may have been progressive elimination. If there were some such system, there might only be two or three athletes left for the final element and since there are references to wrestling as the deciding element, it would make sense for there not to be numerous bouts to decide the winner. There is another assumption implicit in the last statement: that there were a reasonably large number of entrants rather than a restricted number of contestants for the whole event. We simply do not know how many would enter, or how many might be selected during the preliminary training in Elis. The evidence for the order of events can be tantalizing. For example, a fragmentary inscription from Rhodes of the first century BC or AD suggests that the long jump followed the discus: 'Let the man who threw the discus furthest jump […]'. But whether this can be used as evidence for what happened at Olympia some 400 years or so earlier is far from certain.

In 364 BC there was a battle at Olympia actually during the games. The Eleans were attempting to regain control of the festival from the Arcadians (Xenophon, *Hellenica* 7.4.28–9).

5.3 The Arcadians strengthened the garrison at Olympia and because an Olympic year was coming round again, they made preparations to run the Olympic Games with the people of Pisa, who claim to have been in charge of the sacred site originally. When the month came round in which the Olympics are held and the days during which the crowds assemble, at that point the Eleans, who had made their preparations openly and had invited the Achaeans to join them, marched along the road to Olympia. The Arcadians thought they would never march against them and along with the people of Pisa were busy organizing the crowded festival. They had already held the equestrian events and the **foot race** of the pentathlon. Those who had reached the wrestling were no longer competing in the stadium, but between the stadium and the altar.

> 1 What does this passage suggest about the order of events at the Olympic Games?
> 2 Does it tell us anything about the order of events within the pentathlon?
> 3 Is it clear enough to be reliable evidence?

Herodotus (*Histories* 9.33) explains how Tisamenes of Elis came to be a Spartan citizen through his abilities as a prophet of military success. However, when the Delphic oracle told him he would win five victories, he initially thought the god was referring to the pentathlon. In the following extract Pausanias also tells the story, but with a little more detail about Tisamenes' athletic experience (*Description of Greece* 3.11.6).

5.4 Tisamenes of Elis, a member of the **Iamidae**, received an oracle that he would win five particularly famous contests. So he trained for the pentathlon at the Olympic Games, from where he departed in defeat even though he was in fact first in two events, since he beat Hieronymos of **Andros** in the foot race and the long jump. But when he was beaten by Hieronymos in the wrestling and failed to achieve victory, he understood that the oracle meant that the god was giving him **victories** by prophecy in five military conflicts.

> • What does this passage contribute to our understanding of the way that victory in the pentathlon was achieved?

---

foot race usually understood to be a *stadion* race, but there is no specific indication of what distance the foot race was in the pentathlon. The Greek here might be taken to mean 'stadium events' or 'events of the race track'.

Iamidae a priestly family in Elis: see **2.2**, esp. the note on the oracle of Olympian Zeus.

Andros an Aegean island.

victories the first was the battle of Plataea, in which the Greeks defeated the Persians, in 479 BC.

This extract (Bacchylides, *Odes* 9.21–39) is from a poem written to celebrate the victory of Automedes of Phlius in the pentathlon at the Nemean Games (date unknown). Phlius was a small town west of Nemea. Bacchylides was writing in the fifth century BC, but his *epinikia* (odes in praise of victors) were lost until a manuscript consisting of about 200 fragments with the remains of some 14 *epinikia* and six other poems was discovered in Egypt and bought by the British Museum in 1896.

5.5   From those honoured games at **Nemea** men become famous if they garland their **fair** hair with a **crown** awarded **every other year**. On this occasion of Automedes' 25 victory the god has given him the crown, since among the competitors in the pentathlon he stood out like the bright moon outshining the light of the stars on a night in the **middle of the month**. That is how he displayed his marvellous physique in front of the huge surrounding crowd of Greeks when throwing the 30 wheel-shaped discus and he brought a roar from the spectators when launching from his hand the shaft of dark-leaved elder high in the air, or when wrestling 35 with a flashing move at the end; with such great spirit and strength he brought strong-limbed bodies to the ground. Then he came to the dark, swirling waters of the **Asopos**.

---

1   What does this passage suggest about the order of events in the pentathlon?
2   Why are only three disciplines mentioned? Is it because Automedes only won these three? What would that suggest about deciding the winner of the pentathlon?
3   How vividly does Bacchylides evoke the atmosphere at the games?
4   Does it make a difference that this is an *epinikion* rather than a different literary genre?
5   In celebrating Automedes' victory, what does Bacchylides choose to focus on?

Nemea   the sanctuary of Zeus in the north-east Peloponnese, site of one of the four 'crown' games (see glossary).

fair   commonly used to describe heroes' hair.

crown   a crown of wild celery was traditional at Nemea (see **8.2**). For other rewards an athlete might receive, see pp. 126–32 and p. 171.

every other year   the Greek says 'in the third year', counting inclusively. The games at Nemea and the Isthmus were held every two years, those at Olympia and Delphi every four years.

middle of the month   i.e. when the moon is full.

Asopos   i.e. he came home. The Asopos flows through Phliasia to the Gulf of Corinth. Note the importance given to the return of the successful athlete to his home city (see **8.3**).

In this short extract from *Nemean Ode* 7 celebrating the victory in the boys' pentathlon of Sogenes of Aegina, Pindar makes a comparison between overstepping the mark with his tongue and a foul throw with a javelin. The precise meaning of these lines (70–6) is not absolutely clear.

5.6 Sogenes from the clan of the Euxenidae, I swear that I did not overstep the line when letting my swift tongue go like a bronze-bladed **javelin** that disqualifies the strong neck from wrestling and sweat before the body is exposed to the heat of the sun. If struggle there was, greater is the joy that follows. Do forgive me. If, to please the victor, I got carried away and raised my voice to excess, I am not too mean to pay my due.

> 1 What does this passage contribute towards establishing the order of events in the pentathlon?
> 2 Does it reveal any rules for deciding the winner of the pentathlon?
> 3 Does it reveal any rules about throwing the javelin?

The following satirical epigram by Lucillius (first century AD) celebrates an athlete who manages the worst possible performance in the pentathlon (*Greek Anthology* 11.84).

5.7 Among the competitors, not one was thrown quicker than me, and no one at all ran the *stadion* slower. With the discus I didn't come anywhere close and I never had the strength to lift my legs in the jump. A man with a crippled arm threw the javelin better. In five events I was **first** – to be announced five times a loser.

> 1 What does this epigram suggest about the way in which the pentathlon was conducted to establish a winner?
> 2 Is this type of evidence in any way reliable? For example, could we conclude from this that disabled athletes took part in competitions?

Discus

Throwing the discus did not exist as a separate event in athletic games but was only contested as part of the pentathlon, except in the mythical world of epic. Its origins may lie in competitions to throw weights the furthest, since, without a

---

javelin compare **5.14**, where Pindar uses a slightly different javelin metaphor, hoping his throw is within bounds.

first the position of the word at the beginning of the last line highlights its satirical effect.

target to hit, it was concerned with distance rather than accuracy. At Patroclus' funeral games in the *Iliad* (23.826–49), the iron weight is considerably bigger and bulkier than a discus. But Homeric heroes inhabit a different world, where their feats of strength far exceed those of ordinary mortals. Even in the Phaeacian games where a discus is used, Odysseus throws a much bigger discus further than the others (**1.9**).

Some facts are not in dispute about the discus competition, but there are a number of problems which remain unresolved because evidence is either missing or not sufficiently clear. The first of these concerns the size and weight of the discus itself. Although a number of discuses have been found, it is not always clear for what purpose they were designed. Some may have been specifically made as impressive thank-offerings to the gods, some may have been created for the men's competition, some for the boys' and some simply for practice, when precise size or weight would not be as significant as in a competition. The discus handled by Anacharsis (**5.9**) may have belonged to this last category, in contrast to the three possibly official examples stored in the Sicyonian Treasury at Olympia, which Pausanias mentions (**5.10**). As the length of the stadium varied from site to site, it seems likely that weights and sizes of discus were similarly inconsistent. Surviving metal examples vary considerably in size and weight from approximately 1.25 kg (2lb 12oz), 16.5 cm (6.5 in) diameter to approximately 5.7 kg (12 lb 9 oz), 34 cm (13.4 in). By comparison, the standard modern Olympic discus for men weighs 2 kg (4 lb 7 oz), with a diameter of 22 cm (8.7 in) and 1 kg (2lb 3 oz), 18 cm (7.1 in) for women.

The most contentious problem in this event concerns the method of throwing. Some scholars have favoured a style similar to that used by modern athletes, which involves spinning the body for one and a half turns within a 2.5-metre circle to get the maximum momentum. Others argue that the athlete drew his right arm back to the position exemplified by Myron's statue of the ***Diskobolos*** (discus-thrower) and then launched it forward with just a half turn of the body (**5.8**). Aesthetic considerations might support this view if the *Diskobolos* of Myron is depicted at the point where he is poised to make the throw, his body wound up and ready to spring into action. Although it is possible to arrange poses found on vase-paintings into a sequence which would apparently confirm this interpretation, it is not possible to treat this type of evidence as if it were a sequence of freeze-frame photographic studies of movement. One obvious problem lies in the fact that the viewer does not usually see the relationship between the pose and the starting line and so cannot determine which way the athlete is facing. In the modern discipline the thrower faces away from the landing area to start.

In the modern games, the area for throwing the discus is carefully marked and the throw must land within a 35-degree trajectory. We know from Antiphon (**5.16**) that an area was marked out for the javelin, and it is reasonable to assume that the same was done for the discus. Does the presence of the three discuses in the treasury at Olympia (**5.10**) suggest that each athlete had three throws, possibly using a different weight for each throw? A fragmentary inscription from Rhodes, if correctly restored, hints that there may have been five throws allowed. The distances recorded for throwing the discus are not usually precise, although they were marked with a peg and measured. In Homer's *Odyssey* (**1.9**, lines 186–98) Athene places a marker to record Odysseus' throw. In Statius' *Thebaid* (**5.11**) too no precise distances are mentioned, although Phlegyas practises by throwing his discus across the River Alpheios. The one precise distance recorded comes from an epigram in the *Greek Anthology* (**5.20**). For comparison, the current Olympic record set in 1996 is 69.4 metres, although the winning distance at the first modern Games in 1896 was only 29.15 metres, remarkably close to the ancient throw of Phayllos.

 5.8

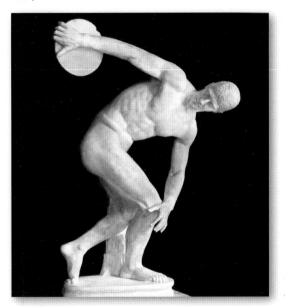

Copy of the Diskobolos *of Myron (original* c. *450 BC).*

- The side view of this statue has been criticized as confused and unsatisfactory. Why do you think the sculptor chose this pose to represent a discus thrower?

Lucian wrote in the second century AD, but the following extract (*Anacharsis* 27) is from a dialogue set in the sixth century BC. His account probably reflects practice in his own day, but it may not be very different from earlier athletic training, even as far back as the time of Solon.

Anacharsis, a Scythian nomad, has travelled to Athens especially to talk with the famous law-giver Solon so that he can find out about the laws and customs of the Greeks and discover the best form of constitution. The main focus of the dialogue is the athletic training given to the young and how that makes them better citizens and soldiers. Anacharsis maintains an uncomprehending and critical attitude throughout the dialogue.

5.9   SOLON You saw another object in the gymnasium, round and made of bronze, like a little shield without a handle or straps. In fact, you tried it out as it was lying in the open and you thought it was heavy and hard to hold because of its smoothness. Well, they throw that up into the air and for some distance, competing to be the one who goes furthest and beats the others with his throw. This exercise gives strength to their shoulders and puts muscle power in their limbs.

> 1 Compare the description of the discus in this passage with the account in Statius' *Thebaid* (**5.11**). What characteristics of the discus made it hard to throw?
>
> 2 Was the development of physical strength a more valid justification for athletics in the sixth century BC than it would be today?
>
> 3 Compare Solon's justification with the arguments of the critics of athletics (pp. 146–50).

In Pausanias' description of the treasuries on the terrace at the foot of the hill of Cronos (see plan, p. 38), he refers briefly to three discuses which may have been used in the competitions (*Description of Greece* 6.19.4).

5.10   In **this treasury** are stored three discuses, the number which they use for the event in the pentathlon.

Statius was a Roman poet of the second half of the first century AD who came to prominence during the reign of Domitian (AD 81–96) and published his epic poem the *Thebaid* in 91–2. It tells the story of the conflict between the sons of Oedipus. Adrastus was leading his army from Argos to Thebes to support Polynices against his brother. On the journey they reached Nemea, where Adrastus celebrated funeral games for the infant Opheltes who had been killed by a snake. This was one of the myths that explained the origin of the Nemean Games (*Thebaid* 6.668–721).

5.11   Phlegyas from **Pisa** starts the business and everyone's eyes were immediately drawn to him: such was the promise of his masculine prowess when they saw his body. First he roughens the discus and his hand with soil, then shakes off the 670 dust and turns it round, skilfully assessing which side fits into his fingers and sits

---

this treasury   of the Sicyonians, dedicated by Myron, tyrant of Sicyon to commemorate his victory in the chariot race in 648 BC.

Pisa   the state closest to Olympia in the north-western Peloponnese and often associated with the games (see Chapter 2, especially **2.3**).

more securely on the middle of his forearm. This sport was his constant passion, not just when he was attending the festival for which his country is renowned, but he habitually took the measurement of the **Alpheios** from bank to bank and, where it was at its widest, used to throw his discus across the river without ever getting it wet. And so, confident in what he is doing, he does not take the measure of the rough expanse of ground straight ahead, but looks along his right arm to the sky. Then, exerting pressure on the ground from each knee, he gathers his strength and sends his discus spinning above him, making it vanish in the clouds. It rapidly gains height and accelerates upward, as an object would if falling, until it finally loses impetus and returns more slowly from its high point to the ground, where it buries itself in the field. 675 680

[*Four lines are omitted here in which a simile compares this to Thessalian witches drawing down the moon in an eclipse.*]

The Greeks applaud, though you, **Hippomedon**, do not look on calmly: a longer throw is expected with a level trajectory. 690

But all at once Fortune intervenes – she enjoys wrecking extravagant expectations. What possibility does a man have of competing against the gods? He was making ready for an immense distance, his neck already twisted round and the whole side of his body now drawing back, when the weight slipped and fell at his feet, making him abandon his throw and let his hand drop down fruitlessly. Everyone groaned, while a few took pleasure at the sight. Next comes Menestheus for his turn, showing greater caution and lacking confidence in his skill. After many appeals to you, **son of Maia**, he tries to neutralize the slipperiness of the discus's solid mass with dust. It leaves his mighty hand with much more good fortune and comes to rest after traversing no small part of the course. There is applause and the place is marked by planting an arrow. Third to put his strength to the test comes Hippomedon, ponderously slow since he took seriously to heart the warnings from Phlegyas' disaster and Menestheus' success. He lifts up the discus to which his right hand is attuned. Then, stretching high, he looks to his tautly poised side and strong arms and sends it spinning with a vigorous twist, following through himself. With an awe-inspiring impetus the discus flies through the air and though now far away it remains true to its aim and stays on course. There was no doubting where it landed, with none near it, as it went beyond that of Menestheus, who was well beaten. Far beyond its rival marks it came to land … 695 700 705 710

Alpheios   the more important of the two rivers whose confluence is beside the sanctuary at Olympia. The river bed is wide and the river itself forms channels which can change position within the bed (see map on p. 57).

Hippomedon   who is about to compete, hence his anxiety.

son of Maia   Hermes.

Statius concludes with a highly exaggerated description of the discus making the ground tremble like **Polyphemus** hurling a rock at Odysseus' ship, or the **giants** piling up mountains to attack the gods on Olympus.

> 1 What evidence does this passage provide about the nature of the discus itself and the importance of a secure grip?
> 2 Does the description of the event here complement or contradict that of Philostratus (**5.12**)?

Philostratus' *Imāginēs* ('Pictures') are descriptions of panel paintings in the house of his host near Naples, where he has come for the local games. In describing a painting of Hyacinthus, who was accidentally killed by a discus thrown by Apollo, Philostratus first begins to talk about the story and the flower before rather flippantly changing direction (*Imāginēs* 1.24).

5.12   Since we have come not as critics of the myths nor ready to disbelieve, but only to view the paintings, let us take a close look at the picture, and firstly at the place for throwing (***balbis***) the discus. A *balbis* is separated off, small but with enough room for one person to stand in, only **giving support to the back** and the right leg, with the front of the body leaning forward and taking the weight off the other leg, which must help give upward thrust by moving in coordination with the right hand. When it comes to the thrower's pattern of movement, he must turn his head to the right and hunch his back just enough to see his ribs. Then he must make his throw by drawing himself up and putting everything into it with the whole of his right side. Apollo launched his discus like this and couldn't have thrown it in any other way.

> 1 Does the fact that the author is describing a picture of the event (and a mythical one, too) rather than an actual athlete in action invalidate this as evidence for the method of throwing?
> 2 It is sometimes said that Philostratus based his description on the famous *Diskobolos* of Myron (**5.8**). Would you agree?

Polyphemus   the Cyclops blinded by Odysseus in Homer, *Odyssey* 9.

giants   the giants Otus and Ephialtes are said to have made this attempt on the gods by piling Mount Ossa and Mount Pelion on top of Mount Olympus.

giving support to the back   the text here is not clear and is often emended. Some take this to mean the *balbis* is not marked off at the back, unlike the modern throwing circle. Others take it to refer to the back of the body in contrast to the front leaning forward. This awkward translation is meant to leave it unclear whether back leg or back is meant.

Javelin

In this element of the pentathlon, the athletes competed to throw the javelin, not at a target, but to achieve the greatest distance. The javelin (*akōn* or *akontion*) was thin, light and made of elder wood, if Bacchylides' reference to it (**5.5**) can be taken as representing the norm. The javelin had a bronze tip (**5.14**), several examples of which have been found, although the perishable shafts have left no trace, leaving us to rely on the representations on vases to assess the length of the ancient javelin. For comparison, the modern javelin must be between 2.6 and 2.7 metres in length and weigh a minimum of 800 grams for Olympic competition. However, the technique of throwing the javelin was very different from the modern style, because a thong (*ankylē*) was used to spin the javelin as it was thrown. Vase-paintings make it clear that the thong was wound round the shaft and held firmly in place by tension exerted by the fingers. It appears that the thong was folded double and wound, not tied, onto the shaft, leaving a loop into which two fingers were inserted, although there are representations which show only one finger being used. As the javelin was thrown, the thong made the javelin spin, helping it to fly more smoothly and achieve a greater distance. The modern javelin has a cord grip at the point of balance to give the athlete a firm hold and reduce the risk of a misdirected throw.

The area into which the javelin was thrown must have been carefully indicated both in competitions and in the gymnasium in order to avoid serious accidents. The dangerous nature of this event is made all too clear in the speeches of Antiphon (**5.16**). The athlete ran up to the mark to throw, although there may not have been room for a 30-metre run-up, the length allowed in the modern competition. It is often assumed that the starting line (*balbis*) for the foot races also served for the javelin and the discus, although Philostratus' description of the *balbis* for the discus (**5.12**) indicates at least side limits to the throwing area too.

Detail from a Panathenaic amphora, c. 530–520 BC with four pentathletes, showing the use of the ankyle.

The following **kylix** (**5.13**) shows four stages of the javelin throw. One youth prepares his javelin, two are running with the javelin held high, and the fourth is poised to throw.

5.13

Attic *red-figure kylix by the Carpenter Painter, 515–510 BC.*

1　Look carefully at the way the youths are handling the javelin. How does the action of pushing against the point relate to the *ankyle*?

2　Does it suggest that the bronze point was not fitted (contrast Pindar and Antiphon)?

3　Compare the run-up taken by modern athletes and the positions in which they hold the javelin.

4　Is the length of javelins depicted similar to those used in the modern Olympics?

In the following short extract from Pindar's ode for the victory of Hieron's chariot at the Pythian Games of 470 BC (*Pythian* 1.41–5), Pindar compares his praise to a javelin throw.

5.14　The gods are responsible for every means of achieving human excellence and whether men are wise or eloquent or have strong hands. Eager as I am to praise that man, I hope, metaphorically speaking, not to throw the bronze-tipped **javelin** I shake in my hand outside the competition space, but to outstrip my opponents with a long throw.

> During the funeral games in the *Thebaid* (see **5.11**), a course for chariot racing is being laid out and Statius offers this observation on the distance between the turning posts (*Thebaid* 6.353–4).

5.15　Between the two ends [of the course] was a distance one might cover with four throws of a javelin or three shots of an arrow.

---

javelin　compare **5.6**, where Pindar uses a slightly different javelin metaphor, hoping not to overstep the line.

1 What evidence do these short extracts provide for our understanding of the ancient javelin competition?

2 Think of the points of comparison that Pindar is setting up in comparing his venture as a poet with that of a javelin thrower. Who would be his 'opponents' and in what sense does he hope that his poem will not go astray?

3 How reliable is Statius as evidence for the distance achieved in throwing the javelin?

The following passages are from a tetralogy (set of four speeches) written by Antiphon. They were not delivered in a law-court but were composed as a teaching aid and are about an imaginary accident in a gymnasium involving the death of a boy. The prosecution delivers the first speech, the defendant replies and then the accuser makes a second speech to which the defence responds again. The prosecution states the basic facts of the case in the first speech about which there is no disagreement, but the defendant seeks to demonstrate that the fault, and responsibility, lies with the victim. Antiphon thus involves us in a real legal puzzle, albeit not an actual case (*Second Tetralogy* 1.1–2 and 2.3–5).

5.16   In the gymnasium my son was struck in the ribs by a javelin thrown by this young man and he was killed on the spot. I am accusing him not of deliberate but accidental killing, although for me personally his involuntary action has resulted in no less a tragedy than if it had been a deliberate act. (1.1–2)

I was of the opinion that by training my son in these pursuits from which the **state derives** particular **benefit**, some good would result for both of us. But it has turned out quite contrary to my expectation. For it was not through any anti-social or unrestrained behaviour, but when practising throwing the javelin with lads of his own age in the gymnasium that he actually hit someone, although he killed no one, at least if the true nature of his action be told. But he has incurred charges from an involuntary act of another who committed the error that affected himself.

If the javelin had wounded the boy after going beyond the boundaries of its designated area to hit him, we would have recourse to no argument to deny responsibility for the death. But since the boy ran into the path of the javelin and put his own body at risk, my son was prevented from hitting his **target area** and the

---

state derives … benefit   an example of *captatio benevolentiae* or securing the goodwill of a jury, here by suggesting his action benefits the state. Contrast the critics of athletics (see e.g. **8.26** and **8.27**) with the assumption here that javelin practice is beneficial, whether simply to aid fitness or to develop a skill with a military application.

target area   the Greek word could mean 'target' or 'thing aimed at', but as with the modern javelin, there appears not to have been an actual object to hit, but an area reserved for the javelin (to prevent the kind of accident at issue here). Otherwise the distance of the throw would not be at issue.

boy got in the way of the javelin and was hit, causing us to be held to account when the fault is not our own. It was because he ran into its path that the boy was hit and the young man is being unjustly charged since he didn't hit anyone standing outside the target area. If it is clear to you that the boy was struck, not while standing still, but when, of his own volition, he ran into the path of the javelin, it becomes clearer still that he died as a result of his own mistake, since he wouldn't have been hit if he had kept still and not run across. (2.3–5)

> 1 What does this speech tell us about the rules concerning the javelin?
> 2 Does it offer any clue about the importance attached to this event?
> 3 Whom would you hold responsible for the death? What other information would help you reach a decision?
> 4 What dangers do athletes have to face in modern athletics? Are any events potentially fatal? If so, what safeguards are put in place?

In his biography of Pericles, the most prominent politician of fifth-century Athens, Plutarch is recounting stories about the difficult relationship between Pericles and his son Xanthippus, who was supposed to have spread unflattering gossip about his father, including the following accusation of time-wasting (*Life of Pericles* 36.2–3).

5.17   Xanthippus began to abuse his father. First, to provoke laughter, he made public his time-wasting at home and the conversations he had with **sophists**. For example, he said that when a pentathlete had accidentally hit **Epitimus of Pharsalus** with a javelin and killed him, Pericles spent an entire day with **Protagoras** debating whether the javelin, the athlete who threw it or the judges (*agonothetai*) had to be considered responsible, in the strictest sense, for the incident.

> 1 Compare the issues debated here with the way a similar accident is debated in Antiphon (**5.16**). Is this obviously satirical?
> 2 Are these reports indicative of a widespread problem, or is the number of cases too few to know how prevalent accidents were with javelins?

---

sophists   teachers of philosophy and rhetoric who were often subjected to the type of criticism Plutarch reports Xanthippus using here – conducting fruitless intellectual debate on trivial topics. Aristophanes' *Clouds* is the most obvious example of the mockery of sophistic teaching.

Epitimus of Pharsalus   otherwise unknown. Pharsalus was a city in Thessaly which became famous as the site of the battle in which Caesar decisively defeated Pompey in 48 BC.

Protagoras   a prominent sophist who visited Athens on several occasions and was associated with Pericles. His most famous doctrine was 'man is the measure of all things'. It is unlikely that this conversation actually happened, although Plato did mention that Protagoras was known for an interest in precision of meaning.

Long jump

The only jump in Greek athletic competition was the long jump (**halma**). While there are few written sources for the long jump and it does not feature in Patroclus' funeral games in the *Iliad* and is only mentioned briefly in the *Odyssey* (see **1.9**, line 103), there are numerous depictions of the event in various stages on vase-paintings, allowing a fairly confident reconstruction, although not without problems. Two issues have been particularly prominent: first, the technique of jumping (especially whether athletes used a standing start or a run-up), and second, the distance that they managed to jump. There are also the usual difficulties in relying on the evidence from vase-paintings. Can we be sure they are accurate representations of the athletes' movements? For example, a striding or running figure fits the circular shape of the tondo (interior base) of a cup much better than a figure with legs together. Arranging the various poses depicted on vases into a sequence also raises problems of interpretation, although in most cases it is clear enough where they belong.

The most distinctive feature of the Greek sport was the use of jumping weights (**haltēres**) to enhance performance. Two basic varieties of jumping weights can be observed in use on vase-paintings, and examples survive. A third type is known from an example from Rhodes (now in the British Museum) and representations in later art. Shaped like a dumb-bell with a carved finger-grip, this third type may have had another use as suggested by Philostratus (**5.23**). The weights which survive vary in size from 1 to 4.5 kg (an exceptionally large example).

Those who think there was a standing start might point to a vase-painting where an athlete with jumping weights seems to be standing beside a turning post which may have marked the starting point for the jump, on the reasonable assumption that the starting line for runners (*balbis*, see **6.3**, **6.8**) was also used as the launching place (**batēr**, see **5.24** and discussion below) for the long jump, javelin and discus. If so, it might be argued that he is preparing himself for a standing jump. Those who think that the athletes ran up are also supported by vase-paintings. A Roman mosaic from Tusculum shows an athlete in the long jump apparently running, and a kylix (drinking cup) in Boston likewise shows an athlete running with jumping weights (*halteres*) and another pushing off with one leg (as in **5.25**). But Quintilian's explicit statement (**5.18**) might possibly tip the balance in favour of a run-up. Even if one concludes that a running jump was the norm, this does not exclude the possibility that standing jumps were used in training.

The place from which the athletes jumped was called the *bater* (thing on which one treads), about which we know nothing for certain. Drees thought it was 'a sort of sill or threshold which afforded additional purchase for take off' (p. 74), although all that can confidently be said is that it was at the beginning of the **skamma** (a dug-up area of loosened soil). The Byzantine lexicon (**5.24**) might suggest it was a stone sill, like a door threshold, and vase-paintings which show the athletes jumping beside a turning post might specifically point to the stone sill (*balbis*) for runners. From there the athlete jumped into the *skamma*. If the *bater* was identical with the *balbis*, care would have to be taken not to dig up the area used for running. In vase-paintings representing the pentathlon, a pick-axe is regularly included with which the athletes created a *skamma* of loose soil so that their feet left a clear impression when they landed. Philostratus (**5.23**) makes it plain that the footmarks had to be perfect for the jump to be valid. Valid jumps were marked with pegs fixed in the *skamma*, as can be seen in the black-figure vase-painting of an athlete about to land (**5.27**).

Pipe music provided a rhythmical accompaniment for the athlete, possibly to help him coordinate the movement of his legs and arms. This might have been particularly important at take-off, when the weights must be swung forward to enhance the momentum of the run.

The recorded distances achieved in the long jump have caused considerable speculation. The 55 feet (16.8 metres) recorded in **5.20** is approximately twice the distance achieved by modern athletes. Some have explained this as a simple mistake; others have thought that the jump must have been like the modern triple jump, although there is very little evidence to support this theory. Perhaps the entry in the Byzantine *Lexica Segueriana* (**5.24**) might be used to support the idea of a *bater* in the middle of the *skamma*, but it is hard to envisage an area for that which would be suitable, unless it consisted of a movable board. Besides, the Byzantine compiler thought this explanation of *bater* less satisfactory.

> Quintilian, writing about the art of rhetoric in the first century AD, is here giving advice about perfecting style and has just stated the need for frequent and careful revision during the process of writing (*Training in Oratory* 10.3.6).

5.18   Apart from creating better links between previous and subsequent sections by doing this, that ardent engagement in thinking which has had time to cool down in the process of writing recovers its vigour afresh, and acquires impetus, as it were, in revisiting the area. It's what we see happen in the long jump competition in order to go for a longer attempt and to run to that area where the competition takes place. Likewise in throwing the javelin we draw back our arms, and when about to fire arrows we stretch the bow-strings back.

> 1 Does this passage offer conclusive proof that athletes took a run-up before jumping?
> 2 Can it be used in conjunction with vase-paintings as evidence for what happened in Greece some 500 years earlier?

> Pausanias gives a mythological explanation for the use of pipe music to accompany the long jump (*Description of Greece* 5.7.10).

5.19   Some say that Zeus wrestled Cronos himself **here** for supremacy, and others claim that he put on games in honour of his victory. Among the winners Apollo is said to have outrun Hermes in a race and to have beaten Ares at boxing. This is why they say Pythian **pipe** music was introduced for the long jump in the pentathlon, because pipe music is sacred to Apollo and Apollo won Olympic victories.

> 1 What other evidence shows that the double pipe (*aulos*) accompanied the long jump?
>
> 2 Why do you think it was used to accompany the long jump in particular?
>
> 3 How does music contribute to modern athletics?

The athlete Phayllos of Croton (in Italy) is mentioned by Herodotus as the commander of the only ship from Croton to join the Greek fleet in its struggle against the Persian invasion (480 BC).

As Phayllos is mentioned in two plays of Aristophanes by old men who recall either running behind him or catching up with him in their youth, his fame as a runner must have endured over half a century at least. But his fame seems to have rested principally on his achievement in the long jump. Plato uses the phrase 'beyond the dug-up area' figuratively to mean 'to excess', and the tenth-century AD lexicon the *Suda* says the expression came from Phayllos' jump because he jumped beyond the 15-metre limit of the area of loosened earth equivalent to the modern sand-pit (*skamma*). However, Gardiner says of Phayllos' record: 'The sporting story is notorious, and the sporting epigram is even less trustworthy than the sporting story' (*Athletics of the Ancient World*, p. 152). The following brief epigram is quoted by an ancient commentator on Aristophanes and it also appears in the *Greek Anthology* (Appendix 297).

5.20   Phayllos made a jump of fifty-five feet [16.8 metres]

and threw the discus five feet short of one hundred [29 metres].

> • The modern Olympic record for the long jump of 8.9 metres (about 29 feet) caused a sensation when it was set in 1968, but it is far shorter than Phayllos' leap. Paradoxically, his discus throw is much shorter than modern athletes achieve. Is there an explanation for this apparent discrepancy?

---

here   Olympia.

pipe   the *aulos*, a wind instrument consisting of two cylindrical tubes with finger-holes. The mouthpiece held a reed, probably like that of the modern oboe.

Jumping weights (*halteres*)

Aristotle had a very wide range of interests, including botany, zoology, constitutional history, politics, rhetoric and literary criticism. But the *Problems* attributed to him were almost certainly not written by the great philosopher and scientist. The questions may well have been asked by Aristotle, but since the quality of the answers is so inconsistent, it is likely that they are in fact a compilation, perhaps made by his followers. In *Problems* 5.8 the use of *halteres* is discussed.

5.21 Why is it more tiring for the arm to throw with an empty hand than when throwing stones? Is it because throwing empty-handed is more like a convulsion? The reason may be that one doesn't have anything to exert pressure on, as a thrower does on the projectile in his hand. In a similar way the pentathlete uses the *halteres* and the runner his arms when pumping them. This is why the one achieves a bigger jump with the *halteres* than without them and the other runs faster when pumping his arms than when not.

> 1 Is it actually more tiring to throw empty-handed than to release an object such as a ball when throwing with the same force?
> 2 Do you think this offers a reasonable explanation of why weights were used for the long jump?

Among the many statues described by Pausanias at Olympia is a scattered group, mostly of deities, dedicated *c.* 460 BC by one Micythus of Rhegium (in southern Italy) in thanks for the recovery of a son from a wasting disease. One of the statues depicts Agon (Contest) who is characterized by carrying jumping weights (*halteres*) (*Description of Greece* 5.26.3).

5.22 These *halteres* are shaped like this: they form a semicircle, but rather more oblong and not precisely circular, and are made in such a way that the fingers go through them as through the handle of a shield.

In the following extract Philostratus (*Gymnasticus* 55) describes the function of the *halteres* as well as their shape.

5.23 The jumping weight (*halter*) is an invention of the pentathletes, invented for the long jump (*halma*) from which it takes its name. The rules recognize that the long jump is more difficult than the other disciplines in the event and allow the jumper extra help with the double pipe (*aulos*) and extra lift with the weight (*halter*) because it is a sure guide for his hands and produces a firm take-off and a well-shaped landing. The rules make it clear how important this is by not allowing a jump to be measured unless the foot marks are perfect. The long weights exercise shoulders and hands, while the round ones exercise fingers. They should be used in all athletic training, for light and heavy events alike, except for a relaxation exercise.

1 If athletes in every discipline did in fact use *halteres* in training as Philostratus recommends here, how would that affect the interpretation of vase-paintings showing them in use?

2 What do the written sources not tell us about *halteres*?

The *bater*

This entry from a Byzantine dictionary of the eleventh century AD, the *Lexica Segueriana*, refers to two earlier authorities.

5.24 *Batēr*: the front edge of the pentathletes' dug-up area, from which they jump at the beginning. **Seleucus**. But **Symmachus**: the middle from which they take off when jumping. Seleucus is better. It also means a door threshold which Homer calls a *bēlon* and the tragic poets a *bālon*.

1 What does the meaning 'threshold' suggest about the nature of the *bater*?

2 If Symmachus defined it correctly, how would that affect our understanding of how this event was performed?

3 What limitations are there on the value of this as evidence?

The vase-painting in **5.25** shows an athlete with two *halteres*. His right leg is raised, possibly to fill the circular space, but possibly indicating a particular movement.

5.25

Fragment of a kylix (cup), c. 510 BC.

Seleucus   first century AD.

Symmachus   second or third century AD.

1 What point in the jump does this represent?
2 Is this pose suited to a standing or running start?

In **5.26**, the athlete on the left looks on while possibly exercising in preparation for a jump. The central figure stretches hands and feet forward to achieve the best distance. The trainer or judge on the right looks down, presumably to ensure that the landing is 'well shaped'.

5.26

Kylix by Onesimos,
c. 500–490 BC.

In this vase-painting showing the long jump (**5.27**) the three vertical lines below the athlete are probably meant to indicate markers from previous jumps. Compare Athene's action after Odysseus' discus throw (**1.9**). Both his trainer on the far right and the athlete with two javelins hold out their hands, perhaps to congratulate him as he seems to have jumped furthest. The figures are all named.

5.27

Attic amphora,
c. 540 BC.

- In **5.23** Philostratus says that the jumping weights (*halteres*) help the athlete to achieve a well-shaped landing. Does this vase-painting show such a landing? How are the *halteres* deployed?

6 Track events

In the modern Olympics there are competitions at eight distances for runners, as well as the steeplechase, hurdles, relays and road-walking. The ancient Olympics, by contrast, recognized only three track events: the *stadion* (roughly 200 metres), the *diaulos* (roughly 400 metres) and the long-distance race (*dolichos*). Two descriptions of races are given in Chapter 1 (**1.8** and a shorter one, **1.9**, lines 120–5). While conditions in the heroic age of Homeric epic are very different from those in the stadium at Olympia, these descriptions come as close to a commentary on a foot race as we get from antiquity. The race in the *Odyssey* has a clear winner and is over as rapidly as the sprint itself, but it still contains some graphic detail, such as the dust kicked up by the runners. The race in the *Iliad* is full of exciting detail and an amusing surprise provided by a passing cow.

The foot race (*stadion*)

The word *stadion* was originally a unit of measurement, later applied to the race track of that length and then the race. However, since the Greeks had no standard measurements, the length of *stadia* is somewhat variable. At Olympia, for example, the track is 192.17 metres, while at Delphi it is 177.5 metres.

Without the 60-metre or 100-metre sprint, the *stadion* (equivalent to our 200 metres) was the fastest event. Representations of foot races on vase-paintings do not usually have any explanatory text and we have to judge which type of race they represent from the postures of the athletes. Athletes taking part are depicted taking long strides and raising their knees high while pumping energetically with their arms to secure greater momentum and balance, as in the following example (**6.1**).

6.1

Panathenaic amphora, c. 530 BC, by the Euphiletos Painter.

1 Compare these athletes to the modern sprinter. Do they have a similar
   physique and technique?
2 Look carefully at the figures of the athletes. What is unnatural about the way
   these runners are depicted? Why do you think the artist has painted them in
   this pose?

The following remark by Pausanias at Olympia indicates the need for heats
(*Description of Greece* 6.13.4).

6.2   The victors in each heat run again for the prize. So he who is crowned in the foot
      race (*stadion*) will be victorious twice.

1 What makes it necessary to hold heats in the modern Olympics?
2 What does this remark suggest about the number of competitors and the size
   of the stadium?

The double *stadion* (*diaulos*)

Diaulos in Greek means a double pipe and a double course. Athletes ran to
a turning post (**kamptēr**) at the far end of the stadium and then back to the
start. It is difficult to distinguish runners competing over one or two lengths
of the track, but a fragment of a Panathenaic amphora is conveniently labelled
diaulodromo eimi ('I am a competitor in the *diaulos*').

It is also difficult to know whether the runners in the *diaulos* kept in lane for
the whole race and each had their own turning post, or whether there was just
one post for all the athletes. Ancient evidence is not conclusive, since vase-
painters may show only one post for economy and the archaeology is open to
different interpretations.

In **6.3** the starting line (*balbis*) and foundations for the starting gate (*hysplex*,
see p. 97) can be seen extending across the stadium. The stone base in the
centre of the track a few yards in front of the *balbis* may have supported the
kampter. Alternatively, the posts set in the holes in the *balbis* may be used as
turning posts (*kampteres*) for each lane.

6.3

*The starting line (*balbis*) and starting gate (*hysplex*) in the stadium at Nemea.*

> • Are there any reasons for preferring one turning post, or more than one?

The distance race (*dolichos*)

The length of this race seems to have varied (distances range from 7 to 24 stades). It is most likely that the single turning post (*kampter*), for which a possible support is visible in **6.3**, was used for this race.

The following anecdote about Diogenes the Cynic (fourth century BC) suggests that distance runners accelerated, as modern runners do, when they approached the end of the race (Diogenes Laertius, *Lives and Opinions of Eminent Philosophers* 6.34). Compare Philostratus' comment in **6.6**.

6.4 In reply to those who said, 'You are an old man. Take it easy now,' he said, 'What if I were running in the distance race (*dolichos*)? Should I take it easy towards the end and not make an extra effort?'

Panathenaic amphorae usually depict an athletic event on one side; in **6.5**, the *dolichos* or distance race. See Chapter 9 (especially p. 174) for more detailed information on these amphorae.

6.5

Panathenaic amphora, 333 BC.

1 How can we tell that these athletes are competing in a long-distance race?
2 Compare the build and musculature of these runners with those in the *stadion* race (**6.1**).
3 Compare the physique of modern sprinters and distance runners. Do you find them similar to or different from the depictions on Greek vases?
4 Can we draw any conclusions about distance running in Greece from this?

In this extract Philostratus describes the types of physique needed for runners in various races and for those who compete in all (*Gymnasticus* 32–3). As an example of a versatile athlete he selects Leonidas of Rhodes, whose achievements are mentioned by Pausanias in **6.13**.

6.6   The best runner of the *dolichos* should have strong shoulders and neck just like a pentathlete, but his legs should be nimble and lightly built like runners in the *stadion*.

[…] For they propel their legs into a sprint with the help of their hands, as if their hands were giving them wings. The runners of the *dolichos* do this near the finishing line, but for the rest of the time they move almost as if they were striding along, holding up their hands '**on guard**' – hence their need for strong shoulders.

Nobody draws any distinction between a runner in armour or a competitor in the *stadion* or *diaulos* ever since the time when **Leonidas of Rhodes** won these three events at four Olympiads, but even so, those who are entering the events

---

… there is possibly a gap in the text here.

on guard   the defensive position in boxing.

Leonidas of Rhodes   see **6.13**.

individually should be distinguished from those entering them all together. A competitor in the race in armour (*hoplitodromos*) should have a ribcage of good length, a shoulder well developed and a well-rounded muscular thigh so that, with these holding up his shield, it is carried well.

The runners in the *stadion*, the lightest event in the games, are very good when they have a physique of good proportions, but better than them are men who are not too tall, but a little taller than the well-proportioned, since excessive height is deficient in strength, just like plants that grow too tall. They should be of firm build since the basic requirement for running well is having a good stance. Their build is like this: their legs in proportion with their shoulders, their chest of quite small proportions and internally robust, their thigh nimble, their lower leg straight, their hands proportionately large, and they should also have moderate muscles since excessive musculature puts a restriction on speed.

Competitors in the *diaulos* should be stronger than those for the *stadion*, but of lighter build than those for the **hoplitodromos**. Those who compete in the three events should have the best combination of qualities which they need for the individual events. In case anyone thinks this is not practical, there were runners like this even in **our day**.

> 1 Compare what Philostratus has to say about the runners in the *stadion* and *dolichos* with the vase-paintings in **6.1** and **6.5**.
>
> 2 How does the physique of modern athletes compare with Philostratus' ideas?
>
> 3 Do his ideas about optimum physique have any validity?

Starting the race

> Modern athletes pay careful attention to getting a good start, particularly in sprints, and use a crouched position and starting blocks. The tension is high as they wait to spring into action and false starts are not uncommon. The following anecdote from Herodotus (*Histories* 8.59) shows that false starts happened in ancient competitions too. The conversation took place as the Athenian Themistocles tried to persuade the other Greeks to remain with their ships at Salamis (480 BC; see timeline, p. 6).

6.7   Once the generals had assembled and before **Eurybiades** had the chance to raise the issue for which he had brought them together, Themistocles spoke with some

---

hoplitodromos   see **6.14–17**.

our day   third century AD.

Eurybiades   the Spartan general who was in overall command of the Greek fleet assembled to resist Xerxes' invasion.

urgency, since his need was great. But before he finished, the **Corinthian** general Adeimantus, son of Ocytus, said: 'Themistocles, at the games those who start too soon are **beaten with rods**.' But he defended himself with the riposte, 'Yes, but those who are left behind do not win crowns.'

> 1 What does this passage tell us about the importance of the start of the race?
> 2 What are the rules governing false starts in modern athletic competitions?
> 3 How reasonable do you think it is for competitors to be beaten for making a false start?

In the following extract from Aristophanes' comedy *Knights* (lines 1158–61) two characters are about to compete in pampering Demos (a figure who represents the People), and the way in which they start shows the importance the Greeks attached to ensuring fair competition.

6.8

SAUSAGE-SELLER	Do you know what you should do?
DEMOS	I will if you tell me.
SAUSAGE-SELLER	Start him and me off from the *balbides*, so that we have an equal opportunity to pamper you.
DEMOS	We must do this. Go on.
PAPHLAGONIAN AND SAUSAGE-SELLER	Right.
DEMOS	Run.
SAUSAGE-SELLER	No cutting in.

It is usually assumed that the athlete depicted in **6.9** is taking up the normal position for the start of a race. Most representations of athletes show a similar stance and the starting lines at Olympia, Nemea and elsewhere seem to confirm this.

At Nemea there are early starting lines with holes for toes to grip, with the left foot forward as in the statuette. The later starting lines at Nemea (**6.3**), Olympia and other sites have two grooves which may have been gripped by the toes at the start.

Corinthian   Corinth had a large contingent at Salamis.

beaten with rods   see p. 53 for beating as a punishment of athletes.

balbides   the Greek word *balbis* (pl. *balbides*) has been applied by archaeologists to the starting lines discovered at Olympia, Nemea and other sites (see **6.3**).

Excavations at Nemea and elsewhere have yielded evidence of starting gates (*hyspleges*) to prevent false starts. These ingenious devices were developed over time and three variations have been identified. At Nemea the track seems to have been divided into 12 lanes by posts in the starting line (*balbis*): the holes to support them are visible in **6.3**. Besides the parallel grooves and sockets for posts, at each end there is a projecting stone base which held the mechanism of the starting gate. In this version, the mechanism was the same as that of a catapult. Posts at either end of the *balbis* were held upright under tension. When released they snapped to the ground, bringing with them the two ropes stretched between them in front of the competitors, who were now able to leap forward (see **6.17**).

 6.9

Bronze statuette from Olympia, c. 500 BC.

Victorious runners

Instead of simply recording the information about a dedication of a statue of Hermes, this epigram takes the form of a dialogue with the statue. Written by Philippus (first century AD), it is recorded in the *Greek Anthology* (6.259).

6.10   Q Who set you up, beardless **Hermes**, beside the starting gates (*hyspleges*)?
       A Hermogenes.
       Q Whose son?
       A Daimeneus.

Hermes   usually depicted as beardless, sometimes with winged sandals.

Q Where from?

A Antioch.

Q For what reason does he honour you?

A Since I helped him in sprint races (*stadia*).

Q Which ones?

A At Isthmia and Nemea.

Q He was running there, was he?

A And came first.

Q Who did he beat?

A Nine boys. And he flew as if with my feet.

> The order in which the foot races were held is revealed by Pausanias in his account of the achievement of a runner called Polites from Keramos in Asia Minor (*Description of Greece* 6.13.3).

6.11   This Polites from Keramos in Caria gave a display of every form of excellence in running at Olympia. From the longest race requiring most stamina, he conditioned himself after the briefest interval for the shortest and quickest. On the same day he won victories in the *dolichos* and, immediately afterwards, the *stadion*, before adding a third for the *diaulos*.

> This victory ode, written by Pindar for Xenophon of Corinth (*Olympian* 13.35–9), celebrates Xenophon's victories in both the *stadion* race and pentathlon at the Olympics of 464 BC. Clearly athletic ability was a family characteristic, since these lines celebrate his father's double victory at the Pythian Games.

6.12   By the waters of the Alpheios, his father Thessalus
is remembered for his glorious victories.
And at **Delphi** he won the *stadion* and *diaulos* on a single day.
In the same month in **rugged Athens**
A day of foot-racing saw him crowned for **three fine victories**.

---

1 How difficult an accomplishment is it to win two track events, or even three, as Polites did, in the modern Olympics?

2 What can you deduce about the fitness of men like Thessalus and Polites?

Delphi   the site of the Pythian Games held in late August.

rugged Athens   possibly at the Panathenaia, held in the month Hecatombaion, approximately August. The crags of the Acropolis give Athens the epithet *rugged*.

three fine victories   an ancient commentator (scholiast) informs us that the events were *diaulos*, *stadion* and race in armour (*hoplitodromos*).

Pausanias records other athletes who won all the foot races at particular festivals, an achievement which would be impossible to emulate today.

6.13   However, Leonidas of Rhodes has the greatest fame for running. He maintained his fitness and speed for **four Olympiads**, achieving a total of 12 victories in foot races.

> • How does Leonidas' achievement compare with that of Polites (**6.11**)?

The race in armour (*hoplitodromos*)

> The race in armour (*hoplitodromos*) seems to bring the games to an end, perhaps because of its late addition to the programme (not until 520 BC – see **2.4**), although Philostratus (**6.14**) offers a more ingenious explanation. This event varied in length, but at Olympia it was the same as the *diaulos*.
>
> In his discussion of the origin of the *hoplitodromos*, Philostratus firstly considers an occasion when the Eleans won a battle during the Olympic festival and a **hoplite** ran into the stadium with news of victory. However, since a similar story is told at Delphi, Argos and Corinth, Philostratus is sceptical and offers a different explanation (*Gymnasticus* 7).

6.14   What I say is that, while it was established for a military reason, it was admitted into the competitions to mark a beginning of hostilities, with the shield showing that the truce (**ekecheiria**) has ended and weapons are needed. If you listen to the herald attentively, you see that at the end of all events, he announces that the competition that dispenses prizes is over and that the trumpet is signalling the business of **Enyalios** by calling young men to arms. This announcement also gives the order to pick up and take away the olive oil, not for anointing, but indicating the cessation of anointing.

> During his description of Sparta, Pausanias specifically states that the *hoplitodromos* brought the athletic events to a close (compare **6.14**) (*Description of Greece* 3.14.3).

6.15   You will see a *stele* on which are inscribed the victories for racing which Chionis, a Spartan, won at Olympia and elsewhere. There were seven Olympic victories,

---

four Olympiads   164, 160, 156, 152 BC.

Enyalios   a name of Ares, god of war.

stele   a stone slab for an inscription.

four in the *stadion* and the rest in the *diaulos*. The race with the shield at the end of the games was **not yet** part of the programme.

Pausanias reveals some details about the equipment used in the race when he is describing the statues at Olympia and the contents of the great temple of Zeus (*Description of Greece* 6.10.4 and 5.12.8).

6.16   Demaretos of **Heraia**, his son and grandson, each won two victories at Olympia. Demaretos won at the 65th Olympiad [520 BC] – when the race in armour was first held – and he repeated his success at the next Olympiad. His statue represents him holding a shield as they do in our day, but also with a helmet on his head and greaves on his shins, equipment which has been withdrawn from use in the race over time by the Eleans and the rest of the Greeks. (6.10.4)

Here too are located 25 bronze shields which are carried by the men armed for the race. (5.12.8)

This vase-painting (**6.17**) from Athens shows two runners in the *hoplitodromos* (a third runner is painted to the right – his right leg is just visible). On the left an upright post can be seen, with two blocks joined by what looks like rope at its base; two ropes are stretched horizontally from it.

6.17

Panathenaic amphora from Athens, fourth century BC.

---

1   What stage of the race does this depict? How can you tell?
2   Is the *hysplex* system illustrated on this vase?

---

not yet   the *hoplitodromos* was introduced in 520 BC.

Heraia   a town in Arcadia, not far from Olympia.

Here   inside the temple of Zeus.

7 Combat sports

The three combat sports were wrestling, boxing and the *pankration*. The Greeks called them the '**heavy events**' because there were no weight divisions, and bigger men therefore dominated the competitions (but see **7.37**).

This passage of Pausanias (*Description of Greece* 6.15.3–5) makes it clear that the order of events could be changed, but it also reveals the normal order for the heavy events in the late third century BC.

7.1 The statue of Kleitomachos of Thebes was set up by his father Hermokrates, and the following achievements brought him fame. At the Isthmus he won the wrestling for men and on the same day he defeated in combat the competitors for boxing and the *pankration*. All three of his victories at Delphi were for the *pankration*. At Olympia this Kleitomachos was the second man (after **Theagenes of Thasos**) to be proclaimed victor in the *pankration* and boxing. He won his victory in the *pankration* first, at the 141st Olympiad [216 BC]. The next Olympiad had this Kleitomachos competing in the *pankration* and boxing, but also had Kapros of Elis ready to compete in both wrestling and the *pankration* on the same day. When Kapros had already secured victory in the wrestling, Kleitomachos told the judges (*Hellanodikai*) that it would be fair for them to call in the *pankration* before he received wounds from boxing. His request was reasonable and the *pankration* was announced in that order. Even though he was beaten by Kapros, against the boxers he fought with a strong will and unflagging stamina.

> 1 Would you agree that Kleitomachos' request was fair?
> 2 What does this passage suggest about the damage that could be sustained in the heavy events?

Wrestling

After the running events, wrestling (***palē***) was the first sport introduced at Olympia both as a separate discipline and as part of the pentathlon at the 18th Olympic competitions in 708 BC (see **2.4**), an indication of the esteem in which it was held. In mythology Herakles was a noted wrestler, particularly for his bout with the giant Antaeus. The history of wrestling can be traced back to around 2000 BC in Egypt. It is the least violent of the combat sports and success depended as much on skill as sheer strength, as is shown in the bout between Ajax and Odysseus in the *Iliad* (**1.7**). The wrestling competition at Olympia and elsewhere probably took place in the stadium where a dug-up area (*skamma*) was created for the event (see **7.7**).

Theagenes of Thasos　see **8.22** on this famous boxer.

Organizing the wrestling and *pankration* competitions

In this extract from Lucian (*Hermotimos* 39–40), Lycinos is trying to convince Hermotimos that he should not accept one set of philosophical teachings without first examining the others. He uses the analogy of the lottery for selecting pairs of contestants in combat sports: when there was an odd number, one would be given a bye and Lycinos argues that the organizers would have to examine all the lots to find the one not paired. After this passage, he is forced to concede that at Olympia where letters on the lots were used in alphabetical order, if there were nine contestants, the one drawing **epsilon** (the fifth letter) would be immediately identified as the odd one, even when the other letters had not been revealed.

7.2   LYCINOS   Hermotimos, I think you have often seen athletic competitions.

       HERMOTIMOS   You are quite right, often and at many venues.

       LYCINOS   Well then, did you ever have a seat close to the judges themselves?

       HERMOTIMOS   Oh yes by Zeus, just recently at Olympia on the left of the judges (*Hellanodikai*). Euandridas of Elis kept a seat for me among his fellow citizens because I was keen to get a close look at everything that happened among the judges.

       LYCINOS   So you must also know how they draw lots to determine the competitors to face each other in the wrestling and the *pankration*.

       HERMOTIMOS   Yes, I know.

       LYCINOS   Then you can explain better what you have had a close view of.

       HERMOTIMOS   In the old days, when Herakles was a judge, bay leaves …

       LYCINOS   Not ancient history, Hermotimos! Tell me what you witnessed in close proximity.

       HERMOTIMOS   A silver urn sacred to the god is placed before the judges. Into this are thrown small lots the same size as a bean, and inscribed. Two have alpha written on them, two have beta, two more have gamma and so on in succession if there are more competitors, so that there are always two lots with the same letter.

Each of the competitors comes forward and with a prayer to Zeus puts his hand in the urn and takes out one of the lots. Then another takes his turn after him. An official (*mastigophoros*)

---

epsilon   the Greek alphabet begins alpha, beta, gamma, delta, epsilon (a, b, g, d, e).

mastigophoros   literally 'whip-bearer', one of the officials often seen on vase-paintings supervising games and ready to punish anyone breaking the rules. See **3.26, 6.7, 7.4, 7.27**.

stands beside each one and holds up the competitor's hand, not allowing him to read the letter he has drawn. Once they all have one, a chief official (*alytarchēs*) I think, or one of the judges themselves (I no longer remember this detail), goes round examining their lots as they stand in a circle and in this way he matches one in possession of an alpha with the one who has drawn the other alpha, whether for wrestling or the *pankration*. Likewise the ones with beta and the others with the same letter he assigns by the same method.

That's what happens if there is an even number of competitors, say eight, four or ten, but if the number is too big – five, seven or nine – an extra letter written on just one lot is thrown in with the others, although it has no matching letter. The man who draws this lot **sits it out**, waiting until these bouts are over, because he has no matching letter. And it is no small stroke of luck for the athlete that he is due to fight tired opponents when he is fresh himself.

- Is drawing lots still the best means of pairing opponents in sport?

Beginning the bout

The marble relief in **7.3** shows two wrestlers in the so-called 'ram' position, in which the wrestlers push against each other with their heads and each tries to secure a grip on his opponent's arm. In this depiction the wrestler on the right has secured a grip with both hands on the left arm of his opponent, who counters by pushing against his left shoulder. The other figures represented on this face are: (left) a runner about to start (his hands are visible here), and (right) a youth preparing to throw a javelin (visible, bottom right).

---

alytarchēs   the official in charge of the *mastigophoroi* and other officials who were responsible for drawing lots, crowd control and punishing athletes who were breaking the rules.

sits it out   when an athlete won without having to fight it was called 'dustless' (*akoniti*). Compare **7.9**.

7.3

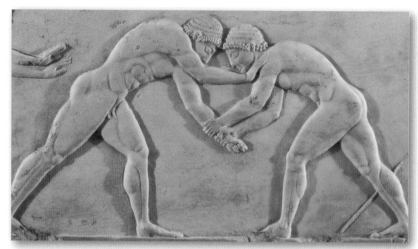

Detail of the relief sculpture on the marble base for a statue; Athens, c. 510 BC.

> 1 Compare this representation of wrestlers with what Anacharsis says in **7.7**.
> 2 Do they offer a convincing illustration of the start of a wrestling match?

In the vase-painting shown in **7.4** the trainer leans forward, pointing with his right hand as if giving instruction to the two wrestlers. The wrestler on the right seems to hold his arms up to allow his companion to secure a hold around his waist. Other vase-paintings and statuettes reveal that the wrestler then lifts his opponent and turns him over to throw him down head first.

7.4

Detail from an Attic wine-cooler (psykter), c. 520–510 BC, painted by Phintias.

In **7.5**, a clothed trainer with rod is visible in the top left. The wrestler on the right seems to have attempted to grasp his opponent around the waist, but his bearded opponent has seized his left arm and slips his own left arm underneath it.

Detail of an amphora, c.525 BC by the Andokides Painter.

1 Is the wrestler on the left poised to achieve a throw as in **7.6**?

2 It has been suggested that the wrestler on the right has avoided his opponent's attempt to seize him by the waist by stepping to the right. How easy is it to determine the sequence of moves that led to this position?

7.6 shows a throw across the shoulder. The wrestler on the left goes down on one knee as he completes a shoulder throw. The judge, holding a rod in his hand, is in position to watch for a fall.

Attic cup, c. 530 BC.

Lucian, writing in the second century AD, set his dialogue *Anacharsis* in the sixth century BC (see **5.9** for further details). Anacharsis has come to Athens especially to talk with the famous law-giver Solon to find out about the laws and customs of the Greeks. Here he is surprised by wrestling (*Anacharsis* 1–2 and 28).

7.7   ANACHARSIS   Solon, why are your young men acting this way? Some of them are twined together attempting to trip each other and some are throttling and twisting each other and getting all entangled as they roll around in the mud like pigs. Yet to start with, as soon as they took off their clothes – I did actually see this – they put on a generous amount of **oil** and perfectly peacefully rubbed each other down in turns. After that I've no idea what has come over them, but they bring their heads together and push each other and use their foreheads to butt like rams. Now look! That one there has picked up the other by the legs and has thrown him to the ground. Now he has dropped down on top of him and won't let him up as he pushes him down into the mud. To cap it all, he has now wound his legs round his waist and thrust his forearm up under his throat, strangling the poor man, who is slapping him on the shoulder in supplication, I presume, in order not to be choked to death. With no regard for the oil, they don't hesitate to get dirty, but rub off their ointment and get defiled with filth while pouring with sweat and making themselves look ridiculous – at least in my eyes – like eels slipping out of each other's hands.

Some others are doing the same thing in the uncovered part of the court. These actually aren't in mud, but they have spread this deep layer of sand in the pit they have dug and they are sprinkling each other and of their own accord piling it on themselves in the manner of cockerels. Their intention, I suppose, is to make it less easy for them to escape in clinches, since the sand removes the slipperiness and gives a firmer grip on dry skin. (1–2)

SOLON   My strange friend, listen to the reason why the mud and dust, which you thought quite ridiculous at first, are put down. The first reason is to prevent them having to fall on a hard surface, allowing them to

---

oil   see pp. 160–1 and **8.51**. Athletes rubbed themselves down with olive oil before taking part in a competition or before practice. After exercise, they scraped the oil, sweat and dirt from their bodies with a ***stlengis*** or *strigil*.

fall safely on a soft surface. Secondly there is an inevitable increase in slipperiness when they are sweating in the mud which made you liken them to eels, but which is neither pointless nor ridiculous. Actually, this makes no small contribution to their strength and muscle tone when, with both of them in this condition, they have to get a firm grip and hold on as their opponent tries to slip free. Don't think it is an easy task to pick someone up in the mud when they are sweaty and oiled and doing their best to escape and slip through your hands. As I said before, all these things are useful for wars, in case there's a need to pick up a wounded friend easily and carry him out of danger or even to grab an enemy and get back carrying him off the ground. This is why we train to excess, setting harder tasks so that they undergo lesser tasks with far more ease. (28)

1 Is it possible to distinguish whether Lucian is describing wrestlers or pankratiasts?
2 How valid is the point Solon makes in the last sentence?
3 Does any part of this description match any of the positions in the illustrations?
4 How does a wrestler signify submission in the first of these two passages?

In this epigram (Philippos in *Greek Anthology* 16.25), the 'sand' which served as the surface on which athletes wrestled is clearly distinguished from the 'dust' which the athletes rubbed on their bodies.

7.8   If you have heard of Damostratos from Sinope who won the pine at Isthmia six times, he's the one you are looking at. In tortuous wrestling his back never left an impression in the sand (*psammos*) from a fall. Look into his face with its wild, animal spirit, how it still preserves the old competitive urge for victory. The bronze says, 'Let my base set me free and, as if alive, I will cover myself in dust (*konis*) for the seventh time now.'

• Does this epigram help to clarify the description in *Anacharsis* (7.7)?

Deciding the winner

The winner of a wrestling bout could be determined not only by submission, but also by falls. Exactly what constituted a fall is a matter of controversy: although the sources do mention falling on the knees and the back, it is not clear whether one knee or two touching the ground would constitute a fall (see **7.6**). It is clear from numerous passing references in antiquity that to decide a bout three falls had to be achieved. This suggests that a maximum of five falls would be needed to decide a winner. A fall only required the relevant part of the body to touch the ground, unlike in modern freestyle wrestling where an opponent has to be manoeuvred so that both shoulders are in contact with the mat. There was no system of points-scoring similar to that used in the modern Olympics to reward successful holds or moves. However, getting the opponent into a position in which he was rendered helpless was also considered a fall. There is an anecdote about Alcibiades in his youth (Plutarch, *Alcibiades* 2) in which Alcibiades bites his opponent, who has him in a hold, to prevent a fall. When his opponent accuses him of biting like women, he retorts, 'No, like lions!' Biting was clearly against the rules, although the anecdote serves to illustrate Alcibiades' quick wit rather than the rules of the sport.

> This satirical epigram from the *Greek Anthology* (Anon., 11.316) may not refer to the famous Milo of Croton (see **8.18–21**) since this story is not told about him by any other author.

7.9   On one occasion Milo was the only wrestler to come to a sacred competition. The supervisor (*athlothetes*) summoned him to give him the crown immediately, but as he came forward, he slipped and fell onto his hip. There was an outcry against crowning this man if he had taken a fall when unopposed, but he stood up in front of everyone and shouted back, 'Aren't there three? I've taken one fall. Now let someone throw me the other times.'

> **1** What impression of Milo does this epigram give?
> **2** Why might he have been the only contender?
> **3** What does this epigram tell us about the way the event was conducted?

> It seems strange that Leontiskos was allowed to use the following technique (Pausanias, *Description of Greece* 6.4.3), since breaking fingers was explicitly forbidden on a late sixth-century BC inscription on a bronze tablet at Olympia. Unfortunately the tablet is badly damaged and the precise context for the ban cannot be established.

7.10   Next to [the statue of] **Sostratos** is one of an adult male wrestler, Leontiskos, who was a Sicilian by birth, from Messene, on the strait. It is said that he was crowned **by the Amphictyons** and twice by the Eleans and that his [method of] wrestling was just like the *pankration* technique of Sostratos of Sicyon: he didn't know how to throw his opponents and he used to win by breaking their fingers.

Sostratos see **7.36**.

by the Amphictyons the Amphictyons were representatives of the league of neighbouring states that controlled the Sanctuary at Delphi.

Boxing

It is hardly surprising that Homer called boxing 'painful' (*Iliad* 23.653), since it is a violent and potentially fatal sport. The injuries described by writers such as Homer, Theocritus (**7.16**) or Apollonius (**7.17**) and the damage, especially to boxers' faces, represented in both art and literature (**7.14**) offer graphic illustration of just how painful this sport could be. The precautions taken in modern boxing seek to minimize the potential hazards and far exceed the protection offered to combatants in Greek athletic festivals. Amateur boxers at the modern Olympics are protected by a whole raft of rules. There are eleven weight divisions to ensure even contests, in contrast to the Greek practice of only distinguishing between men and boys (as in **1.1**). The length of each bout has been restricted (since the year 2000) to four two-minute rounds, separated by a minute's break. The Greek bouts only ended by knock-out or submission. Protective headgear is now standard for amateur boxing, and the Greeks appear to have had some protection for the ears, at least for sparring. The modern ring is 6.1 metres square, with four ropes and padded corner-posts to confine the bout in a reasonably safe way. The Greeks had no ring as such, but there seems to have been a method of confining the space for fighting. References to a *klimax* (literally, 'ladder') and a vase-painting showing a horizontal bar being held up behind two boxers are tantalizing glimpses of what may well have been regular practice, since it would not be practical for a spectator sport not to be confined. Modern referees have the power to stop a fight when one boxer is taking too much punishment or is deemed unable to continue safely. A cut can stop a contest and doctors are always at the ringside with the power to halt a bout for medical reasons. A fighter's corner can also prevent their fighter from unnecessary suffering by throwing in the towel. Even so, modern boxers can push themselves to the limits of physical endurance, as happened in the 1975 'Thriller in Manila' between Joe Frazier and Mohammed Ali, when Ali collapsed in the ring after Frazier did not come out for the final round. Modern boxing gloves afford considerable protection to the wearer's hands and his opponent's skin. International rules stipulate they must weigh 284 g (10 oz), with padding making up at least 50 per cent of the weight. While there is some evidence for padded gloves used in sparring, for actual bouts Greek boxers wore *himantes*, leather strips tied around the wrists and hands which were sometimes nicknamed 'ants' because of their sting.

With no weight divisions and no rounds, boxing in antiquity was dominated by men of substantial strength, stamina and skill.

The origin of boxing

Philostratus explains why the Spartans invented boxing (*Gymnasticus* 9).

7.11 Boxing was a Spartan invention which at some time reached the barbarian **Bebrykes**. **Polydeukes** was its best exponent. These facts explain why poets sang of him. The Spartans of old began boxing for the following reasons. They had no helmets and they did not think it in keeping with their native traditions to fight while wearing one, but they had a shield which served instead of a helmet if it was skilfully deployed. And so, to protect themselves from blows to the face and to withstand being hit, they practised boxing and got their faces used to enduring blows. But as time went on, they abandoned boxing and likewise the *pankration*, because they thought it shameful to compete in these events where Sparta could be accused of lacking courage if one man surrendered.

> 1 Would you approve of the Spartans' reasons for practising the sport or for abandoning it?
>
> 2 What is your attitude to boxing as a school sport?

This epigram from the *Greek Anthology* (6.256) celebrates the awesome appearance of a boxer called Nikophon of Miletus, who served as a magistrate in AD 11–12. It was written by Antipater of Thessalonica (first century BC to first century AD).

7.12 The **Milesian giant**'s sinew thick as a bull's, his shoulders iron like **Atlas**', his hair and majestic beard like Herakles', and his lion's eyes – not even Olympian Zeus saw these without trembling when Nikophon won the men's boxing at Olympia.

In the following extract Philostratus sets out his ideas for the most suitable physique for a boxer (*Gymnasticus* 34).

7.13 The boxer should have long hands, solid forearms, powerfully built upper arms, strong shoulders and a long neck. Thicker wrists deliver heavier blows but less thick wrists are supple and strike with ease. He should be supported on firm hips because holding hands out on guard makes the body unbalanced unless it rests on strong hips. I don't think that having thick calves is of any value in a competitive event, least of all in boxing, because they are sluggish when set against opponents' legs and are easily caught when an opponent attacks. He should have a straight lower leg and one in proportion to his thighs which should be unconstrained and set apart, since the boxer's shape is better suited for attack if his thighs don't

Bebrykes a tribe who lived in Mysia (north-west Turkey), on the eastern shore of the Hellespont (see **7.15**).

Polydeukes better known by his Roman name Pollux. In the usual version of the myth he was the son of Zeus and twin brother of Castor, whose father was Tyndareus, a mortal. The two together were known as the Dioscuri.

Milesian giant Nikophon.

Atlas the deity who supported the sky on his shoulders in myth.

touch. The best stomach is contracted because men like that are nimble and their breathing is good. Even so, a boxer has some benefit from a paunch because such a belly prevents blows to the face by impeding the striker's delivery.

> • Would you agree with Philostratus' notion of a boxer's physique?

Lucillius, the author of a substantial number of satirical epigrams in the *Greek Anthology*, wrote several parodies of the sort of epigrams which celebrated the achievements of athletes. This one (11.75) 'celebrates' the physical damage to the boxer's face in the exaggerated manner of comedy. Olympicus is an obviously invented name for an athlete.

7.14   **Augustus**, Olympicus here, who's like this now, used to have a nose, a chin, an eyebrow, little ears, and some eyelids. Then he entered the lists as a boxer and lost everything. He didn't even get a share of the inheritance from his father because his brother produced a likeness of him that he had and he was judged to be a stranger since he didn't look anything like it.

> • How far do you think these descriptions of the physical attributes of boxers are realistic?

In the following two extracts from Theocritus, the twin Dioscuri have joined the expedition for the Golden Fleece on Jason's ship the *Argo*. En route to Colchis the Argo has landed in the country of the Bebrykes, just south of the Bosporos facing modern Istanbul. The Dioscuri, who have wandered off on their own, come across Amykos, the monstrous king of the Bebrykes, beside a spring. He is described as a typical boxer (*Idyll* 22: 'Hymn to the Dioscuri, Castor and Polydeukes' 45–50).

7.15   Terrible to look at, his **ears bruised** from the blows of hard fists, his mighty chest 45
and broad back bulged with flesh of iron like some colossal statue of wrought metal. Just below his shoulders the muscles in his solid arms stood out like round boulders which a river, swollen in winter, has rolled and smoothed in its strong 50
currents.

Augustus   Lucillius, writing in the first century AD, addresses the emperor, probably Nero (Augustus was the first Roman emperor, but like Caesar, the name was used generally to mean 'emperor').

ears bruised   compare Plato, *Gorgias* 515e where Callicles refers to Spartan sympathizers as 'men with bust-up ears' because of their devotion to boxing. A Greek bronze statue of the first century BC found in Rome depicts a seated boxer with ears badly swollen and bleeding (copper inlay is used for the blood).

Amykos proves to be most inhospitable and before he will let them drink from the spring, he challenges Polydeukes to a boxing match. Polydeukes, son of Zeus and Leda, excelled at boxing and is described as 'fearsome to challenge at boxing when he has bound his hands round the middle with oxhide thongs' (*Idyll* 22.2–3).

Although the reward for victory is to drink from the spring, Theocritus makes Polydeukes show a typical Greek interest in what prizes are at stake (see **1.3** for prizes offered by Achilles). Amykos' uncompromising reply that the loser shall belong to the winner emphasizes his barbaric nature. When the Bebrykes and the Argonauts have assembled, the contest begins (*Idyll* 22.80–134).

7.16   When they had strengthened their hands with strips of oxhide and had wound   80
the long thongs around their forearms, they came together on the middle ground, breathing with intent to kill each other. Then they had a great struggle in their eagerness to get the sunlight at their back, but it was you, Polydeukes, who   85
outwitted the big hulk by your skill, and the sun's rays fell full in Amykos' face. But he, with anger in his heart, charged forward aiming blows with his fists, and as he came on, the son of Tyndareus struck him on the point of his chin, which made him more riled than before. He mixed up the fight and pressed home a   90
strong attack with his head down. The Bebrykes shouted encouragement while the heroes on the other side cheered on mighty Polydeukes, fearing that the man **the size of Tityus** would overwhelm him by crowding him in the narrow space.

But the **son of Zeus**, stepping aside this way and that, kept lacerating him with   95
both fists in turn and stalled his attack, confident though the **son of Poseidon** was. Amykos, groggy from the blows, came to a standstill and spat out red blood, while all the heroes shouted at the sight of the painful wounds around his mouth and   100
jaw. His face was puffed up and his eyes were narrowed. The lord Polydeukes kept confusing him, feinting with his fists from every direction. But when he realized that his opponent was at his mercy, he delivered a blow down on his brow above the middle of his nose and gashed open the whole forehead to the bone. From   105
that punch Amykos was stretched out flat on his back over the lush vegetation. He got up again and then it turned into a bitter battle. Hitting each other with the hard thongs, they were out for the kill. The chief of the Bebrykes kept landing his fists on the chest and below the neck, but undefeated Polydeukes kept messing up   110
his whole face with disfiguring blows. As Amykos sweated, his flesh began to cave

---

the size of Tityus   a giant of vast size who tried to rape the goddess Leto and was punished for eternity in Hades by having his liver consumed by vultures.

son of Zeus   Polydeukes. Myths about the Dioscuri do not agree about their parentage. In the best-known version, Zeus seduced Tyndareus' wife Leda in the form of a swan and fathered Polydeukes, while Tyndareus fathered his twin Castor.

son of Poseidon   Amykos was son of the sea-god Poseidon and a local nymph.

in and he was soon reduced from his giant size. But as the struggle intensified, his opponent was acquiring ever more stout limbs and a **better complexion**. 114

… Well, Amykos was keen to pull off a major coup and from his guard position 118 he leant across and grabbed Polydeukes' left hand in his own left. Stepping 120 forward with the opposite foot he swung his broad fist from his right side. If he had connected, he would have hurt the **king of Amyklai**, but he ducked his head down, at the same time landing a blow below the left temple with a strong right hand and putting his shoulder into it. Dark blood quickly poured from the gash 125 in his temple. With his left he struck his mouth and the rows of his teeth were rattled. All the time he was raining sharper, hurtful blows on his face until his cheeks were pulverized. Losing his senses he sprawled full length on the ground and **raised both his hands**, refusing to fight on as he was close to death. 130

In your victory over him, boxer Polydeukes, you behaved with no arrogance, but he swore you a great oath, calling on his father Poseidon from the sea, that never again would he give trouble to strangers.

> Apollonius of Rhodes, like Theocritus, was a poet writing in Alexandria in the third century BC. The encounter of Polydeukes and Amykos also features as an episode in his epic poem *Argonautica* (Voyage of the *Argo*). In this extract he describes the same fight, but with variations (*Argonautica* 2.67–98).

7.17   When, standing apart, they were equipped with leather thongs, at once they raised their heavy fists in front of their faces and advanced fiercely on one another. Then, in the same way that a fierce crest of a wave at sea rears up against a swift ship, 70 but she only just escapes through the skill of her clever pilot as a wave surges up to flood over her sides, so did the king of the Bebrykes begin to stalk the **son of Tyndareus**, trying to intimidate him and allowing him no respite.

But he avoided every onslaught by his craft and remained unhurt. He was quick 75 to weigh up his opponent's rough boxing, where he was invincibly strong, and where he was weaker. Then he stood his ground without wavering and traded

---

better complexion   this might seem strange, but appearances can change quickly during a fight, as this description from the famous fight in 1974 between Mohammed Ali and George Foreman (the so-called 'Rumble in the Jungle') shows: 'Foreman came out for the sixth looking like an alley cat with chewed up brows. Lumps and swellings were all over his face, his skin equal to tar that has baked in the sun. When the bell rang, however, he looked dangerous again, no longer a cat, but a bull' (Mailer).

king of Amyklai   Polydeukes. Amyklai was just south of Sparta, the city from which the Dioscuri originate.

raised both his hands   vase-paintings show boxers surrendering by raising the index finger of one hand.

son of Tyndareus   Polydeukes. See **7.16n.**

blow for blow. As when carpenters forcefully drive home a ship's timbers that 80
resist the sharp nails by striking with their hammers, and the noise resounds time
after time without let-up, that was the sound from the cheeks and jaws of them
both: and there was an unspeakable crunching of teeth. Standing toe to toe, they
didn't stop exchanging blows until a debilitating shortage of breath overcame 85
them both. They **stood a little way apart** and wiped plenty of sweat from their
brows, wearily panting for breath. Then they rushed at each other again, like
two bulls furiously competing for a grazing heifer. At that point Amykos raised 90
himself up on his toes like a **man who kills an ox**, and stretching up from his feet,
he brought his heavy fist down on his opponent. Polydeukes resisted the attack
by moving his head to the side and taking a slight blow from the forearm on his
shoulder. He stepped in close, getting his knee past Amykos' knee and in a rapid
move struck him above the ear, breaking the bones in his head. Amykos dropped 95
to his knees in pain. The **Minyan heroes** shouted in triumph, and Amykos' life
slipped away all at once.

1 How far do these accounts of the fight agree?
2 Where do they differ?
3 Do they tell us anything about the tactics used by boxers?
4 What does the passage by Theocritus (**7.16**) imply about attitudes to body shots?

In this extract the historian Polybius, who lived in the second century BC, compares the change of feelings of the people towards the Macedonian king **Perseus** with this change of support by the crowd for two boxers (*Histories* 27.9.3–13).

7.18 When a low-ranking and much inferior opponent faces a famous and seemingly
unbeatable athlete, the crowd immediately switches its support to the inferior
man. They shout encouragement and impulsively get behind him. If he even
lands a glancing blow to the face and makes a mark with it, they all respond with
immediate involvement. Sometimes they even try to mock the other man, not
because they hate him or don't rate him, but rather surprisingly because they
feel sympathy for the underdog and instinctively shift their support to him. But
if somebody gets their attention at the right moment, they are quick to change

---

stood a little way apart   there were no rounds in Greek boxing.

man who kills an ox   at a sacrifice the ox was killed or stunned with a blow to the head
before its throat was cut.

Minyan heroes   the Argonauts.

Perseus   king of Macedonia from 179 BC until defeated by the Romans at the battle of
Pydna in 168.

side and instantly correct their mistake. This, they say, is what Kleitomachos did. He had the reputation of being invincible in athletic circles and his fame was at its height all over the world. The story goes that King **Ptolemy** wanted the credit for destroying his reputation and so he had the boxer Aristonicos trained with ambitious thoroughness, since he appeared to have a superior talent for this sport, and then sent him off.

When Aristonicos arrived in Greece and came face to face with Kleitomachos at Olympia, immediately, it would seem, the crowd was inclined to support Aristonicos and cheered him on, thrilled that someone had the courage, at least briefly, to face Kleitomachos. When it became apparent in the course of the bout that he was a match for his opponent and he even inflicted some serious damage, there was applause and the crowd began to get carried away with excitement, shouting encouragement to Aristonicos. It was at this moment that they say Kleitomachos backed off briefly to catch his breath and turned to the crowd, asking them why they were cheering Aristonicos and giving him their full support. Had they noticed Kleitomachos fighting unfairly in the bout or were they not aware that he was now fighting for the honour of Greece and Aristonicos for that of King Ptolemy? So, did they want an Egyptian to beat the Greeks and carry off the Olympic crown or a Theban and Boeotian to be announced as the boxing champion? When Kleitomachos finished speaking, they say there was such a shift of feeling among the crowd that with this reversal Aristonicos was beaten more by the crowd than by Kleitomachos.

> 1 In this and the passage from Apollonius (**7.17**), what makes formal rounds unnecessary?
> 2 How much influence does the support of the crowd have in modern spectator sports? What do we mean by 'home advantage'?

Practising

> In this extract from Plato's *Laws* (829e–830c) about the type of citizen needed by the state, athletic training, especially boxing, is considered important for producing men fit for military service.

7.19   Well then, what sort of men am I to train up, when the organization of the state is complete? Shouldn't they be athletes, those who compete in the greatest contests where they face countless opponents? 'Absolutely right,' would be the correct response. So, what follows? If we were training boxers or pankratiasts or athletes in some other similar event, would we enter the actual contest without previously practising combat with an opponent on a daily basis? Say we were boxers, we

---

Ptolemy   king of Egypt.

would surely spend endless days before the contest learning how to fight, and working out, practising by imitation all the skills we were going to use when the time came for us to fight to win. We would get as close to actual combat as possible, wearing padded gloves (*sphairai*) instead of leather thongs (*himantes*), so that punching and slipping punches were practised to the fullest extent required. And if we happened to be very short of sparring partners, would we not have the nerve to hang up a lifeless dummy and practise on that because we were afraid of the laughter of fools? And even if we were on our own with absolutely no sparring partners, alive or inanimate, wouldn't we have taken to fighting against ourselves, literally shadow boxing? After all, what other name would one give to using one's arms like this?

> In one of his moral essays, Plutarch says it is best for a politician to adopt a mild manner and avoid anger when in a dispute. He makes a comparison with practising boxing (*Moralia* 825e).

7.20   For they bind gloves (*episphairai*) round the hands of men who are fighting **in the palaistra** so that the contest, involving soft and painless blows, does not turn out to be fatal.

> In the following extract Philostratus (*Gymnasticus* 57) discusses punchbags for athletes training for boxing or the *pankration*.

7.21   A **punchbag** should be hung up for boxers, and more importantly for those who regularly practise the *pankration*. The one for boxing should be light, since only the hands of boxers exercise on the punchbag, but the one for the pankratiasts should be heavier and bigger so that they can practise standing their ground against the momentum of the punchbag and exercise their shoulders and fingers by striking against an object of equivalent size. The athlete's head should butt it and he should subject himself to all the upright forms of the *pankration*.

Ear protectors

> There are a few scattered references to ear protectors (*amphōtides*) worn by boxers. The description of Amykos in Theocritus (**7.15**) gives graphic illustration of the damage a boxer's ears could suffer. In this discussion about keeping vice away from the young, Plutarch gives the obvious reason for their use (*Moralia* 38b).

---

in the *palaistra*   directly contradicting Plutarch, *Moralia* 638e.

punchbag   the Greek word literally means 'leather sack'.

7.22   Xenocrates said that ear protectors should be put on children rather than on athletes, on the grounds that the latter have their ears disfigured by blows, while the former have their characters corrupted by words.

Pausanias describes the death and victory of the boxer Kreugas in his *Description of Greece*, 8.40.3.

7.23   I know that the Argives did **something similar** in the case of Kreugas, a boxer from **Epidamnos**. For the Argives gave Kreugas the crown at the Nemean Games when he was dead, because Damoxenus of Syracuse who was fighting against him broke the agreement they had with each other. For evening was about to fall on them while they were still boxing and they agreed within hearing to take turns striking each other. In those days boxers didn't yet have a sharp thong on the wrist of each hand, but still boxed with soft gloves binding them under the hollow of the hand so that their fingers were left exposed. Thin thongs of raw oxhide plaited together made up the soft gloves. Anyway, on this occasion Kreugas aimed his blow at Damoxenus' head, but Damoxenus told Kreugas to hold up his arm and when he did this, Damoxenus struck him under the ribs with straight fingers. Because of the sharpness of his nails and the force of the blow, he thrust his hand into his opponent's body. He took hold of the guts, dragged them out and broke them off. Kreugas died instantly and the Argives expelled Damoxenus for breaking the terms of the agreement by using many blows on his opponent instead of one. They awarded victory to the dead man Kreugas and had a statue of him made in Argos which in my day still stood in the sanctuary of Lycian Apollo.

> 1   What does this passage tell us about the organization of the bouts?
> 2   This is clearly an unusual situation. On what technicality was Damoxenus disqualified?

Equipment

In this extract from *Gymnasticus* 10, Philostratus explains the change in style of the boxing gloves (*himantes*).

7.24   Equipment for boxing in the early days was like this. The four fingers were put into a strap and projected beyond the strap just enough to make a fist when they were clenched tight. They were held together by a thong which they had built up like a support from the forearm.

---

something similar   Pausanias tells this story after that of Arrhachion the pankratiast when he sees the latter's statue at Phigalia (see **7.33**).

Epidamnos   a city in Illyricum on the east coast of the Adriatic, later called Dyrrhachium.

But nowadays it has changed, since they knead hides of the fattest cattle and make a boxing glove (*himas*) which is sharp and projects. The thumb does not give any assistance to the fingers in punching so that wounds are kept in proportion, since the whole hand is not engaged. That is why they exclude the *himantes* (gloves) of pigskin from the stadia, as they consider blows from these painful and hard to heal.

> In the twelfth century AD Eustathius taught and wrote in Constantinople before becoming bishop of Thessalonica. The following brief extract from his work, *Commentary on Homer's Iliad* 1324.18, perhaps adds a little to our understanding of why leather thongs/gloves (*himantes*) were worn.

7.25 The leather *himantes* of the boxers are wound around their hands, making some contribution to their blows and keeping the fingers together while making them hard and round like a club.

> The vase-painting in **7.26** shows two boxers. Note how each hand and wrist is bound by a leather thong (*himas*). The boxer on the left has blood pouring from his nose. Boxers in art display typical wounds such as a flattened nose, cuts to the face and swollen or bleeding ears.

7.26

Detail from an amphora, c. 530 BC, with the inscription 'made by Nikosthenes'.

1 Is the physique of these boxers like that described by Philostratus in **7.13**?
2 Is their pose realistic for fighting toe to toe or has the vase-painter shown more interest in design? Read **7.39** before answering.
3 Why do the boxers stand with their legs apart?

The vase-painting in **7.27** shows two youths boxing. The one on the right signals his submission with a raised finger as he turns to the naked man on the right. He is possibly the trainer since he makes the same signal to the bearded judge on the left, who wears a garland and a cloak and holds a forked stick.

7.27

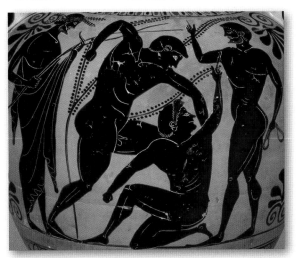

Amphora attributed to the Leagros *group, 515–500 BC.*

The art of defence is the main skill a boxer needs to learn. Some modern boxers like the American heavyweight Mohammed Ali or the British middleweight Errol Graham made it a prominent part of their game. Ancient boxers are recorded who could elude their opponents successfully. Among the statues that Pausanias describes at Olympia was one to a certain Hippomachos (*Description of Greece* 6.12.6).

7.28　Kallon, son of Harmodius, and Hippomachos, son of Moschion, Eleans by birth, were winners of the boxing competition for boys. Daippos made the statue of the former, but we don't know who made the statue of Hippomachos. They say that he defeated three opponents without receiving a blow or suffering any injury to his body.

Philo of Alexandria, writing in the first century AD, describes the boxer's techniques for avoiding blows in the following extract from *On the Cherubim* (lines 80–1).

7.29　As the punches are thrown at him, he deflects them with each hand and, by moving his neck from side to side, he takes care not to get hit. Often he stands on tiptoe and lifts himself up to his full height or makes himself compact by drawing himself in, forcing his opponent to throw punches at thin air and do something close to shadow boxing.

The following brief anecdote is related by Aelian in his selection of miscellaneous facts which he put together in the early third century AD. This work only survives in abbreviated form and this passage (*Historical Miscellany* 10.19) has no particular context.

7.30 Eurydamas of Cyrene was victorious in boxing. Although he had his teeth knocked out by his opponent, he swallowed them so that his adversary wouldn't notice.

In Philostratus' *Heroicus*, written in the third century AD, the dialogue is between a vine dresser and a Phoenician stranger at the shrine of hero Protesilaos. In this extract (II.16) they discuss the advice the hero gives to two boxers.

7.31
VINE DRESSER	I expect you have heard of the skilful Ploutarchos?
PHOENICIAN	I have – I guess you mean the boxer.
VINE DRESSER	Yes, and on his way to his second Olympiad for the men's competition, he begged the hero to give him an oracle about victory. The hero told him to pray to **Achelous**, who presided over the games.
PHOENICIAN	So, what was the riddle?
VINE DRESSER	At Olympia he was fighting Hermeias the Egyptian for the crown of victory. They were exhausted, one from his wounds, the other from thirst, since it was high noon for the boxing. A cloud burst over the stadium and Ploutarchos, the thirsty one, sucked in the water which the fleece around his forearms had absorbed. And by thinking over the oracle's response, as he said after the event, he gave his confidence a boost and he won the victory. You may equally admire Eudaimon the Egyptian if you have come across him boxing somewhere. When he asked how he would not be defeated, the oracle said, 'By despising death.'
PHOENICIAN	And in fact he obeys the oracle, Vine dresser, because by making himself ready in this way he appears hard as iron and like a god to the crowd.

---

1 What does this passage reveal about the equipment used by boxers?
2 Are there modern equivalents?
3 How important is morale in a combat sport like boxing?

Achelous the name of several rivers in Greece, but also used simply to mean water, as the solution of the riddle shows.

The *pankration*

The name *pankration* (all power/victory) indicates that every form of fighting was allowed, but in fact there were some restrictions. It is often said to be a mixture of boxing and wrestling, and it can be difficult to distinguish these various disciplines in images depicting combat sports.

The *pankration* does not feature in the games described by Homer. In the lists of Pausanias and Philostratus it is a late introduction into the Olympic Games, the men's competition first appearing at the 33rd Olympiad (648 BC) and the boys' as late as 200 BC in the 145th Olympiad (**2.4**).

> Pindar wrote *Isthmian* 4 for Melissos of Thebes, winner of the *pankration* at the Isthmian Games. He has mentioned the honour bestowed on Ajax by Homer and now hopes the Muses will aid his praise of the successful athlete. Pindar's description of Melissos is frank enough for some to have thought he knew his fellow citizen (lines 43–51).

7.32   May we find the Muses sympathetic to light that torch of song for Melissos too, the descendant of Telesias, as a crown worthy of the *pankration*. In spirit he is as 45 bold as wild, loud-roaring lions during combat, and in cunning he is a fox who sprawls on her back and holds off the eagle's stoop. One must do everything to put one's opponent in the shade.

Melissos is not blessed with the physique of **Orion**, but while disregarded for his 50 appearance, his strength makes him a hard opponent in close combat.

> •   What does this passage tell us about the qualities needed by a successful pankratiast?

Arrhachion the pankratiast

> Pausanias tells the story of an athlete being awarded victory despite being killed in combat. He has come to the town of Phigalia in Arcadia, not far from Messenia in the southern Peloponnese, where he sees the statue of Arrhachion (*Description of Greece* 8.40.1).

7.33   In their market place the Phigalians have a statue of Arrhachion the pankratiast. It is archaic in style, particularly in its posture. The feet are not far apart and the arms hang down by the side as far as the hips. The statue is made of stone and they say an inscription was written on it. Although this has disappeared with

---

Orion   a giant hunter, immortalized as the constellation Orion.

time, Arrhachion won two Olympic victories at festivals before the **54th** and at this one he won, both because of the fairness of the *Hellanodikai* and because of his own ability. For, when he was competing for the wild olive against the only competitor still left, whoever this opponent was got a hold first and held Arrhachion in a grip with his legs and at the same time he squeezed his neck with his hands. Arrhachion dislocated one of his opponent's toes but died from the stranglehold, while the one strangling him surrendered at the same time because of the pain from his toe. The Eleans crowned Arrhachion's corpse and declared him the winner.

> The *Imāginēs* are a series of descriptions of works of art, a type of literary composition that can be traced back as far as Homer's detailed account of the shield of Achilles in *Iliad* 18.478–608. Probably composed by Philostratus, this description of the crowning of Arrichion (as Philostratus spells the name) in *Imāginēs* 2.6 includes some general remarks about the *pankration.*

7.34   Now here you are at the actual Olympic Games, and at the finest event of those at Olympia, the men's *pankration.* Arrichion is receiving the crown despite dying at the moment of victory and he is being crowned by this *Hellanodikes* here – let the judges' epithet 'precise' be given him for his careful attention to the truth and because of his depiction 'as one of them'. The topography provides a stadium in a single depression of sufficient extent and the river Alpheios is flowing by – lightly, which is why, as you know, it is the only river to flow **on the surface of the sea.** Growing around it are lovely olive trees looking grey-green and with the curliness of parsley.

After the stadium we will take a look at these and many other things, but let us examine the action of Arrichion before it is over. He seems not only to have overcome his opponent, but also to have won over the Greek crowd. At any rate they have leapt out of their seats shouting, and some are waving their hands, some their clothes, some are jumping off the ground and some are joyfully embracing the men next to them. The truly amazing event is just making it impossible for the spectators to contain themselves. Is anyone so lacking in feeling as to not cheer for this athlete? The two victories he had already won at Olympia were a great achievement, but this present victory is greater as he obtained it at the cost of his life, being conveyed, dust and all, to the land of the blessed. Don't let this be put down to chance, since some very shrewd calculation preceded his victory.

54th   564 BC.

on the surface of the sea   the river-god Alpheios fell in love with the nymph Arethusa, but Artemis rescued Arethusa from his pursuit by transforming her into a spring at Syracuse in Sicily. Alpheios is said to have flowed beneath the sea until he mingled with her waters at Syracuse. Philostratus seems to allude to this myth, but offers a variation with the water of Alpheios flowing on the surface of the sea.

And the wrestling? My dear boy, those who practise the *pankration* also use a dangerous type of wrestling. They must take blows to the face that are not considered safe for the wrestler, and they must wrestle in ways in which one must be able to win despite a fall. They also need the skill to employ different strangleholds at different times. The same men wrestle with the ankle and twist the arm as well as delivering blows and jumping on their opponent. These are actions belonging to the *pankration*, but biting or gouging are not. The Spartans allow even these, because they are training themselves for battle, I presume. The Elean games exclude these while giving approval to strangling. As a result, Arrichion's opponent who already had a hold round his middle determined to kill him and now pressed his forearm into his throat, stopping his breathing. He slotted his legs into Arrichion's groin and slipped the ends of his feet behind each knee. By choking him he gained the initiative as the resulting drowsiness of death pervaded Arrichion's senses. But when he applied less pressure with his legs, he failed to anticipate Arrichion's counter move. Arrichion kicked out with the sole of his foot and as a result exposed his opponent's right to danger since his knee was unsupported. He gripped his opponent with his upper legs as he was no longer evenly balanced and put his weight on the left side. He held his opponent's foot firmly with his knee and by twisting violently outward, he made the ball of the ankle unable to stay in its socket. As Arrichion's soul departed from his body, it made his body feeble, but gave him the strength for what he wanted to do.

The man choking Arrichion is painted to resemble a corpse and is signalling surrender with his hand. Arrichion, on the other hand, is painted like victorious athletes with his blood in full bloom and his sweat still fresh, and he is smiling like the living when they sense victory.

The vase-painting in **7.35** shows, on the left, two boxers fighting. The boxer on the right has a face disfigured by blows. In the centre two pankratiasts are fighting, watched by their trainer wielding his forked stick. Behind them hangs a discus in its carrying bag, and a bunch of boxer's thongs (*himantes*) can also be made out, despite the damage to the pot.

7.35

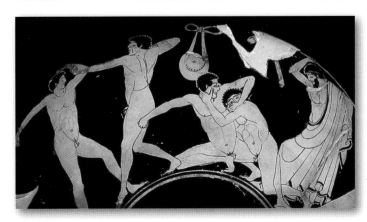

Attic cup (kylix) by the Foundry Painter, c. 490 BC.

- What foul is being committed here, according to Philostratus in **7.34**?

Techniques of the pankratiasts

> Among the statues described by Pausanias at Olympia, there is one of Sostratos of Sicyon, a pankratiast with an unusual technique which he shared with the wrestler Leontiskos (**7.10**) (*Description of Greece* 6.4.2).

7.36 He had the nickname **Akrochersites** because he used to take hold of his opponent's fingers and break them, not letting go until he saw him surrender. His combined victories at Nemea and Isthmia came to twelve, but at Olympia and Delphi, he had two at the latter and three at Olympia. The **104th Olympiad**, the one at which Sostratos won his first victory, is not recorded by the Eleans because they did not stage the games themselves, but the Pisatans and Arcadians did instead.

> In Philostratus' *Heroicus* (II.6), a vine dresser and a Phoenician stranger discuss a pankratiast with a particular technique suited to his build.

7.37 VINE DRESSER   I'm sure you've heard of the Cilician pankratiast whom our fathers used to call *halter* since he was small, and much more so than his opponents.

PHOENICIAN   I know him from the evidence of his statues, of course – there are many places where he stands in bronze.

VINE DRESSER   He excelled both in skill and fighting spirit, and the suitability of his physique gave him considerable strength. On arriving at the shrine here while sailing direct to Delphi to compete in the games, he asked Protesilaos what he should do to defeat his rivals and the reply was 'by being trodden on'. Not surprisingly, the athlete was immediately disheartened, as if floored by the oracle. But after first discovering the way to kick out with the heel in a contest, he later realized that Protesilaos was telling him not to let go of the opponent's foot, because a man fighting with the heel is inevitably trampled on constantly, and to lie underneath his opponent. By using this tactic, this athlete acquired a famous name and was never defeated.

> In Lucian's *Anacharsis* 3, the Scythian visitor has seen wrestlers in the gymnasium and now comments on the athletes practising the *pankration*.

Akrochersites   'Fingerman'.

104th Olympiad   364 BC, when armed conflict reached the Altis itself. See **5.3**.

halter   jumping weight: see **5.21–3**.

7.38   Those standing up, who are themselves covered with dust too, are fighting by
        hitting and kicking each other. This unlucky one, it seems, is even going to spit
        out his teeth, his mouth is so full of blood and sand. As you see, he has taken a
        blow to the jaw from a fist. But this official isn't separating them or stopping the
        fight – I can tell he is one of the officials from his purple robe – in fact he is even
        urging them on and praising the one who landed the blow.

> Aulus Gellius, writing in the late second century AD, describes here the stance
> adopted by pankratiasts when beginning a bout (*Noctes Atticae* 13.28). He
> is discussing the need for the mind to be constantly alert and ready to face
> life's troubles and dangers, and he compares the need for pankratiasts to be
> mentally sharp. Compare **7.26**.

7.39   When they are summoned to fight, they stand with their arms held high in front
        of them and they protect their head and face by creating a defence with their
        hands like a rampart. Before the fight gets underway, all their limbs are ready to
        avoid blows or to deliver them.

> 1 Which of the combat sports do you think was the most violent and
>   dangerous?
> 2 Which one required the greatest skill?
> 3 What are the closest modern equivalents?

> Marcus Aurelius, the Roman emperor and Stoic philosopher, suggests that
> by analysing aesthetic pleasure we are no longer captivated by it and in this
> extract he urges a similar analytical approach to life (*Meditations* 11.2).

7.40   You will despise delightful songs, dancing and the *pankration* if you split up
        the harmonious melody into its individual notes and for each one ask yourself
        whether you are under its spell. Actually you will be baffled, as you will if you do
        the equivalent for dance, movement by movement, pose by pose, and likewise for
        the *pankration*. Therefore on the whole – apart from virtue and what comes from
        virtue – remember to go directly to the constituent parts and come to despise
        things by dividing them up. Apply this same approach to the whole of life too.

> 1 Is aesthetic pleasure what attracts an audience to sport?
> 2 Do you think that watching the *pankration* would give the same sort of
>   pleasure as watching dance?
> 3 Do you share Marcus Aurelius' attitude to the *pankration*?

8 Athletes

This chapter examines some aspects of the athletic experience in Greece beyond the actual competitions. Preparation and training were of vital importance for an athlete to achieve the level of fitness and skill to make him a worthy competitor at athletic festivals. If an athlete was successful, the consequent rewards could significantly enhance his status. In some cases, athletes became famous for their exploits and occasionally became heroes, though in a very different sense from the modern concept of a hero. Those who failed to win perhaps did not all have to 'suffer disgrace' as Epictetus observed about unsuccessful Olympic competitors (see **3.13**), but they receive very little mention in comparison with the praise accorded to the victors.

Prizes

Prizes were an essential element of Greek athletics, as their vocabulary proclaims: **athlon** is the Greek for 'prize', **athlos** for 'competition for prizes' and **athlētēs** for 'competitor for prizes'. This language may seem mercenary and not in accord with the ideal of participation in sport for its own sake, an ideal still influential and seemingly embedded in the ancient Olympics and the other Panhellenic 'crown' games, whose prizes were of no monetary value. Even the modern Olympic medals are of far greater symbolic worth than the value of the metal used to make them. The earliest recorded prizes are those in Homer. At the funeral games of Patroclus in the *Iliad* Achilles offers prizes of considerable value. In **1.3** they are brought out in advance of the competitions and they are then announced before each event. These prizes have an affinity with the exchange of gifts of friendship between the heroes, where reciprocal generosity functions as a form of social bonding to the advantage of both donor and recipient. These contests in the *Iliad*, though announced as if an open challenge, are necessarily the preserve of the warrior elite, who recognize their fitness to compete without any formal process of selection. Only Thersites in *Iliad* Book 2 stands out from the otherwise silent ranks of the common soldiers, and he is put firmly in his place by Odysseus. One possible exception is the boxer Epeios, whose self-confessed inferiority in battle (*Iliad* 23.670) and risible attempt at throwing the iron weight (*Iliad* 23.826–49) are indicative of his status on the periphery of the elite. In such circumstances, offering prizes for all participants secures the greatest advantage by cementing bonds of friendship within the highest social rank. Only one event (throwing the iron) has a single prize. Later, the standard practice at the 'crown' games and elsewhere was to give only the winner a prize, although there is an inscription in Athens (**9.2**) which lists second prizes for a whole range of events, and up to five prizes for singing to the lyre (**kithara**).

During the Archaic period there was a transition from the individually sponsored games such as we see in the *Iliad* to the Panhellenic 'crown' games, which awarded wreaths woven from the leaves of wild plants, and local civic games, some of which awarded substantial prizes (see **9.2**) and some distinctive rewards. Among prizes listed by Pindar are woollen cloaks from Pellene in Achaea (*Nemean* 10.44).

One way of explaining how the 'crown' games came to have prizes of no monetary value, is to consider the god as the donor of prizes. In the following passage from Aristophanes' *Wealth* the comic playwright plays with this idea. In a debate over whether poverty is the source of all good things, Aristophanes mentions the lack of monetary value in the Olympic crown (*Wealth* 583–9).

8.1   POVERTY   Of course, Zeus is poor, and I'll give you clear proof of that now. For if he were rich, why would he personally put on the Olympic Games at which he assembles all the Greeks every fourth year, and then, on proclaiming the victorious athletes, crowns them with a wreath of wild olive? Yet, if he were wealthy, he ought rather to be crowning them with gold.

CHREMYLOS   Not so. Obviously by doing this he is showing that he honours wealth because he's parsimonious and unwilling to squander any of it. By crowning the victors with worthless stuff he keeps wealth to himself.

> • Can this argument from a comedy be used as evidence that the Greeks thought of the crowns as prizes from the gods?

In his travel narrative, Pausanias describes the town of Tegea in Arcadia and includes a brief digression on the victory crowns and their origins (*Description of Greece* 8.48.2–3).

8.2   In the section **on Elis** I have already explained the reason why the winner is given a crown of wild olive at Olympia and I will reveal **later** why it is one of laurel at Delphi.

---

on Elis   in which Pausanias describes how Herakles (one of the Idaean Daktyls or Curetes, not the famous Herakles) brought wild olive from the far north and crowned the winner of a race at Olympia. See p. 23.

later   Apollo fell in love with Daphne, who fled from his advances. When Apollo was just about to catch her, she begged her father, a river-god, to change her and spoil her beauty. He transformed her into a laurel tree which Apollo then claimed as his tree.

At the Isthmus it was pine and at Nemea it was wild celery that were used in honour of the sufferings of **Palaimon** and **Archemoros**. But most games have a crown of palm and everywhere a palm branch is placed in the winner's right hand. They say that the custom arose because on his way back **from Crete** Theseus held games on Delos in honour of Apollo and crowned the winners with palm.

Other rewards

Prizes, however, were far from the only rewards available, especially on the athlete's return to his city. Vitruvius (**8.3**) highlights the athlete's triumphal return and the enduring financial rewards. At Athens Plato (**8.28**) mentions free meals in the *prytaneion* for victors in equestrian events, and Xenophanes (**8.27**) talks of successful athletes being given a 'conspicuous front seat at competitive events', 'meals at public expense' and gifts. Besides other passing references in literary texts, an inscription of the mid-fifth century BC has a decree granting free meals for life in the *prytaneion* for victors in the four 'crown' games. In his *Life of Solon* (23.3) Plutarch tells us that in Athens a victor at the Isthmian Games was paid 100 drachmas, while an Olympic victor received 500 drachmas. These were very substantial sums of money in the sixth century BC and it is worth asking why Athens (and other cities) should offer this sort of largesse to successful athletes. When the victor was announced at the 'crown' games, his city of origin was announced too and thus secured some of the fame and glory of the victory. How much this meant can be seen from several stories about athletes who were bribed to change their country of origin (**8.4**) or from the discussions of Alcibiades' success at Olympia (**4.3–5**) or from statements like Pindar's 'the finest of crowns [from Olympia and Delphi] glorify the mother city' (*Olympian* 9.19–20).

Vitruvius, the Roman author of *On Architecture*, was writing in the age of the first Roman emperor Augustus (31 BC–AD 14). In the opening sections of his ninth book (9.1–2) he expresses the view that the honours given by the Greeks to athletes would have been better deserved by writers such as Pythagoras, Plato or Aristotle. Compare the section on critics of athletics, pp. 146–50.

Palaimon   Melikertes, killed by his mother Ino, but later transformed into a sea-god, Palaimon. His uncle Sisyphos, king of Corinth, founded the Isthmian Games in his honour.

Archemoros   Hypsipyle, a slave, was entrusted with the care of the royal heir Opheltes, whose health depended on him not touching the ground before he could walk. When she laid him on a bed of wild celery, he was killed by a snake and renamed Archemoros.

from Crete   after killing the Minotaur.

8.3   For famous athletes, who had been victorious in the Olympic, Pythian, Isthmian or Nemean Games, the ancestors of the Greeks established such great honours that not only do they receive an accolade along with their palm branch and crown as they stand before the crowd, but, when they return with their victory to their own country, they ride in triumph on a four-horse chariot into their native city and for the rest of their lives they enjoy a fixed income from the state. When I consider this, I am surprised that the same or even greater honours have not been awarded to writers who provide all peoples with an endless supply of useful things for all time. This would have been more worthwhile to institute because, while athletes improve the strength of their own bodies by exercise, writers improve not only their own faculties but everyone's by the teachings provided in their books for learning and sharpening the mind.

For what use to mankind was Milo of Croton just because he was undefeated, or indeed any other champions of the kind, except that while they were alive, they enjoyed some celebrity among their fellow citizens?

---

1   How does the treatment of athletes described by Vitruvius compare with the ways in which modern athletes are treated?

2   Do you agree with Vitruvius' opinion of their worth? Would you prefer to see intellectuals receive higher pay instead?

In *Description of Greece* 6.13.1, Pausanias describes some famous athletes who had left memorials at Olympia. Among them was Astylos, who was remarkable for changing his city.

8.4   [The statue of] Astylos of **Croton** is the work of Pythagoras. Astylos won victories in the sprint (*stadion*) and *diaulos* **three times** in succession at Olympia. Because in the last two he called himself a Syracusan to gratify **Hieron son of Deinomenes**, the people of Croton sentenced his house to be a prison and took down his statue that stood beside the temple of **Lakinian Hera**.

Croton   on the south coast of Italy. Founded from Achaea *c.* 710 BC, it was at the height of its power when Astylos was victorious.

three times   488, 484, 480 BC.

Hieron son of Deinomenes   regent of Gela in Sicily until 478 BC, after which he was tyrant of Syracuse. He was one of the most important figures in the region and a patron of Greek poets and festivals.

Lakinian Hera   Lakinion was a headland to the south of Croton on which there was an important sanctuary of Hera.

1   What does this short passage tell us about the relationship between athletes and their cities?

2   Is there a similar attitude in the modern games?

Fame and victory monuments

One way of celebrating victory was to leave a lasting memorial in the form of a statue, whether at the athlete's home city or at the festival site. This could be an expensive undertaking and not every victorious athlete, even among the most distinguished, made a dedication of this sort. It seems that permission was required from the authorities, as we hear at Olympia when there are special circumstances (**8.37** and **4.17**). But the huge number of statues that Pausanias describes at Olympia is vivid testimony to the desire for permanent commemoration of athletic achievement. Although the statues have virtually all been lost, inscribed bases often remain and Pausanias catalogues a selection of the ones which were identifiable in the second century AD. Other sites too were rich in votive offerings and victory monuments. At Delphi for example, Polyzalos of Gela commemorated his victory in the chariot race with a bronze chariot and team of which only the famous charioteer and some fragments survive (**4.10**). Some statues, such as Polycleitus' *Doryphoros* or the *Diskobolos* of Myron (**5.8**), which we know from Roman marble copies, might have once commemorated victories, but without an inscription to put them in context they can only suggest the sort of monuments which once adorned Greek cities and sanctuaries. Paintings, statuettes and other offerings were also available options to commemorate and offer thanks for a victory, but these either have not survived or cannot be identified as such.

Inscriptions accompanied the statues to convey the essential information: the athlete's name, those of his father and his city, and his sporting achievements. Pausanias records the following inscription (*Description of Greece* 6.9.9).

8.5   Next to Gelon's chariot a statue of Philon is dedicated, the work of Glaukias of Aegina. Simonides, son of Leoprepes wrote a very skilful elegiac couplet for this Philon:

> My fatherland is Corcyra and Philon is my name. I am the son
>
> Of Glaukos and I won the boxing at two Olympiads.

Statues could be dedicated by the athletes themselves or (in the equestrian events) by the owners of the horses, and sometimes this is recorded (Pausanias, *Description of Greece* 6.10.6–8).

8.6 Next to Pantarkes is the chariot of Kleosthenes of **Epidamnos**. This work is by Ageladas and stands behind the Zeus dedicated by the Greeks from the spoils of the **battle of Plataea**. Kleosthenes was victorious at the **66th Olympiad** and he set up a statue of himself and his charioteer together with his horses. The names of the horses are also inscribed, Phoinix and Korax and those on each side of the yoke, Knakias on the right and Samos on the left. This elegiac couplet is on the chariot:

> Kleosthenes, son of Pontis, from Epidamnos set me up,
>
> after victory with his horses in Zeus' fine games.

This Kleosthenes was the first of those breeding horses in Greece to dedicate a statue at Olympia.

> Cities could also set up statues to their athletes (Pausanias, *Description of Greece* 6.13.11).

8.7 The People of Athens dedicated the statue of Aristophon, son of Lysinos, who was victorious in the men's *pankration* at the Olympic Games.

> In Lucian's *Anacharsis* 10, Solon tries to defend the practice of giving wreaths for victory. Afterwards Anacharsis remains unconvinced that the suffering endured by the athletes (particularly pankratiasts) is worth it, especially when there is only one winner.

8.8 My dear friend, we don't pay any attention to the mere items presented. These are just tokens of victory indicating the winners. It is the fame that accompanies them that is worth everything to the victors, and for that, even being kicked is acceptable to those who are pursuing glory by their physical exertions. Fame cannot be acquired without a struggle, but the man who is eager for it must endure many difficulties initially and only then expect from his efforts a profitable and enjoyable result.

---

1 Is modern sponsorship of sport in any way comparable to the rewards given to athletes by Greek cities?

2 What returns do modern sponsors of sport hope for?

Epidamnos   in northern Greece on the Adriatic coast.

battle of Plataea   479 BC.

66th Olympiad   516 BC.

An athlete's fame may earn him respect beyond his own city, although as this story in Pausanias reveals, it was not to be relied upon (*Description of Greece* 6.7.4–6).

8.9   Dorieus, son of Diagoras, besides **his Olympic victories**, had eight victories at Isthmia, one less than that at Nemea, and he is said to have won 'without dust' at Delphi. Peisirodos and he were announced as citizens of **Thurii**, because they had been chased from Rhodes by their opponents and had gone to Thurii in Italy. Dorieus later returned to Rhodes. Of all men he was the one most obviously sympathetic to the Spartan cause, even fighting against the Athenians with his own ships until he was captured by some Athenian warships and taken alive to Athens. Before Dorieus was brought before them, the Athenians were angry with him and threatened him, but when they gathered in the assembly and saw such a great man, who had achieved such fame, in the role of prisoner, their attitude towards him changed and they allowed him to go free without any unpleasant treatment, although they were in a position to inflict serious punishment and justly so.

The story of Dorieus' death is told by **Androtion** in his Attic History: the king of Persia's fleet was then in **Kaunos** under the command of **Conon** and the people of Rhodes were persuaded by Conon to switch allegiance from the Spartans and join the alliance of the king and the Athenians. At the time Dorieus was away from Rhodes, somewhere in the central Peloponnese. He was caught by some Spartans, taken to Sparta, convicted by the Spartans of wrongdoing and given the death penalty.

---

1   Do you think the Athenians or Spartans act more sensibly towards Dorieus?

2   Xenophon (*Hellenica* 1.5.19) says the Athenians had previously condemned Dorieus and his family to death, but now took pity on him and set him free. He does not mention Dorieus' athletic achievements. Do you think the Athenians are more likely to have been influenced by pity or by Dorieus' athletic achievements?

3   Why did the Greeks value fame so highly? Was it of any more practical value beyond Dorieus' experience?

---

his Olympic victories   three at consecutive Olympiads (432, 428, 424 BC) for the *pankration*.

Thurii   a city in southern Italy, founded by colonists from Athens in 444 BC.

Androtion   a fourth-century BC chronicler of Athenian history.

Kaunos   a town on the coast of Asia Minor (modern Turkey), north-east of Rhodes.

Conon   an Athenian in command of a fleet of allied Persian ships with mainly Greek crews, in 396 BC.

Pindar and victory odes

Another important medium for commemorating victory was poetry. This could take the form of a dedicatory epigram as in **8.5** and **8.6** or a more elaborate (and more expensive) victory ode commissioned by the athlete, his family or his city.

Simonides, Pindar (*c.* 518–*c.* 438 BC) and Bacchylides are the three most important composers of *epinikia* or victory odes for successful athletes. Pindar's poetry has survived in greater quantity than that of any other Greek lyric poet and is best represented by the 45 *epinikia* which have come down to us arranged by festival in four books. As we have seen (p. 74), 14 *epinikia* by Bacchylides were discovered on a fragmentary papyrus roll which arrived in the British Museum from an unknown location in Egypt in 1896. Simonides belongs to the generation before Pindar and Bacchylides, but only a few scraps of his *epinikia* survive. The genre seems to have gone out of fashion during the fifth century BC, although there are some possible indications of the tradition continuing (see **4.4**).

The highly elaborate odes of Pindar reflect the sophisticated clientele for whom they were written. As can be seen in *Pythian* 10 (**8.10**), they were commissioned by the elite of Greek society – aristocrats and rulers – for performance at victory celebrations, probably at banquets (*symposia*) and on more than one occasion. Short odes with no myth are likely to have been composed for immediate celebration at the games. For an example, see Bacchylides, *Odes* 4 (**4.6**). They would have been accompanied by music and probably dance, as Pindar mentions happening among the Hyperboreans (see **8.10**, lines 38–9). The group of performers is called a ***kōmos***, hence the English 'encomium' (formal/elaborate praise). Besides details of the event and the successful athlete (or, for the equestrian events, the owner), there is praise of his family and his homeland. A relevant mythological story helps to embellish the ode and give variety to the praise, but can also offer opportunities to draw on common moralizing subjects arising from athletic success such as mortality, fortune or the relationship between men and gods.

Composed for the victor in the boys' *diaulos*, Hippokleas of Thessaly, at the Pythian Games of 498 BC, *Pythian* 10 is the earliest victory ode by Pindar.

Hippokleas, son of Phrikias, came from Pelinnaion in Thessaly. His victory song was commissioned by Thorax from the aristocratic Thessalian family of the Aleuadai (sons of Aleuas). He and his brothers are mentioned as upholders of the law. The ode was performed by men of Ephyra (i.e. Thessaly), but exactly where and when it was sung is a matter of speculation. It is likely to have been at a celebratory ***symposion*** when the victorious athlete returned to Thessaly, but it is also likely to have been sung on more public occasions appropriate for praising the Thessalian aristocrats mentioned in it, perhaps at other games where it might also have helped Pindar advertise his poetic skill.

8.10   [*1–9 Pindar praises Thessaly because he is invited to celebrate Hippokleas' victory at Delphi.*]

Fortunate is **Sparta, blessed is Thessaly**: both are ruled by the **descendants of one father**, the supreme warrior Herakles. Why am I boasting? Is it inappropriate? Not so, but **Pytho** and Pelinnaion and the **sons of Aleuas** are calling me, wishing to bring   5 for Hippokleas **the splendid voices of men in festive celebration**. For he enjoys the taste of victory. **The gorge of Parnassus** has declared him to the neighbouring people as winner of the *diaulos* for boys.

[*10–30 Pindar attributes success to Apollo and inherited ability. After a prayer for their future prosperity, he emphasizes the distinction between men and gods.*]

Apollo, men's completion of things and their beginning grow to be sweet with a   10 god's backing. No doubt it was through your agency that he achieved this, but his natural talent too has trodden in the steps of his father, twice Olympic victor **in the war-sustaining weapons of Ares**. The contest in the deep meadow under the rock   15 of **Kirrha** made Phrikias victorious in a foot race. May fortune also accompany them in days to come for their magnificent wealth to bloom. They have been given no small share of the pleasurable things in Greece but may they not encounter   20 resentful reversals of fortune from the gods. A god may have no trouble in his heart. Happy and praised in song by the wise is that man who achieves victory with his hands or through his speed of foot and wins the greatest of prizes with his daring and strength, and still lives to see his young son deservedly win Pythian crowns.   25 Never can he go up to bronze heaven, but as for the triumphs we, the mortal race, achieve, he reaches the furthest limit on his voyage. But not by ship or by going on foot would you find the wonderful road to the **Hyperboreans**' company.   30

Sparta, blessed is Thessaly   Sparta and Thessaly were allies at the time this ode was composed. Thessaly, the victor's homeland, is given the more flattering, quasi-divine epithet 'blessed'.

descendants of one father   the 'descendants of Herakles' spread from northern Greece into the Peloponnese.

Pytho   the oracle at Delphi.

sons of Aleuas   the aristocratic family of Thessaly who commissioned this poem.

the splendid voices of men in festive celebration   the poem has been written to be sung by a chorus of men from Pelinnaion.

The gorge of Parnassus   Delphi, set in a gorge on the lower slopes of Mount Parnassus.

in the war-sustaining weapons of Ares   i.e. in the *hoplitodromos* (see **6.14–17**).

Kirrha   the port on the Corinthian Gulf just below Delphi. Phrikias has won a foot race in the Pythian Games.

Hyperboreans   a mythical people who lived in the far north, beyond the river Ister (Danube). Apollo was closely associated with them and visited them in winter. They were beyond the reach of ordinary mortals, but are visited here by Perseus. In *Olympian* 3, Pindar tells the story of Herakles bringing the sacred olive tree to Olympia from the Hyperboreans.

[31–50 Mythological digression: Perseus' visit to the Hyperboreans. This section amplifies the comparison of men and gods.]

Perseus, leader of the people, once feasted with them when he entered their homes. They were offering splendid hecatombs of asses to the god when he met them. Apollo takes particular pleasure in their constant festivities and worship and laughs 35 when he sees **the rampant lewdness of monstrous asses**.

The Muse is not absent from their customary celebrations, but resounding everywhere are choruses of girls, the sounds of the lyre and the shrill noise of the *aulos*. They bind their hair with **golden** laurel and enjoy feasting together. No 40 diseases, no destructive old age are present among this sacred race, but they live apart from work and fighting, escaping the severe justice of Nemesis.

Once the **son of Danae**, guided by Athene and breathing with a bold heart, came to 45 this company of blessed men. He slew the Gorgon and came carrying her head with its hair a tangle of snakes, a stony death for the **islanders**. Nothing seems to me too incredible to admire if the gods have done it. 50

[51–4 Pindar addresses himself to bring the digression to a close.]

Stop rowing and firmly fix the anchor from the prow in the seabed for protection against low-lying rocks. For the finest of praise songs flits **like a bee** from one topic to another.

[55–72 Pindar hopes he will enhance Hippokleas' victory celebration and ends the ode with praise of the aristocratic family that commissioned the ode.]

While the **Ephyraeans** around the **Peneios** pour out my sweet music, with my 55 songs I hope to make Hippokleas even more admired for his victory crowns among his contemporaries and older generations too, and the darling of young girls.

Perseus   Pindar briefly mentions the famous story of how Perseus killed the Gorgon Medusa and brought back her head to the island of Seriphos, where he turned the king Polydectes and his followers to stone in order to rescue his mother Danae. Perseus has connections with Thessaly because it was there that he accidentally killed his grandfather Akrisios when throwing a discus. He was also an ancestor of Herakles, from whom the sons of Aleuas claimed descent.

the rampant lewdness of monstrous asses   this wording is commonly used for a phrase which literally says 'upright arrogance of monsters' and is taken to refer to the sexual excitement of the asses. Why Apollo should find this amusing is not explained.

aulos   the double pipes used to accompany choral song – and the long jump (see **5.19**).

golden   not only a sign of wealth, but everlasting.

son of Danae   Perseus.

islanders   of Seriphos.

like a bee   Pindar's imagery for his poem changes abruptly from boat to bee.

Ephyraeans   Thessalians.

Peneios   the main river in Thessaly.

Love of different things excites different people's minds. If each man gets what he 60
strives for, let him grasp his heart's desire that is there to be taken. But to foresee
what is a year away is baffling.

I trust the kind hospitality of **Thorax**, who has been active on my behalf, yoking
this four-horse chariot of the Muses, showing friendship to a friend and kind 65
guidance to a guide. Under examination gold shows its nature by the touchstone,
as does an upright mind. We shall praise the **noble brothers** then because they
carry on high and glorify the law of the Thessalians. On good men depends the 70
hereditary good government of cities.

---

1 In lines 10–30, what two reasons does Pindar give for Hippokleas' success?
2 How does he rate the success of Hippokleas?
3 What contrast does he make between mortals and gods?
4 In lines 31–50, how is the life of the Hyperboreans similar to and different
   from that of humans?
5 What does Pindar hope that his ode achieves?

Awards ceremonies

When were victorious athletes crowned? Were ceremonies held after each
individual competition was completed, as happens in the medal ceremonies at
the modern Olympics? Or was there, as some think, a final awards ceremony
on the final day of the festival before the banquet provided for the victors in the
Prytaneion? The response of Lichas (**3.27**), who tied a ribbon on his charioteer,
suggests that instant recognition was given, at least in some form.

> Pausanias briefly mentions a banquet held in the Prytaneion for the Olympic
> victors (*Description of Greece* 5.15.12).

8.11   The Eleans have a banqueting hall too. It is inside the **Prytaneion**, opposite the
room with the **hearth**, and in it they feast the Olympic victors.

> In his account of games after a procession in Rome, Dionysius of
> Halicarnassus, writing in the age of Augustus (31 BC–AD 14), has described
> the chariot racing before turning his attention to athletics (*Roman Antiquities*
> 7.73.3–4).

Thorax, noble brothers see introduction to the ode, above.

Prytaneion, hearth see **10.11**.

8.12   When the equestrian events were completed, then those who were competing with their own bodies (runners, boxers and wrestlers) came forward. These three events were current among the ancient Greeks, as Homer shows at the funeral of Patroclus. In the intervals between events, they observed a custom that is quintessentially Greek and the most excellent of all, by holding crowning ceremonies and proclaiming the honours which they were giving to their benefactors, as used to happen at the Dionysia festivals, and they would make a display of the spoils of war for those who had assembled for the spectacle.

1 Is this good evidence to suggest that victors were crowned after their event?
2 Does the reference to Homer invalidate this as evidence for the practice at Olympia?

In this vase-painting (**8.13**) the athlete, perhaps a victor in a boys' event, has ribbons on his arm and leg, a garland round his neck and a sprig of vegetation in his hands; an older man ties a ribbon round his head. Modern athletes are presented with bunches of flowers as well as their medals at the Olympics.

8.13

Attic hydria (water jar) c. 500 BC.

1 Is the fact that the athlete is naked an indication that he is being crowned immediately after his victory?
2 Compare **3.27**. Does the action of Lichas resemble this vase-painting?

Olympic victor lists (*Olympionikai*)

The origin of the Olympic athletic competitions and the date at which they began will probably never be ascertained with certainty. The date of 776 BC for the first Olympics is almost universally accepted, though perhaps more through convenience than conviction. This date receives its main support from Olympic victor lists, which show a reasonable degree of unanimity. When and where records were first kept remains unknown. There are references to lists on display at Olympia (**8.14**) and Pausanias refers to 'Eleans' written records of Olympic victors (**3.27**), which suggests an official list by his time (second century AD), but the earliest known list was compiled in the late fifth century BC by Hippias of Elis.

From then onwards there appears to have been a continuous tradition of compiling and updating such lists until the fifth century AD. Compilers tended to add additional records of historical events, so that the lists became a chronological record of more than the Olympic Games. By the fifth century BC the independent Greek city states were developing their own systems of identifying years, usually by the name of a magistrate such as the eponymous **archon** (**8.17**) at Athens. This made it hard to communicate chronological information other than locally, and for historians and others who were seeking a wider audience for their work, a Panhellenic system was needed. The Olympic victor lists fitted this bill. Gradually improvements were made to the system: Aristotle introduced the numbering of Olympiads, making a quick calculation of the date possible, and Eratosthenes refined it by adding the numbers 1–4 to mark the years within each Olympiad.

> Among the statues Pausanias describes at Olympia is that of a boy from Elis called Lastratidas, whose father left an interestingly different memorial.

8.14 Paraballon, Lastratidas' father, happened to win the *diaulos* race and he left for those coming after him something to aspire to, by having inscribed in the **gymnasium** at Olympia a list of Olympic victors.

> In discussing the problems of dating for the reign of an early king of Rome, Plutarch makes the following comment in the opening chapter of his biography of Numa (*Numa* 1.4).

8.15 It is difficult to fix dates precisely, particularly those derived from the Olympic victories, the list of which they say Hippias of Elis published without any compellingly trustworthy source.

---

gymnasium   if this refers to the gymnasium that survives at Olympia, Paraballon's list cannot have been made before the third century BC, when the building was started.

The following list of victors at the 76th and 77th Olympiads (476 and 472 BC) is selected from a longer list probably dating from the third century AD. Found at Oxyrhynchus in Egypt (*POxy* II 222), it was written on the back of a financial account. The entries are written in a format found elsewhere: the events are listed in the order in which they were introduced to the programme, except that the *gymnikos agon* is listed before the *hippikos agon*.

8.16   76th   Scamandros of Mytilene   *stadion*

Dandis of Argos   *diaulos*

[...] of Sparta   *dolichos*

[...] of Tarentum   pentathlon

[...] of Maroneia   wrestling

Euthymos of Locri in Italy   boxing

Theogenes of Thasos   *pankration*

[...] of Sparta   boys' *stadion*

Theognetos of Aegina   boys' wrestling

Agesidamus of Locri in Italy   boys' boxing

[...] yrus of Syracuse   **hoplitēs**

Theron of Akragas   four-horse chariot

Hieron of Syracuse   horse race

77th   Dandis of Argos   *stadion*

[...] of Epidaurus   *diaulos*

Ergoteles of Himera   *dolichos*

[...] amos of Miletus   pentathlon

[...] menes of Samos   wrestling

Euthymos of Locri in Italy   boxing

Kallias of Athens   *pankration*

[...] sandridas of Corinth   boys' *stadion*

[...] kratidas of Tarentum   boys' wrestling

Tellon of Mainalia   boys' boxing

[...] gias of Epidamnus   *hoplites*

Argos, the people   four-horse chariot

Hieron of Syracuse   horse race

The following extract is from a list from Egypt which was probably made in the third century AD. The list's emphasis is on recording historical events; only the number of the Olympiad and the winner of the *stadion* are concerned with athletics. It also records the archons at Athens in the four years of the Olympiad, before a chronicle of events in each year. This section from the 108th Olympiad of 348 BC is cut short by a gap in the papyrus, but the format should be clear enough.

8.17   In the one hundred and eighth Olympiad Polykles of Cyrene won the *stadion*. At Athens the **archons** were Theophilos, Themistocles, Arkhias and Euboulos.

In the first year of this Olympiad Plato the philosopher died and Speusippos took his place as head of the school.

In the second year Philip [...

---

1   How do these records differ from those kept by the International Olympic Committee's website or modern authors such as David Wallechinsky in *The Complete Book of the Olympics*?

2   What other records of individual victories were there?

3   Why did the Greeks attach importance to recording the names of winners, their cities of origin and the events they won?

4   How much do these lists contribute to our understanding of Greek athletics?

Milo of Croton

There are a number of athletes whose success was so awesome that they achieved legendary status. Of these the most famous was Milo of Croton. Stories of his prowess might seem exaggerated, but there is a modern parallel in the giant figure of the Russian Greco-Roman wrestler Alexander Karelin. Not only did he achieve fantastic success in competition (12 European, 9 World and 3 Olympic titles), remaining unbeaten for 13 years, but a story similar to Milo's feat of carrying his statue is recorded in D. Miller's *Official History of the Olympic Games*: 'he once carried a large refrigerator, unaided, up eight flights of stairs at his Siberian home when the elevator was out of action' (p. 338).

---

archons   magistrates in Athens. The eponymous archon gave his name to the year he served.

[...   the papyrus has a gap here because it was trimmed down when the reverse was used for another purpose.

The same source says of the American who deprived Karelin of his fourth Olympic crown in 2000 that he used to carry new-born calves on his shoulders. These anecdotes may be more authentic than the stories that grew up around Milo, but they are similar in that they add colourful detail to enhance the stature of these heroes. It should cause no surprise to find a television commentator comparing Karelin to Hercules (Greek Herakles). But, unlike Milo, whose demise became a cautionary tale, Karelin entered politics and became a Russian MP.

In this extract Pausanias is describing statues of famous athletes at Olympia (*Description of Greece* 6.14.5–8). Milo won his first Olympic crown in the boys' competition in 540 or 536 BC. He went on to win five Olympic crowns in the men's competition.

8.18 Milo, son of Diotimus, is the work of Dameas who was also from Croton. Milo achieved six victories for wrestling at Olympia, one of them in the boys' competition, and at Delphi six in the men's competition and one in the boys'. He also came to wrestle at Olympia for a seventh time, but he could not throw Timasitheus, a fellow-citizen of his and a young man in his prime who, on top of that, was reluctant to face him at close quarters.

Milo is also said to have personally carried the statue of himself into the Altis. There are stories about his exploits with both a pomegranate and a discus. He would hold a pomegranate in such a way that nobody could extricate it by force while he caused it no damage with his tight grip. He used to stand on an oiled discus and make a fool of anyone who tried to grapple with him and push him off the discus. He also used to present other demonstrations like this. He used to tie a cord around his head in the same way as he put on a victory headband or crown. Holding his breath inside his lips and filling the veins of his head with blood, he would break the cord by the strength of his veins.

Another anecdote has it that he would hold his right arm from shoulder to elbow down by his side and stretch out the part below the elbow horizontally, turning up his thumb while his other fingers were set one on top of another in a row. His little finger was therefore at the bottom, but there was nobody who succeeded in forcing it from its place.

They say he was killed by wild animals. In his land of Croton he came across a log which was drying and in it were wedges that held it open. Milo over-confidently pushed his hands into the log, but the wedges slipped and Milo was held fast by the wood until discovered by wolves, an animal found there in large numbers. Such was the end that overtook Milo.

The following learned conversation comes from Athenaeus' huge work of the early third century AD, *The Learned Banqueters* (10.412e–f).

8.19   Milo of Croton, according to Theodorus of Hierapolis in his work on athletic contests, used to eat 20 *mnas* of meat and the same amount of bread and used to drink three **jugs** of wine. At Olympia he put a four-year-old bull on his shoulders and carried it round the stadium. After that he cut it up and ate it on his own in one day. Titormos of Aitolia ate a bull for breakfast in competition with him, as Alexander of Aitolia reports. Phylarchos in the third book of his histories says that Milo ate a bull while reclining in front of the altar of Zeus and as a result the poet Dorieus wrote the following for him:

> Such was Milo when he lifted the weight, the four-year-old bull at the festival of Zeus, and easily carried the huge beast like a new-born lamb through all the assembled crowd. That was astonishing, but he performed a greater marvel before the altar at **Pisa**. The unyoked bull which he had paraded, he cut up into joints of meat and then devoured the entire animal on his own.

Milo was not without his critics in the ancient world. In the following two extracts (*On Old Age* 27 and 33), Cicero relates an anecdote not found elsewhere and poses a rhetorical question which implies a critical attitude to the celebrity of the strongman.

8.20   What statement could be more worthy of contempt than that of Milo of Croton? When he was now an old man and saw athletes exercising on the race track, he is said to have looked at his own muscles and with tears in his eyes said 'But these are dead already.' (27)

Milo is said to have entered the stadium at Olympia while carrying an ox on his shoulders: which would you prefer to be given, his strength of body or Pythagoras' strength of intellect? (33)

Diodorus Siculus (*c.* 90–30 BC) was a Sicilian Greek of the first century BC who went to live in Alexandria and later Rome. He compiled a universal history in 40 books, some of which, including Book 9, only survive in excerpts and quotations. The first excerpt from his work portrays Milo as a mighty warrior fighting in the front ranks in the war between Croton and Sybaris in southern Italy, which led to the destruction of Sybaris in 510 BC (*Historical Library* 12.9.5–6). The second quotation poses an ancient equivalent of Milton's question, 'What is strength without a double share of wisdom?' (*Historical Library* 9.14.1).

---

mnas   the *mna* varied as a measurement of weight, but was somewhere around 500 g, which gives Milo a prodigious appetite of about 10 kg of meat (at a sitting?).

jugs   the word for jug here (*chous*) was a unit of measurement equivalent to approximately 3 litres.

Pisa   Pisa was very close to Olympia and sometimes used as an alternative name.

8.21   When the Sybarites marched against them with 300,000 men, the people of Croton deployed 100,000 against them, with the athlete Milo at their head. Because of the superiority of his physical strength he was the first to rout those who faced him. This man, six times an Olympic victor and possessing the strength to match his physique, is said to have gone into battle wearing his Olympic crowns and dressed in the costume of Herakles with a lion skin and club, and to have won the admiration of his fellow citizens by being responsible for their victory. (12.9.5–6)

It is not the possession of strength (of whatever sort) that is a great thing, but the appropriate use of it. What benefit did Milo of Croton get from his vast physical strength? (9.14.1)

> 1   What points could be made to offer a positive answer to Diodorus Siculus' question?
> 2   Does his tale of Milo in battle have any credibility?
> 3   If so, does he answer his own question?

Athletic heroes

In Diodorus' story of Milo in battle, there is an obvious association with the mythical hero Herakles. But for the Greeks there was another specific meaning of 'hero' which was defined by Walter Burkert as 'a deceased person who exerts from his grave a power for good or evil and who demands appropriate honour' (p. 23), and several athletes became heroes in this sense. Lucian mentions that the statues of Theagenes and Poulydamas at Olympia had healing powers.

Theagenes or Theogenes of Thasos

It is recorded on an inscription that Theagenes was undefeated in boxing for 22 years and won well over a thousand victories. Pausanias relates his story in *Description of Greece* 6.11.2–9.

8.22   Not far from **the kings** I mentioned stands the statue of Theagenes, son of Timosthenes, from Thasos. The people of Thasos say that he isn't the son of Timosthenes, but that Timosthenes was a priest of Thasian Herakles and that a **phantom of Herakles** in the guise of Timosthenes had intercourse with

---

the kings   of Macedonia.

phantom of Herakles   echoing the myth of Herakles' conception when Zeus slept with Alkmene in the guise of her husband Amphitryon.

Theagenes' mother. They say that when he was eight, a bronze statue of a god set up in the agora took his fancy on his way home from school. He took down the statue, put it on one of his shoulders and carried it home. The citizens were angry with him for what he had done, but one of them, a respected citizen of advanced age, stopped them from killing the boy and told him to take the statue back from his home to the agora. On doing so, the boy instantly acquired considerable fame because of his strength, and his feat became celebrated all over Greece. My work has already described Theagenes' most notable achievements at the Olympic Games, how he defeated Euthymos the boxer and how a fine was imposed on him by the Eleans. On that occasion a man from Mantinea called Dromeus is said to have been the first man (of those we know) to have achieved victory in the *pankration* '**without dust**' (*akoniti*).

Theagenes won the *pankration* at the next Olympiad. At Delphi too he achieved three victories for boxing. At Nemea he won nine victories and at Isthmia ten, some for the *pankration* and some for boxing. At Phthia in Thessaly he gave up his keen pursuit of boxing and the *pankration*, and turned his attention to becoming famous among the Greeks for running. In fact he beat the competitors in the *dolichos*. In my opinion, this ambition related to **Achilles**: to win a victory in running in the land of the swiftest of those called heroes. In all he had 1,400 crowns. When he departed from mankind, one of his enemies from when he was alive used to come every night to the statue of Theagenes and whip the bronze as if he were hurting Theagenes himself. The statue put an end to the mistreatment (*hybris*) by falling on him. The man died and his sons prosecuted the statue for murder. The Thasians threw the statue into the sea, following the opinion of **Draco** who wrote homicide laws for the Athenians and prescribed banishment even for lifeless objects if one of them actually killed a man by falling on him.

But as time went by and the land stopped producing crops for the Thasians, they sent envoys to Delphi. The oracular reply they received from the god told them to take back those who were exiled. Responding to this oracle, they received back the exiles but without achieving a cure for the crop failure. Therefore they went to Delphi a second time, saying that they had done what the oracle had told them, but the wrath of the gods remained. This time the Pythia responded, 'You have neglected your great man, the forgotten Theagenes.' They were in a quandary over how to recover Theagenes' statue when, they say, some fishermen who had put to sea to fish got the statue entangled in their net and brought it back to land. The Thasians set it up where it originally stood and it is their custom to

---

without dust   unopposed.

dolichos   distance race.

Achilles   see **1.8**, line 776, where Achilles has his regular epithet 'swift-footed'.

Draco   Athenian law-giver to whom Athenian homicide laws were often attributed. As the origin of the English word 'draconian' his name has become a byword for severity.

sacrifice to him as a god. I know many other places, both in Greece and among foreigners, where statues of Theagenes are dedicated and he both cures diseases and receives honours from the locals. The statue of Theagenes is in the Altis, the work of Glaukias of Aegina.

Kleomedes of Astypalaia

This extract about the boxer Kleomedes is from Pausanias, *Description of Greece* 6.9.6–8. Plutarch tells the same story, omitting the reason for Kleomedes' madness given by Pausanias, but adding that he broke the column with his fist!

8.23   At the **previous Olympiad** they say that Kleomedes of **Astypalaia** killed Ikkos, a man from **Epidaurus**, in a boxing match. When he was found guilty of wrongdoing by the *Hellanodikai* and stripped of his crown, he went out of his mind with grief and returned to Astypalaia. There in an assault on a school of around sixty children, he overturned the column which supported the roof. When the roof fell down on the children, he was pelted with stones by the people of the town and took refuge in the temple of Athene. He climbed into a chest which was dedicated in the temple and closed the lid. The Astypalaians struggled to no effect in their attempts to open the chest until finally they split the wood – only to find no Kleomedes, dead or alive. They sent some men to Delphi to ask what had happened to Kleomedes, and this is the oracular reply they say the Pythia gave:

> Kleomedes of Astypalaia, last of the heroes,
>
> As he is no longer mortal, honour him with sacrifices.

And so the people of Astypalaia have paid honours to Kleomedes as a hero ever since.

---

1   Do these stories of athletes as heroes have any common features?
2   Do they bear any relation to the hero-worship of sporting celebrities in the modern world?

---

previous Olympiad   492 BC.

Astypalaia   an island in the southern Aegean.

Epidaurus   city famous for the sanctuary of Asklepios, on the coast of the Saronic Gulf facing Athens.

Hellanodikai   see pp. 45–55.

Critics of athletics

From Tyrtaeus in the seventh century BC to Vitruvius (**8.3**) or Plutarch under the Roman empire, there is a coherent critique of the usefulness of athletics, especially as distraction from training for warfare. Tyrtaeus was a poet writing in Sparta in the seventh century BC. This is an extract from one of the longest fragments of his poetry, preserved in a later anthology (Fragment 12, lines 1–14).

8.24 I would not mention a man or think him of any worth for prowess in running or skill in wrestling, not even if he had the size and strength of the **Cyclopes** and could beat Thracian **Boreas** in running, nor if he were more attractive in looks than **Tithonus** or richer than **Midas or Kinyras**, nor if he were more kingly than Pelops, son of Tantalus, or had **Adrastus' winning way with words**, nor if he had every high regard, but not impetuous might. For a man is no good in war unless he could bear to witness bloody slaughter and stand his ground at close quarters and aim at the enemy. This excellence, this prize among men is the best and most noble for a young man to win.

Dio Chrysostom (late first century AD–early second century AD) was called *Chrysostomos* (golden-mouth) because of his skill as a speaker. His ninth Discourse describes Diogenes the Cynic (a philosopher of the fourth century BC) at the Isthmian Games. Others came to watch the athletics or fill themselves with food, but Diogenes came to observe the folly of his fellow men. When the organizers complained of Diogenes wearing a crown of pine, the mark of victory at Isthmia, he listed his victories over poverty, exile, disrepute, anger, pain, fear and pleasure and asked whether he was more worthy of the crown than the athletes (*Discourses* 9.14–20).

8.25 Later he saw someone leaving the stadium accompanied by a large crowd. He wasn't setting foot on the ground, but was being carried high by the mass of people, some of whom were shouting as they followed, while others were jumping for joy and lifting their hands to heaven, and others were casting garlands and ribbons on him.

Cyclopes a race of one-eyed giants. See Homer, *Odyssey* 9.

Boreas the North Wind. Thrace was to the north of Greece.

Tithonus a handsome Trojan with whom Eos, the goddess of the dawn, fell in love. She obtained everlasting life for him, but forgot to ask for everlasting youth.

Midas or Kinyras Midas, king of Phrygia, is famous for his golden touch (see Ovid, *Metamorphoses* 11), and Kinyras, king of Cyprus, was also noted for his wealth.

Adrastus' winning way with words Adrastus was king of Argos and leader of the Seven against Thebes, the expedition which attempted to win the throne for his son-in-law Polynices. His diplomatic skill in persuading others to join this expedition is probably what Tyrtaeus refers to.

When Diogenes was able to get close to him, he asked what had happened and what the uproar surrounding him was all about. The man replied, 'I have won the *stadion* race for men, Diogenes.'

'So what?' Diogenes said. 'You haven't actually become the slightest bit wiser by beating your competitors in a race, nor have you got more self-control now than before, nor are you less of a coward, nor do you suffer less, nor will you need less, nor live a life more free of pain.'

'By Zeus, that may be so,' he said, 'but I am the fastest of all the Greeks.'

'But not faster than hares,' said Diogenes, 'nor deer – and yet these swiftest of all animals are also the most timid: afraid of men, dogs and eagles, they have a miserable existence. Don't you know that speed is an indication of cowardice? It is natural for the same animals to have the greatest speed and the least courage. For instance, because Herakles was slower than many and unable to catch evil-doers on foot, he used to carry a bow and arrows and use them against those who ran away.'

The man replied, 'But Achilles, the poet says, was quick and the bravest.'

'How do you know,' said Diogenes, 'that Achilles was quick? He couldn't catch Hector though he chased him all day. Aren't you ashamed to take pride in something in which you are naturally inferior to the most ordinary beasts? I don't think you are even capable of beating a fox. In fact, just what was your margin of victory?'

He replied, 'It was slight, Diogenes, and that, you know, was the amazing thing about the victory.'

'And the upshot is,' Diogenes retorted, 'that you attained happiness from one stride.'

'Yes, because we were all the best runners.'

'How much faster than you do larks cover the distance of the *stadion*?'

'But that's because they have wings,' he said.

'Well,' Diogenes said, 'if being swiftest is best, then I dare say it is much better to be a lark than a man. So, there is no need to pity nightingales or hoopoes because they were turned from humans into birds according to **the myth**.'

'But,' he countered, 'I am a man and the fastest of men.'

'So what? Is it not reasonable to assume that among ants one is faster than another? But they don't admire it as a result, do they? Don't you think it absurd for someone to admire an ant for its speed? There again, had all the runners been lame, should you have been proud that as a lame man you beat lame men?'

---

the myth   Tereus, a Thracian king, married Procne from Athens. Later he raped her sister Philomela and cut out her tongue to prevent her telling what happened. After the sisters took revenge by killing Tereus' son Itys and serving his cooked flesh to his father, the three were turned into birds: Tereus became a hoopoe, Philomela a swallow and Procne a nightingale (in the Greek version).

In talking like this to the man, Diogenes made many of those present look down on the activity and he made the man himself depart in sorrow and considerably humbled.

> 1 Would you agree with Diogenes' criticism of athletic achievement?
> 2 How valid do you think his arguments are?

In Book 10 of Athenaeus' *The Learned Banqueters*, during a discussion of gluttony there is a digression on the value of athletics which arises from stories of athletes' prodigious feats of eating (10.412d–14d). Milo of Croton, whose normal fare was 10 kg of meat, 10 kg of bread and three jugs of wine, once carried a four-year-old bull round the stadium before cutting it up and eating it all in one day (**8.19**). Theagenes of Thasos was also said to have eaten a bull on his own. Astyanax of Miletus, winner of three consecutive Olympic crowns for the *pankration*, once ate an entire dinner prepared for nine guests.

8.26　It is not surprising that these men became gluttons because everyone who becomes an athlete is taught, along with physical exercises, to eat a lot too. And so Euripides also says in his first *Autolycus*:

> Of the countless bad things in Greece, there is nothing worse than those
> of the athletic persuasion. Firstly, they neither learn how to live well, nor
> would they be able to. For how would a man who is a slave to his jaw and
> second best to his belly, acquire more wealth than his father? On the other　　5
> hand, they can't bear being poor or handle misfortune because they are used
> to bad habits and find it hard to change in the face of difficulties. In their
> prime they go about as celebrities, the glory of their city, but when bitter　　10
> old age comes their way, they are goners, like threadbare coats that have lost
> their nap. I am critical too of the habit of the Greeks who hold meetings for
> these men and honour them with useless pleasures, all for a feast. For what　　15
> good do they do their home town by winning a crown for wrestling well or
> being a fast sprinter or throwing a discus or delivering a good blow to a jaw?
> Will they fight the enemy with a discus in their hands or will they throw the　　20
> enemy out of their country by delivering punches through shields? Nobody
> stands close to iron weaponry and does these stupid things. In my opinion
> men who are wise and good should be crowned with leaves, and the man　　25
> who is prudent and just and the finest leader in the city, one who by his
> words puts a stop to evil deeds and does away with battles and civil unrest.
> Such things are good for every city and for all Greeks.

Euripides took this from the elegies of Xenophanes of Colophon …

Autolycus　Euripides, fragment 282; the play has not survived.

Xenophanes of Colophon, *c.* 570–478 BC, was a philosopher and poet. This poem in elegiac couplets (Poem 2) is quoted by Athenaeus, who says that Xenophanes made other attacks on athletics (*The Learned Banqueters* 10.413f–10.414c).

8.27 But if someone were to win a victory for speed of foot or for competing in the pentathlon where Zeus' sacred precinct is beside **Pisa's river** at Olympia, or for wrestling or even in the **painful art of boxing** or some terrible contest they call 5
pankration, he would be more glorious for his fellow citizens to see and would win a conspicuous front seat at competitive events and he would get **meals at public expense** from the city and a gift for him to treasure. And even if he won 10
with horses, he would get all these things, though he is not as worthy as me because my poetic art is better than the strength of men or horses. But this is an unreasonable custom and it is not right to privilege physical strength at the expense of intellectual accomplishment. Even if there were a good boxer among 15
the people or a pentathlete or wrestler or fast runner (which takes pride of place among all the feats of strength at the games), for all that, good order would be no more prevalent in the city. It would be but a small gratification for the city if 20
someone were to win a contest by the banks of Pisa, because that doesn't make the city's coffers bulge.

[*Athenaeus continues:*]

Xenophanes makes many other claims about his own art while belittling the idea of athletics as useless and unprofitable. Archaeus of Eretria when describing the good physical condition of athletes says: 'For, naked about the loins, they travel around, their arms glistening and bulging in their prime, their strong shoulders gleaming with the bloom of youth. With a glut of oil they anoint their chests and the hollow of their shields as if they enjoyed luxury from their own estates.'

[*At this point Athenaeus returns to the theme of gluttony.*]

1 What are the criticisms which Athenaeus assembles?
2 What do they have to do with his discussion of gluttony?
3 Are there any positives in the portrayal of athletes in these passages?
4 Contrast the opinions in **7.7**, **7.19** and the story of Milo in **8.21**. How useful do you think athletics may have been for military training?

Pisa's river   the Alpheios. Note the ring composition, the way in which the poet recalls the beginning of the poem by repeating the reference to Pisa at the end.

painful art of boxing   an echo of *Iliad* 23.653.

meals at public expense   in Athens meals were provided in the *prytaneion* for Olympic victors and other worthy recipients.

The following extract is from Plato's version of Socrates' defence at his trial in 399 BC for impiety and corrupting the young (*Apology* 36d–e). After he has been found guilty and the prosecution has proposed the death penalty, Socrates at first proposes being fed at state expense, before finally suggesting a fine. He portrays himself as the gadfly of Athens, claiming that he benefited his fellow citizens by trying to make them pursue goodness and wisdom rather than possessions. The jury votes for the death penalty.

8.28   And so, what does a man like me deserve? Something good, men of Athens, if I must truly propose a penalty I deserve. On top of that, it should be a good thing appropriate for me. So, what is appropriate for a poor man, your benefactor who needs to have time free for giving you advice. There is nothing more appropriate than giving such a man free meals in the ***prytaneion***, far more so than for one of you if he has won a **horse** or chariot race (for two or four horses) at Olympia. A man like that makes you appear to enjoy good fortune, whereas I make it a reality. He has no need of subsistence, whereas I do. Therefore, if I must propose a penalty according to my just deserts, I propose just this, free meals in the *prytaneion*.

> • How similar are the opinions of Socrates and Xenophanes about the worth of the Olympic Games?

Among his 'Roman Questions', Plutarch asks why the priest of Zeus is not allowed to anoint himself with oil in the open air. His answer contains the following criticism of Greek practice (*Moralia* 274d).

8.29   The Romans used to look with grave suspicion on rubbing dry with oil and they used to think that nothing was so much to blame for the servitude and weakness of the Greeks as their gymnasia and *palaistrai* which engender considerable *ennui* and listlessness in their cities as well as the misuse of leisure and pederasty, besides destroying the bodies of the young with regimes of sleep, walking, rhythmic movement and strict diet. Under the influence of these they have let their weapons training fall away without thinking and have become content to be called nimble and fine athletes instead of good soldiers and cavalrymen.

> 1 What are the main strands of criticism in these extracts (**8.24–9**)?
> 2 How valid do you think they are?

prytaneion   distinguished Athenians were sometimes awarded free meals here at state expense. Compare the Prytaneion at Olympia (**8.11, 10.11**) and see glossary.

horse   horses were expensive to maintain and only the wealthier citizens could afford to enter the horse races. Socrates therefore chooses the right target to contrast with his poverty.

Trainers

Although Nestor's advice to his son Antilochus before the chariot race in the *Iliad* (23.306–48) might resemble that of a trainer, his actual relationship to him is quite different. For all their athletic prowess, mythical heroes seem to rely more on their innate abilities than training. Antilochus did not really need his father's advice, since he was 'wary enough himself' (line 305). Physical education does not feature prominently in the world of myth. The centaur Cheiron educated a whole succession of young heroes in various skills, the art of medicine in particular, but also some which developed their physique, such as hunting. One aspect of ancient education and training, physical punishment (**8.34**), also appears in a myth which must have delighted pupils. Linus, who tried to teach Herakles to play the lyre, was killed by his unresponsive pupil for beating him.

The earliest known trainer is Eryxias, operating in the sixth century BC (**8.33**). Later, as training increased in importance, strict regimes of training were developed, as suggested by Epictetus (**8.31**). A fragmentary papyrus text found in Egypt has a list of sophisticated moves in wrestling. Unfortunately the text is now badly damaged, but it was neatly written, evidently for publication, which suggests that such books circulated and were used as training manuals. One system of training (the so-called tetrad system) that was much criticized by Philostratus, writing in the third century AD, was practised over a four-day period.

Already by the classical period in Greece trainers might be an essential support for successful athletes, as they have become in the modern world. In modern boxing in particular, the trainer oversees the whole preparation of the athlete and gives advice between rounds, rather like Tisias advising Glaucus (**8.33**). Some successful athletes continued to work as trainers, as Pindar reveals (**8.39**). Greek athletes, like modern footballers, might have enjoyed a relatively short career in their sport, and it is hardly surprising that some continued their involvement by coaching others (as Ikkos, **8.35**).

There are two principal terms for trainers in Greek (***gymnastēs*** and ***paidotribēs***) but their usage is less clear cut than the distinction made by Aristotle between the physical (*gymnastes*) and skills trainer.

For those entering the Olympic Games, the trainer as well as the athlete had to take the oath (**3.18**) and attend the event naked (see pp. 161–5). Trainers were given a special enclosure.

It is difficult to distinguish trainers from judges on vase-paintings. Both carry a forked rod, used for hitting the athletes when they transgress the rules. Trainers appear most commonly on vases which depict 'heavy' events, but they also occur elsewhere (e.g. **5.27**). The amphora in **8.30** shows two naked athletes, supervised by their trainer, preparing for boxing or perhaps the *pankration*. Unusually, one is seen from behind, with the other binding his wrist with leather thongs (*himantes*).

8.30

Amphora by the Kleophrades Painter, c. 500 BC.

Training regimes could be tough. In this discourse of Epictetus, he uses athletics as an example of how important it is to consider what an activity entails before embarking on it (Arrian, *Discourses of Epictetus* 3.15).

8.31 'I want to win a victory at Olympia.' But consider the preliminaries and the consequences of this and only then, if it would be to your advantage, undertake the task. You must obey the rules, follow a **controlled diet**, refrain from fancy foods, train under compulsion at the appointed time in the heat and the cold. You must not drink cold water or wine when they are available. In short you must give yourself up to your trainer as you do to your doctor. Then in the competition you may be gouged, sometimes dislocate an arm, sprain an ankle, swallow mouthfuls of dust and be whipped. And on top of all this you are sometimes defeated. With these considerations in mind, if you are still keen, off you go to train.

> - Why do you think it became acceptable for athletes to be publicly whipped, when such a punishment would normally be used only on the young or slaves?

controlled diet   compare **8.29**. Philostratus (*Gymnasticus* 43–4) contrasts the simple diet (barley and unleavened wheat bread and beef, goat and venison) of earlier times with the later luxury and refinement taken to such extremes that pigs from near rivers are to be avoided because they eat crayfish, and only pigs fed on cornels and acorns are to be eaten. A meat-rich diet might help body-building for the heavy events: according to an anecdote (Diogenes Laertius, *Lives and Opinions of Eminent Philosophers* 6.49), Diogenes the Cynic, when asked why athletes were stupid, replied, 'because they are built of pork and beef'.

The Greek trainer (*gymnastes*) supervised the training of athletes and accompanied them to the games. The following passage from Philostratus, *Gymnasticus* 17 explains why trainers too were obliged to be naked at the Olympic Games.

8.32 At Delphi, Isthmia and everywhere else games are held, the trainer rubs down his athlete with oil while wearing a thin cloak. There is no one who will make him take it off if he doesn't want to, but at Olympia he is in attendance without clothes. In some people's opinion, the Eleans are testing the trainer to see if he has the stamina and can bear the heat at that time of year. But according to the Eleans, Pherenike of Rhodes, the daughter of the boxer Diagoras, was such a tough-looking woman that the Eleans thought she was a man at first. At Olympia she was wrapped up in a cloak and was training her own son Peisirodos. He was a boxer too with fast hands, technically adept and just as good as his grandfather. When they became aware of the deceit they were reluctant to put Pherenike to death because Diagoras and his sons were close to their hearts (the whole family of Pherenike were Olympic champions). But they did pass a law that a trainer must remove his clothes and undergo examination by them.

Four anecdotes from Philostratus, *Gymnasticus* 20–3 give an insight into the psychological tactics of trainers: Tisias gives 'ringside' advice to the boxer Glaucus; Eryxias inspires his fighter, the pankratiast Arrichion, with some extreme advice at the games of 564 BC; Promachos' trainer uses devious means to inspire him to victory; and Mandrogenes' trainer exploits the athlete's emotions.

8.33 There are many ways in which trainers help athletes, whether by encouragement, criticism, threats or subtle tricks, but while there are too many to mention them all, I must give an account of the more notable examples. When the boxer Glaucus of **Karystos** was giving ground to his opponent at Olympia, his trainer Tisias guided him to victory with the advice to use the 'plough shot'. This meant hitting his opponent with the full force of his right hand. Glaucus had such strength in that hand that back in Euboea he once straightened out a bent ploughshare by hitting it with his right hand like a hammer.

Arrichion the pankratiast already had two Olympic victories to his name and he was fighting for the crown at a third Olympiad to add to these. When he reached the point when he was beginning to tire, his trainer Eryxias filled him with a desire for death by shouting out from the periphery that refusing to give up at Olympia makes a fine epitaph.

Karystos   a town on the island of Euboea.

Arrichion   for further details about Arrichion or Arrachion see **7.33** and **7.34**.

The trainer of Promachos of **Pellene** found out that he was in love and, as it was nearly time for the Olympics, he said, 'Promachos, you appear to be in love.' When he saw he was blushing, he said, 'It wasn't to embarrass you that I said this, but to assist you in your love affair. I could talk to your dear lady on your behalf.' He didn't in fact talk to her, but came to the athlete with a false story, but one perfect for the lover. 'She considers you worthy,' he said, 'of being her lover, when you have won at Olympia.' Pumped up by what he heard, Promachos not only won, but even beat **Poulydamas of Skotoussa** – after Poulydamas had overcome some lions at the court of **Ochus**, king of Persia.

I personally heard Mandrogenes of **Magnesia** attribute to his trainer the endurance he possessed in his youth in the *pankration*. He said that when his father was dead and the household was in the control of his mother whose strength exceeded that of a woman, his trainer wrote her a letter like this. 'If you hear that your son has died, believe it, but if you hear that he has been defeated, don't believe it.' He said that he was thrilled by this letter and displayed the utmost courage to prevent his trainer from becoming a liar and his mother from being deceived.

1 Do the actions of the trainers in these anecdotes merely indicate low cunning or could they be called examples of the use of sport psychology?

2 How reliable do you think they are as evidence for trainers' activities?

3 Why might the techniques used by the trainers in Philostratus' account have been particularly effective, given what you know about Greek culture?

The following story is related by Aelian in his selection of miscellaneous facts which he put together in the early third century AD (*Historical Miscellany* 2.6). It illustrates the idea that the judgement of the expert is to be preferred to that of the inexpert public, which Aelian likens to Socrates' attitude in Plato's *Crito*. Aelian also relates a very similar anecdote (14.8) about Hippomachus as an *aulos* (double pipes) trainer.

8.34   There is a story about Hippomachus the trainer that when the athlete trained by him executed a fall and the whole crowd standing around cheered, Hippomachus struck him with his rod and said, 'But you have done badly and not performed as you should what ought to have been better. For these men would not have praised you if you had applied some technique.' His subtext was that those who perform any action well and with finesse must please those with a theoretical appreciation of the actions, not the crowd.

Pellene   a town of Achaia in the northern Peloponnese.

Poulydamas of Skotoussa   was renowned for his physical strength, like Milo of Croton (pp. 140–3). Skotoussa was a town in northern Thessaly.

Ochus   Artaxerxes III, king of Persia 359–338 BC.

Magnesia   a town not far from Ephesus in Asia Minor (modern Turkey).

- Is it reasonable to assume that trainers were more interested in the finer points of technique than winning?

Some athletes avoided sex during training. One Olympic victor, the pankratiast Ikkos, also became a famous trainer and may have recommended sexual abstinence since it apparently worked for him. Of the several anecdotes about the continence of athletes, this extract from Plato's *Laws* (839e5–840a6), in the section on self-control in sexual matters, mentions boys as well as women as potential objects of sexual desire.

8.35   Do we not know from reports of Ikkos of Tarentum because of the competition at Olympia and other games too? On account of his ambition to win and because he possessed the skill and mental determination coupled with self-control, as the story goes, he never laid hands on a woman or for that matter a boy during the entire critical period of his **training**. Much the same story exists about Krison, Astylos, Diapompos and very many others.

In Aristophanes' *Clouds*, there is a debate between two personifications, Right Argument and Wrong Argument, with a focus on education. Right Argument, who speaks the extracts below (lines 973–80 and 1002–14), is advocating the (in his view) superior education in the good old days. His remarks are addressed to Strepsiades, the character who wants an education to equip him with the rhetorical skills to escape from his creditors.

8.36   At the trainer's, when the boys were in the process of sitting down, they had to keep their thighs in front so that they didn't display to those outside anything **cruel**. Then, when they stood up again, they had to smooth out the sand and   975 take care not to leave behind the imprint of their genitals for their lovers. No boy would anoint himself below the navel in those days so that a dewy down bloomed on his genitals as on fruits. Nor would he make his voice soft and tender for his lover and walk along prostituting himself with his eyes. (973–80)

---

training   this anecdote suggests Ikkos' motivation came from his desire to win rather than any precepts from a trainer, but Philostratus, thinking it better to avoid exercise after sex, advised athletes to observe careful limits to exercise after any emission of semen. There is still debate over this issue and some modern sportsmen observe abstinence whether self-imposed (as reportedly by Mohammed Ali before fights) or at the direction of a coach (as when Luis Felipe Scolari banned the Brazil football team from having sex at the 2002 World Cup).

cruel   an unexpected word for tormenting the onlookers with desire by revealing their genitals.

But shiny with oil and blooming you'll spend your time in the gymnasia, not in the **agora** going on about weird, prickly topics like boys nowadays, nor being hauled off to court on some damned-tacky-contentious little matter. No, you'll go down to the **Academy** and set off running under the sacred olives, crowned with grey- 1005 green reed with a chaste friend of your own age, smelling of bindweed, the quiet life and leaf-shedding white poplar, rejoicing in the season of spring when the plane tree whispers to the elm. If you do these things as I tell you and keep your 1010 mind focused on them, you'll always have a chest shining with oil, a gleaming skin, big shoulders, a tiny tongue, a big butt and a **small prick**. (1002–14)

> 1 What is Right Argument's attitude to homoeroticism in the gymnasium? What comic technique is used to reveal his true feelings?
> 2 What details about the Academy can we learn from these extracts?
> 3 The second paragraph is a poetic and idealized representation of the 'right' part that exercise might play in a proper education. What aspects does it idealize?

Among all the statues of successful athletes at Olympia, Pausanias records a special dispensation for a boy wrestler to have a statue of his trainer erected too (*Description of Greece* 6.3.6).

8.37   Kratinos of Aigeira in Achaia was then the most handsome man of his time and he wrestled with particular skill. When he won the wrestling for boys, he was allowed by the Eleans to put up a statue of his trainer as well.

> 1 Why might it have been unusual for a trainer to be recorded on a victory monument?
> 2 Why isn't the trainer's name recorded?

The names of trainers are occasionally mentioned in Bacchylides and Pindar, and Pausanias remarks on an inscription naming the trainer and not the athlete (*Description of Greece* 6.2.9).

agora   the market place and political centre of Athens, a place to discuss contentious issues, as opposed to the gymnasium, a place to enjoy oneself.

Academy   one of the main gymnasia, just outside Athens. Dedicated to the local deity Akademos, it later became associated with Plato and his school of philosophy. See p. 158.

small prick   vase-paintings usually represent athletes (and gods and heroes) in this manner, whereas comic characters have excessively large genitalia.

8.38   The inscription on the Samian boxer says that the man who dedicated it was the trainer Mykon and that the Samians are the best of the Ionians for athletes and in sea battles. This is what the inscription says, but as for the boxer himself, it gives no information.

> Pindar's eighth Olympian ode was written for Alkimedon of Aegina, who won the boys' wrestling in 460 BC (*Olympian* 8.53–66).

8.39   Among men, nothing will be equally pleasing. If for Melesias I traced in my song his glory from [training] beardless youths, let envy not throw a jagged stone 55 at me. For I shall also mention his success in the same event at Nemea and his later combat against men in the *pankration.* It is easier to teach when you have knowledge and stupid not to learn in advance. The minds of the inexperienced 60 carry less weight. But Melesias could speak better than others about that business, the method that will advance a man whose ambition is to win the most desired fame from the sacred games. Now his prize is Alkimedon winning his thirtieth 65 victory.

> 1 What sort of celebrity did trainers enjoy?
> 2 Is it still important for trainers to have practised the sport themselves?
> 3 Why do you think these trainers were mentioned by name?

> In Plato's dialogue named after him, Protagoras has been giving an outline of Athenian education and its civilizing effects. After mentioning the contributions of the *didaskolos* (teacher) and *kitharistēs* (lyre player), he briefly mentions the *paidotribes* (*Protagoras* 326 b6–c3).

8.40   Then in addition to these they send them to a trainer (*paidotribes*) so that, with an improved physique, they may be fit to serve their well-trained mind, and not be compelled to show cowardice in wars or any other activities because of their poor physical condition. These are the things the most able do – the most able are the wealthiest – and their children begin going to the teachers (*didaskoloi*) at the earliest age, and leave at the latest.

> 1 How does Protagoras' opinion of athletic training differ from that of the critics (pp. 146–50)?
> 2 What does this extract reveal about athletics and social class?
> 3 How important is money in launching and sustaining a sporting career in the modern world?

The gymnasium and *palaistra*

Places to exercise and train became important as the practice of physical education began to develop in Greek cities by the sixth century BC. The *gymnasion* ('place for naked exercise') and *palaistra* ('wrestling ground') are the two types of building that eventually emerge for the purpose, although the distinction between them is often unclear, since they have much in common in providing space for physical exercise (see e.g. **3.20**). Some events, such as the javelin, needed specifically designated areas (see **5.16**).

Inevitably they were frequented by those who were wealthy enough to enjoy leisure. The popularity of athletic imagery on vase-painting is evidence of the attraction athletics had for those who could afford to use the pottery at *symposia* (dinner parties). Gymnasia also provided attractive spaces (**8.41**) for social gathering and became centres for learning, culture and erotic attachment (**8.36**). Plato used them as settings for some of his philosophical dialogues: *Euthydemus* at the Lyceum, *Lysis* at a newly built *palaistra* and *Charmides* also at a *palaistra*, a place where Charmides knows he will meet his friends. Two gymnasia at Athens, the Academy and the Lyceum, have become particularly well known because of their association with the philosophical schools of Plato and Aristotle in the fourth century BC. Like the theatre or **agora**, the gymnasium became one of the defining buildings of a Greek city. Vitruvius, the Roman writer on architecture, gives a detailed description of a complex which contains facilities suited to both gymnasium and *palaistra*. From their early, relatively simple form, gymnasia and *palaistrai* became institutions with elaborate systems of management and elected officials to oversee what had by then become a complex combination of religious centre, athletic training ground, social centre and place of learning.

> In the following extract from Plutarch, *Cimon* 13.8, Cimon, a wealthy Athenian politician, provides the essential amenities for the Academy.

8.41 He [Cimon] was **the first** to beautify the city with so-called free and elegant haunts which shortly afterwards were held in extraordinary high regard. The agora he planted with plane trees and the Academy he turned from a waterless, parched place into an irrigated grove provided with cleared running tracks and shady walks.

- Compare what Plutarch and Aristophanes (**8.36**) say about the Academy.

---

the first in the aftermath of the Persian Wars when the Persians had captured and sacked Athens (480 BC).

Theophrastus (*c.* 370–285 BC) was a pupil of Aristotle and became head of the Lyceum. He was a philosopher with a wide range of interests from botany to logic; the *Characters*, sketches of 30 character-types, became his most famous work, although its purpose has been much debated. This passage, from Character 7, is part of a character description which appears to be out of place in the text and is often added to Character 21, Petty Ambition.

8.42   … [he will own] a little *palaistra*, complete with **dust**, and a **ball-court**, and he'll go round lending it to philosophers, **sophists, military instructors** and musicians to perform in. At their displays he himself comes in later when they are all seated, so that members of the audience will say to each other, 'This is the owner of the *palaistra.*'

> Writing in the reign of Augustus (31 BC–AD 14), Vitruvius describes in detail the architectural features of a ***palaestra***. Although he does not use the word *gymnasium*, some of the features he describes would suit such a building (*On Architecture* 5.11).

8.43   Even though the construction of ***palaestrae*** is unusual in Italy, there is a tradition and I think I should make it clear by giving an account of how they are organized among the Greeks. In *palaestrae*, square or rectangular **peristyles** should be built so that they have a circuit to walk round of **two stades** which the Greeks call a *diaulos*. Of these colonnades, three should be laid out as single, but the fourth (facing south) as double so that when there is heavy rain and wind, spray can't reach the inner part. In the other three colonnades, spacious bays should be laid out with seats on which philosophers, teachers of rhetoric and others who take pleasure in learning can sit and exchange views. But the following elements should be located in the double colonnade: in the middle an *ephebeum*, a very large bay with seats, one third longer than it is wide; to the right a *coryceum* and next to it a *consisterium*; beyond the *consisterium*, in the corner of the colonnade, a cold bath

---

dust   for wrestling. See **7.7** and **7.8**.

ball-court   various ball games were popular among the Greeks.

sophists   teachers of rhetoric in particular.

military instructors   the hoplite (heavy infantryman) would need careful training to fight in formation. A display by such an instructor is mentioned at the beginning of Plato's *Laches*, where there is also a discussion about sending sons to learn the art of fighting in armour.

two stades   this may be an exaggeration or a mistake. The *palaistra* at Olympia is about half this size.

ephebeum   room for young men (18–20 years old in Athens).

coryceum   room containing a punchbag for exercise (see **7.21**).

consisterium   room for applying dust (see **7.7**).

---

which the Greeks call a *loutron*; to the left of the *ephebeum*, an *elaeothesium* and next to it a cold bath and from there, a passage into the furnace room at the corner of the colonnade. Next to this, but on the inside behind the cold bath, should be located a vaulted sweat-room, twice as long as it is wide. In one of its corners it should have a *laconicum* constructed to the same design described **earlier**, and opposite the *laconicum*, a hot bath. In the palaestra the colonnades should be laid out in the manner just described.

Outside, three colonnades should be arranged, one as one leaves the peristyle and two with running tracks, one on the left and one on the right. Of these, the one facing north should be made double and of a generous width, the other single. It should be made in such a way that the sides next to the walls and next to the columns have borders to serve as paths not less than three metres wide. The space in the middle should be excavated so that there are steps descending a half a metre from the sides to a level track which is not less than four metres wide. In this way, those who wear clothes and walk around on the paths will not be impeded by those anointed with oil who are taking exercise. This type of colonnade is called a *xystos* by the Greeks because athletes train on covered running tracks during the winter. Next to the *xystum* and the double colonnade should be assigned open-air paths which the Greeks call *paradromides* and our people call *xysta*. In fine weather during the winter the athletes leave the covered track and exercise on these. The *xysta* should be made in such a way that there are groves of trees between the colonnades and among the trees are paths and places to rest made of cement. Behind the *xystum*, a stadium should be designed so that there is plenty of space for crowds of men to watch the athletes competing.

> 1 How do the training facilities for athletes in the modern world compare with those described in these passages?
>
> 2 What do these passages suggest were the essential facilities for Greek athletes?

Olive oil

One of the essential facilities for athletes was a place to rub themselves down with oil before beginning exercise (**7.7**, **8.32**, **8.36**, **8.44**, **8.45**) and to scrape off the oil and sweat after exercise. An athlete would carry a flask (aryballos) of olive oil and a *stlengis* (Latin *strigil*) with which to scrape the oil, sweat and dust from the body when he had finished exercising or competing.

---

elaeothesium   room for applying oil.

laconicum, **earlier**   a hot, dry room described in the previous chapter on baths.

xystos   or *xyston* in Greek (Latin *xystus* or *xystum*). The meaning developed from 'scraped area' (**3.20**) to 'path/walkway' and here it also refers to a covered colonnade.

Philostratus (*Gymnasticus* 18) indicates that oil must be applied liberally, but the benefits from applying oil are not entirely clear. Lucian (**8.51**) suggested it promoted suppleness, while Pliny the Elder said it promoted warmth and protected against cold, yet allowed one to keep a cool head when heated. He also noted that the scrapings from the athletes' bodies (**gloios**) were sometimes sold for huge sums, presumably for the manly essence they contained.

On the left of this vase-painting (**8.44**) a young athlete called Hegesias is pouring olive oil from an aryballos into his cupped left hand in preparation for anointing himself. His cloak (*himation*) lies on a stool while another young athlete folds his cloak. The arm and leg visible on the right belong to a slave in attendance. Beneath Hegesias' left arm is written 'Leagros is handsome', a type of inscription common on Greek vases, attesting to the Greek appreciation of the beauty of boys and youths.

8.44

Detail from an Attic mixing bowl (krater) by Euphronios, c. 510–500 BC.

---

1 What advantages of applying olive oil can you think of?
2 Are there any disadvantages?
3 What substances do we use to anoint ourselves with today, and for what reasons?

Nudity

In the Bronze Age, athletes appear not to have competed naked. Both visual evidence (the boy boxers, **1.1**; compare the figures in **1.2**) and Homer's description of athletic contests (*Iliad* 23.710, 683–5, *Odyssey* 18.66–9, 74 ff.) indicate that some clothing was worn, even if it was only a loincloth.

Vase-paintings begin to depict athletes naked in the late seventh century BC (or earlier) and by the mid-sixth century athletic nudity was very common. A small number of Attic vases of the late sixth century show athletes wearing a loincloth, but it seems that these were intended for the different taste of the Etruscan market, since most have been discovered in Etruria. The loincloths are always added in white paint over the naked figures, rather as an afterthought. Depiction of the naked or partially naked male figure was the norm in Greek art from an early period, and in contexts other than athletic too. Some see this as an expression of appreciation for the physical prowess, courage, fitness, health and beauty of the male body in its prime, and these qualities are exactly those exhibited by athletes in competition.

The literary evidence for the beginning of nudity in athletics presents us with two conflicting opinions. The earliest authors, Thucydides (late fifth century BC) and Plato (fourth century BC), suggest that the practice had been adopted only recently, but later authors such as Dionysius of Halicarnassus (first century BC) preserve a different tradition that an athlete named either Akanthos or Orsippos first ran naked as early as the 15th Olympiad (720 BC).

Attempts to reconcile the evidence have not been entirely successful, since all of it has limitations. Even the depiction of athletic nudity in vase-painting has been questioned as evidence, because vase-painters are not necessarily representing bodies realistically. Depiction of small genitals, absence of body hair, elongated fingers and toes or the posture of runners with the left arm and leg thrust forward together are some of the more obvious unrealistic conventions often adopted by vase-painters. Besides, heroes and warriors are also frequently depicted naked in scenes from battle where they would certainly be clothed. The literary evidence is also questionable. Thucydides' statement must be seen in the context of a rapid historical summary in which 'recent' may be a relative term, and since his reference to naked athletics is hardly central to his discussion, it is perhaps less carefully considered than the events of his main narrative. Plato may possibly have followed Thucydides, though his account varies in detail. Besides, it may be that the practice, like a fashion, caught on gradually at different times in different places until it became a universal characteristic of Greek athletics. The accounts which ascribe the origin of the practice to an individual or specific event may be following a habit manifest in many myths that explain origins by a story. At any rate, the practice of competing naked became the norm and the Greeks were proud of their physiques and contemptuous of the white bodies of foreigners who failed to exercise (**8.52**).

Some naked athletes tied their penis back on itself with a 'dog-leash' (**kynodesmē**: *kuōn*, Greek for 'dog', was also slang for 'penis'). Perhaps this was to protect the penis during energetic exercise or perhaps to inhibit sexual arousal. The practice is known mostly from vase-paintings and late references.

Thucydides opens his account of the Peloponnesian War with a survey of early Greek history. In a digression on costume he turns his attention to nudity in athletics (*Histories* 1.6.4–5).

8.45　The Spartans were the first to adopt the simple form of dress worn to **this day**, and in other ways too the lifestyle of their more affluent citizens was very like that of the majority. They were the first to remove their clothes and, naked in public, give their bodies a liberal application of olive oil during their athletic exercises. In the past, even at the Olympic Games, athletes used to compete wearing a covering around their genitals and it is not many years since they stopped. Among barbarians, particularly in Asia, who currently hold prize contests for boxing and wrestling, they still compete in loincloths.

In Plato's *Republic* Socrates sets out a vision of an ideal state. In Book 5.452c–d he suggests to his interlocutor Glaucon (Plato's brother) that women should have the same initial education as men and observes that one shouldn't ridicule the idea since people used to mock male nudity, which was a recently introduced practice, now fully accepted.

8.46　'... it is not long since the Greeks thought, as the majority of barbarians still do, that it was shameful and ridiculous for men to be seen naked and when the Cretans first began naked exercise and were followed by the Spartans, it provided an opportunity for wits to make fun of all this. Don't you think so?' 'I do.' 'But when, I suppose, it became clear that it is better to remove clothes than to cover up in all such circumstances, then what was ridiculous to the eye ceased to be so when logic revealed it to be best.'

- What details do the accounts of Thucydides and Plato agree and disagree on?

In describing the procession to the Circus Maximus in Rome for the opening of games, Dionysius of Halicarnassus mentions the athletic competitors who are naked except for a loincloth. There follows this digression on nudity in Greek athletics (*Roman Antiquities* 7.72.2–4).

8.47　After **these** came competitors in athletic events, both light and heavy, their bodies naked except for a covering around their genitals. This has remained the custom in Rome even down to **our time**, as it used to be among the Greeks originally.

this day　late fifth century BC.

these　the charioteers.

our time　late first century BC.

The practice became obsolete in Greece once the Spartans put an end to it. The first man to try stripping his body and running naked was Akanthos of Sparta at the **15th Olympiad**. Before this all Greeks were ashamed to reveal their bodies completely naked in the games, as **Homer**, the oldest and most trustworthy of witnesses, attests by making his heroes wear loincloths.

It is clear that the Romans preserved down to our own day this custom that existed among the Greeks long ago. They didn't learn it from **us** later, but never changed it in the meanwhile, as we did.

> This inscription from Megara (IG VII 52) in central Greece was carved sometime after the reign of Trajan (died AD 117), but the poem was probably composed somewhat earlier.

8.48   The Megarians set me up here as a conspicuous memorial to fiery **Orrhippos**, in obedience to the word of Delphi. He was the man who redeemed the furthest borders of the land when **the enemy** were appropriating considerable territory and he was the first to win a crown at Olympia naked, when previous competitors wore loincloths in the *stadion*.

> Pausanias must have seen this inscription when he visited the agora at Megara, where the memorial to Orsippos was situated next to the tomb of Koroibos, whose story he has told. In the following extract from *Description of Greece* (1.44.1) he goes on to mention Orsippos.

8.49   Close to **Koroibos** is buried Orsippos who won the sprint (*stadion*) at Olympia, running naked at a time when the athletes at the games were wearing loincloths in the old tradition. They say that later, in his generalship, Orsippos annexed some of the neighbours' territory. I think he deliberately let his loincloth fall off at Olympia because he realized that a naked man finds it easier to run than a man wearing a loincloth.

15th Olympiad   720 BC.

Homer   Dionysius quotes *Iliad* 23.685, where two boxers are wearing loincloths, though he introduces it as if it were line 710, when Ajax and Odysseus are about to wrestle. He also mentions the fight between Odysseus and the beggar Irus (*Odyssey* 18.66–9, 74–5).

us   Dionysius was a Greek.

Orrhippos   Megarian dialect form of Orsippos.

the enemy   Megara's neighbours, the Corinthians.

stadion   the word could signify the stadium or the race.

Koroibos   Koroibos of Argos rescued his city by killing Vengeance, whom Apollo had sent to avenge the death of his child, Linos. When a plague followed, Koroibos was told by the Pythia to take a tripod and build a temple to Apollo at the place where he dropped it. Koroibos' grave was in the agora at Megara.

Isidore of Seville (*c*. AD 560–636) wrote an encyclopedia in Latin called *Etymologiae*. In his discussion of athletics (*gymnicus ludus*) he records yet another version of the origin of athletic nudity (18.17.2).

8.50 In the early days competitors had their private parts covered so that they were not naked, but later a runner's loincloth came loose and he suddenly fell to the ground and died. Therefore by decree of the council the archon Hippomenes then allowed everyone to exercise naked from **that time**.

> 1 Are any of these explanations about the origins of competing naked at all convincing?
> 2 What date for the introduction of nudity is suggested by Thucydides and Plato? Does the evidence from Pausanias and Dionysius contradict this?

Lucian, writing in the second century AD, set this dialogue, *Anacharsis* 24, in the sixth century BC. (See **5.9** for further details.) Anacharsis has come to Athens especially to talk with the famous law-giver Solon, who explains to him the principles of Greek education and offers these observations on their physical training.

8.51 Their bodies, something you were particularly keen to hear about, we train as follows. We strip them, as I said, when they are no longer soft and altogether lacking firmness. In the first place, we think it is right to make them get used to the open air, adapting them to all seasons so that they don't find heat oppressive and don't succumb to the cold. Secondly, we rub them down with olive oil and make them more supple so that they become more vigorous. As we think that leather softened with oil becomes harder to break and much more durable, though it is in fact lifeless by then, it would be strange if we were to suppose that the condition of the living body was not improved by oil.

> • Does Solon offer a convincing justification for nudity in athletics?

During the Spartan king Agesilaos' campaign in Asia (396–395 BC), Xenophon tells us that, in order to inspire contempt for the enemy, he put captured natives up for sale naked (*Hellenica* 3.4.19).

8.52 When the soldiers saw they were white because they never stripped off, and soft and unexercised because they were always in carriages, they thought that the war would be no different from having to fight against women.

---

that time   late eighth century BC.

Women and athletics

We hear very little about women and athletics in ancient Greece from written sources. There are a number of references to Spartan women's participation in athletics, but judging by the few references in Athenian literature, Sparta is likely to have been exceptional. Some inscriptions record girls winning races in various Greek cities, but they are of late or uncertain date. Although there is some evidence of girls running at Brauron, the cult centre of Artemis in Attica, it is not clear whether they are in an athletic competition or performing a ceremony or rite associated with Artemis the huntress, who is also depicted running with a dog on a sixth-century BC plaque from the site. At Olympia it is clear that a separate festival in honour of Hera featured a competition for female athletes, but its programme is very limited in comparison with what seems to have been available for Spartan women. Even the rules concerning female spectators at the Olympic Games have to be pieced together from different contexts in Pausanias, and yet the savage penalty of being hurled over a cliff – and indeed the fact that recourse to it was never needed – suggests a strong prohibition, even though only incidentally recorded (**8.53**). Some scholars have pointed to a similar disparity in the coverage of contemporary sport, with women's events attracting far less attention than the men's. There was in fact one possible way for a woman to compete at the Olympics, and that was as an owner of a team in the chariot race. Kyniska, a Spartan woman, became the first to achieve that distinction (see **4.9**).

> In the following extract from his *Description of Greece* (5.6.7–8), Pausanias, describing the route from Elis to Olympia, reveals the punishment for women caught attending the Olympic Games. However, in his description of the stadium (see **3.3**) he tells us that the Priestess of Demeter and unmarried women were not excluded from watching the Olympic competitions.

8.53   On the road to Olympia, after leaving **Scillous**, but before crossing the Alpheios, there is a mountain called Typaion with a sheer face of high cliffs. If women are detected either attending the Olympic Games, or even just on the other side of the Alpheios on the days women are excluded, the Eleans have a law which sanctions pushing them off this mountain. In fact they say that no woman has been caught with the single exception of Kallipateira (some call this same woman **Pherenike**, not Kallipateira).

Her husband had died before her, and after making herself look exactly like a trainer, she brought their son to fight at Olympia. When Peisirodos won, Kallipateira jumped over the fence of the trainers' enclosure and revealed her body. Although

---

Scillous   a town south of the Alpheios, not far from Olympia.

Pherenike   Philostratus uses this name ('bringer of victory') in his version of the story (**8.32**).

her gender was revealed, they let her off without a punishment in a show of respect to her father, her brothers and her son, all of whom had Olympic victories. But they did make a law for trainers stipulating that in future they attend the games naked.

> • How believable is this story about Kallipateira?

The Heraia

> There are many unanswered questions about the games of Hera at Olympia. Although Pausanias manages to convey a considerable amount of information in a brief description, he does not reveal, among other things, the time of the Heraia, its duration, and whether it was Panhellenic or confined to the women of Elis. He gives the following description of the games during his account of the temple of Hera and its contents (*Description of Greece* 5.16.2–4).

8.54   Every four years the Sixteen Women weave a *peplos* for Hera. Those same women also organize the Heraia games. The competition consists of a foot race for girls, but not, one must say, all girls of the same age. The youngest race first, after them the next age group and finally the oldest girls. They run like this: their hair is let down, their tunic comes down to just above the knee and they bare their right shoulder as far as the breast. They also have the Olympic stadium as the appointed place for their competition, but they reduce the length of the track for them by about **a sixth**. They present the winners with crowns of olive and a share of the cow sacrificed to Hera, besides which they can dedicate **statues** with their name inscribed. Administrative assistants of the Sixteen, when they put on the games, are likewise women. They also trace back the girls' competition to the distant past, saying that **Hippodameia** in thanking Hera for her marriage to Pelops assembled the Sixteen Women and with them became the first to conduct the Heraia. They also put it on record that victory went to Chloris, the only surviving daughter of the **house of Amphion**.

> The following bronze statuette of a girl was probably made in Sparta in about 500 BC. It was found in Epirus in north-west Greece.

---

peplos   a type of dress. Compare the Panathenaia, **9.1**.

a sixth   i.e. shortened by 100 (Greek) feet to 500 feet (approximately by 33 metres to 167 metres).

statues   the Greek word could signify paintings.

Hippodameia   see pp. 23–4.

house of Amphion   Amphion and Niobe had a large family, but when Niobe boasted that she had more children than Leto's two, Apollo and Artemis killed all her children. In some versions of the myth a son and a daughter named Meliboia survived. She was so frightened that she turned pale from fear: hence her name was changed to Chloris ('pale').

8.55

Bronze statuette of a girl, c. *500 BC.*

1 Why does the girl turn her head and lift her dress with her left hand?
2 Do you think the statuette depicts a girl running or dancing?

After relating the origins of the Sixteen Women and their other responsibilities, Pausanias records in the first of these two short extracts how they were selected in his day and how they were purified before they carried out their duties (see **3.23**). He also reveals in his description of Elis that they had a building in the agora (*Description of Greece* 5.16.7–8 and 6.24.10).

8.56   They [the people of Elis] are divided into eight tribes and from each they choose two women. Whatever the appointed tasks for the Sixteen Women or the *Hellanodikai*, they perform none of them before they are purified with a piglet fit for purification and water. (5.16.7–8)

A building has been erected in the agora for the women called the Sixteen, where they weave the *peplos* for Hera. (6.24.10)

1 Why is there so little evidence for women's involvement in athletics?
2 How different from ours were ancient Greek attitudes to women taking athletic exercise?
3 Is there any evidence to suggest that women's games were well organized and of importance?
4 How clear are the rules about female spectators at the Olympics?

Women's athletics in Sparta

In this extract from his biography of the Spartan law-giver Lykourgos (possibly eighth century BC), Plutarch is detailing his regulations for education at Sparta (*Lykourgos* 14.1–2, 4).

8.57 But he [**Lykourgos**] paid every possible attention even to women. He made girls exercise their bodies with running, wrestling, and throwing the discus and javelin so that, as their children take root in the womb, they might get a strong start in strong bodies and enjoy better growth, and so that the women themselves, facing up to the birth of children with strength, might struggle both nobly and easily with the pangs of childbirth. … There was no disgrace attached to the girls' stripping. Instead, done with modesty and no promiscuity, it instilled a simple way of life and a competitive desire for a physical well-being. It also gave women a taste of noble spirit, as they had an equal opportunity to display their worth (*aretē*) and show their ambition.

Although Plutarch goes on to discuss the role of women more generally in Spartan society, Xenophon is in no doubt about the main purpose of their physical education (*Constitution of Sparta* 1.4).

8.58 Lykourgos thought that for free women, the most important thing was having children. First he ordained for the female sex no less physical exercise than for the male. Secondly he established for women competitions against each other in racing and strength, in the same way as for men. His belief was that stronger children would be born from parents who were both strong.

Athenian attitudes to women's athletics

In discussing the education of women in the ideal state, Socrates establishes that if they are to perform the same roles as men, they should have the same initial education, that is 'music' (liberal arts or culture) and physical education. When the question of which new practice seems most laughable arises, the following brief dialogue ensues (Plato, *Republic* 5.452a–b).

8.59 'Which of them,' I said, 'do you see as most ridiculous? Surely the obvious choice is that of women exercising naked in the *palaistra* with the men, and not just the young, but even those now getting on in years, like the old men in the gymnasia who, despite being wrinkled and not a pretty sight, nevertheless enjoy exercise.' 'Yes by Zeus,' **he** said, 'that would seem ludicrous under present conditions.'

Lykourgos   see p. 27.

he   Glaukon. See **8.46**.

When the Spartan Lampito makes her first appearance on stage in Aristophanes' comedy *Lysistrata*, she is welcomed by the Athenian women with some admiration for her physique. In this fantasy where the women of Greece unite to force their men to give up fighting wars by going on sex-strike, differences between the women are treated with wry humour (lines 78–83).

8.60   LYSISTRATA   My dearest Spartan, Lampito, welcome. How lovely you look, my darling, and what a fine complexion you have. How well-built your body is – you could even strangle a bull.

LAMPITO   **By the two gods**, I reckon I could. Anyway, I am in training and do kick-ass jumps.

CALONIKE   Oh, what beautiful tits you've got!

Athenian prejudices could be given a different expression, as in the following extract from Euripides' tragedy *Andromache*. Here Peleus is trying to defend Andromache and her son against the Spartan Menelaus. After reproaching him for Helen's elopement with Paris, he delivers a brief condemnation of all Spartan women based on their participation in athletics (lines 595–601).

8.61   Even if she wanted, a Spartan girl could not be chaste. They leave the house in the company of young men and, with naked thighs and dress undone, they share race tracks and training grounds (*palaistrai*), something I cannot endure. Should it be any surprise then, if you don't bring up women to be chaste?

> 1   How reliable is evidence for Spartan practice when it is taken from plays performed on the Athenian stage, given that Athens and Sparta were inveterate enemies?
>
> 2   What different attitudes towards women are revealed in these passages?
>
> 3   What seems to be the main reason for women to take part in athletics?
>
> 4   Is there any suggestion that they might share the same ideals as the men?
>
> 5   What importance is attached to watching athletes?
>
> 6   What importance do modern obstetricians attach to physical fitness for women?

By the two gods   the Dioscuri (see **7.11** and **7.15**).

9 The Panathenaia

Of the many games which came to be celebrated locally in cities across the Greek world, the best known are those which developed into Panhellenic games at the Panathenaic festival in Athens. As at Olympia there were (equally unreliable) myths about the festival's origin, whether it was attributed to Erichthonius who invented the chariot and first drove his invention at the Panathenaia, or to Theseus who unified Attica (hence *Panathenaia* or 'All-Athenian'), or was celebrated for Athene's victory in the battle of gods against giants. Nor can the later history and development of the festival be reconstructed with any certainty. Initially held on what is often claimed to be the birthday of the goddess Athene, the 28th of the Athenian month Hekatombaion (i.e. in late July), the festival gradually expanded to include recitations of the Homeric epics, music, possibly drama (by the first century AD), athletics, horse racing, and team events for the ten tribes into which the people of Athens were divided on the establishment of the democracy in *c.* 508 BC. As at Olympia, there is a traditional date (566 BC) for the founding of the festival, which is shortly after the establishment of the circuit (*periodos*) of 'crown' games – the Pythian Games at Delphi were founded in 582, the Isthmian Games in 581 and the Nemean Games in 573. The Great Panathenaia was celebrated every four years like the Olympics and Pythian Games at Delphi (the Nemean and Isthmian were held every two years). The Lesser Panathenaia took place on the intervening years, but was still an important occasion in the religious calendar at Athens (see **9.3**).

The most striking differences between the 'crown' games and the Panathenaia concerned the prizes (**9.2**). At the Panathenaia, not only were the prizes of considerable monetary value, but they were also awarded for the runner-up and, in music, for as far as fifth place. Such lavish outlay on prizes must have been aimed at securing the best performers, rather in the same way that golf or tennis tournaments today offer significant prize money to attract the best players. (Wimbledon champions received £1,000,000 in 2010.) Besides the financial rewards, the trophies and medals awarded to modern athletes are of great symbolic significance, as were the crowns, garlands and ribbons awarded to Greek athletes. A tennis player who achieves victory in each of the four Majors in a year to complete a Grand Slam attains a distinction similar to that of the *periodonikēs*, a winner at all four 'crown' games.

The programme of events at the Great Panathenaia can be largely reconstructed from a fourth-century BC inscription detailing the prizes awarded there (**9.2**), but not every part of the inscription survives to give a complete picture. The competition for rhapsodes involved reciting the *Iliad* and *Odyssey*, each of which must have taken about 12 hours for a complete recitation. There were musical contests (**9.2**, **9.3**), and athletic competitions which probably included a very

Marble relief of a chariot in the race for **apobatai**; *fourth century BC.*

similar range of events to those at Olympia, although they are not all recorded on the inscription (**9.2**), and there is also an extra category for 'beardless' youths. Panathenaic vases (e.g. **6.5**, **6.17**) also have representations of events which must have featured in the games. There were the usual equestrian events, some open to all Greeks and others open to Athenians only. Among the latter were some with a very different character, such as throwing the javelin from horseback or the race for chariots with a charioteer and a rider (***apobatēs***) who leapt from the chariot and ran alongside, perhaps for the last stretch of the course.

Radically different from the Olympic competitions were the team events for the ten tribes of the democratic constitution. These had a more obvious military benefit because military units were organized by tribe and the competitions helped to encourage a team spirit and tribal bonding. They included a cavalry event called the ***anthippasia*** (**9.4**, **9.5**), in which the riders seem to have engaged in flight and pursuit and possibly charged through opposing ranks at ever-increasing speeds. How the winners were decided remains obscure. We can get some idea of the pyrrhic dance (a war dance) from Plato (**9.6**), and possibly from sculpture (**9.7**), but the competition for manly excellence (***euandria***) remains a puzzle. It is tempting to regard it as a male beauty competition, as a character in Athenaeus says 'they choose the most beautiful', but that seems unlikely given the nature of the other events and the semantic range of 'beauty' in Greek. The boat race must have been held at sea, but we have no information apart from the prizes listed in **9.2**, where 200 dinners at state expense might suggest the race was between **triremes** – warships with 180 rowers and a further complement of marines and crew. A torch race (**10.12–16**) was held, probably on the night before the great procession along with the all-night celebration (*pannychis*). The procession itself, taking the specially woven dress (*peplos*) (**9.1**) to the statue of Athene on the Acropolis, was the climax of the whole festival. The *peplos* was carried in a ship specially made for the Panathenaic procession. We hear of a number of participants in the procession, such as handsome old men carrying branches (**thallophoroi**), **metics** (resident foreigners) dressed in purple and carrying trays, metic girls carrying parasols or stools, citizen girls carrying baskets; but these special categories were only a minor part of the whole and we do not have any description of the complete procession. Some idea can be obtained from the Parthenon frieze which is generally taken to represent the procession, but its precise relationship to the actual festival is a hotly debated issue. Even what seems to be the climactic moment depicted over the eastern entrance to the Parthenon, which is usually taken to represent the handing over of the *peplos*, is not universally accepted as such. The sacrifice and feast which followed brought the festival to a close.

The *Constitution of the Athenians*, often ascribed by some to Aristotle, provides some information about the administration of the Panathenaia and the prizes awarded.

9.1   They select by lot ten *athlothetai*, one from each tribe. When they have been **vetted**, they hold the post for four years. They organize the procession at the Panathenaia, the music competition, the athletic competition and the equestrian events. They also have the *peplos* made and (in partnership with the *boulē*) the amphorae, and they present the oil to the athletes. The oil is collected from the sacred olive trees. From the owners of the land where the olive trees are, the **archon** collects a tax of **three half-kotylai** from each tree. ... The **treasurers** keep it safely on the Acropolis all the time except at the Panathenaia, when they measure it out for the *athlothetai* who give it to the victorious competitors. Prizes for the victors in the music competition are of silver and gold; for those in the *euandria* there are **shields** and for those in the athletic and equestrian competitions, olive oil.

---

athlothetai   supervisors of the games.

vetted   by a process called *dokimasia* which examined the eligibility of all those selected for office.

peplos   a type of dress.

boulē   a council of 500 men chosen by lot. They represented the democracy in day-to-day affairs.

archon   the *archon eponymos*, so called because he gave his name to the year, was the most important of the archons (magistrates/officers) who had a variety of duties.

three half-kotylai   about 0.4 litres.

...   Aristotle describes changes to the system of collection in the omitted section.

treasurers   ten Treasurers of Athene were appointed by lot to look after the sacred images, treasures, ceremonial equipment and considerable sums of money.

euandria   the competition for manly excellence, about which very little is known.

shields   compare this with the statement on the inscription, **9.2**.

- What insights does this passage offer into the administration required for staging elaborate festivals in the ancient world?

Panathenaic amphorae

Unlike at the Olympics, athletes at the Panathenaia competed not only for crowns, ribbons or garlands but also for prizes of real monetary value. Those for athletics were amphorae (two-handled storage/transport jars) of olive oil, which also had a symbolic and even propaganda value for Athens. The oil came from Athene's sacred olives, indicating that the gift was coming from the goddess in the same way that the crowns of the 'crown' games were divine gifts. The Panathenaic amphorae also depicted the goddess in the paintings with which they were decorated, and usually had an inscription to confirm their origin as a prize from Athens. On the opposite side to Athene was depicted one of the athletic or equestrian events. It is often claimed that these paintings portrayed the event for which each amphora was a prize, but this has been called into question. The amphorae have a distinctive shape with a narrow neck and foot, and usually stand 60–70 cm high. Even after the **red-figure technique** became almost universal, Panathenaic amphorae continued to use the black-figure technique. Their considerable size meant that they could hold almost 40 litres of olive oil and they were therefore valuable prizes.

A Panathenaic amphora, the 'Burgon amphora', inscribed: 'I am one of the prizes from Athens'. It shows Athene, armed, brandishing a spear; a siren appears on the neck of the vase. On the other side is a two-horse chariot. Dating from the mid-sixth century BC, this is probably the earliest surviving example of a Panathenaic amphora.

red-figure technique this technique was introduced around 530 BC and gradually replaced the earlier black-figure technique. The red colour of the clay was now used for the figures, and a slip which fires black was used for the background.

The following inscription (IG² 2311) is incomplete, but preserves with relatively slight damage two columns listing the prizes to be awarded at the Great Panathenaia. It is on a stone *stēlē* found on the Acropolis and dates from the first half of the fourth century BC.

9.2   *Column 1*

For singers accompanied on the *kithara*

    For the first a crown of gold olive leaves of 1,000 **drachmas**
    and 500 drachmas of silver

For the second	[1,]200 drachmas
For the third	600 drachmas
For the fourth	400 drachmas
For the fifth	300 drachmas

For singers accompanied by the *aulos* (men)

For the first a crown of 300 drachmas	
For the second	100 drachmas

For *kithara* players (men)

    For the first 500 drachmas
    and a crown of 300 drachmas
    For the second [...]
    For the third 100 drachmas

[*text fragmentary or missing*]

For the winner of the *stadion* (boys)
    50 amphorae of olive oil
    10 for the second

For the winner of the pentathlon (boys)
    30 amphorae of olive oil
    6 for the second

For the winner of the wrestling (boys)
    30 amphorae of olive oil
    6 for the second

---

kithara   a string instrument resembling a lyre.

drachmas   the drachma was both a unit of measurement of weight (4.36 g) and a silver coin.

aulos   see glossary.

For the winner of the boxing (boys)
> 30 amphorae of olive oil
> 6 for the second

For the winner of the *pankration* (boys)
> 40 amphorae of olive oil
> 8 for the second

For the winner of the *stadion* (beardless)
> 60 amphorae of olive oil
> 12 for the second

For the winner of the pentathlon (beardless)
> 40 amphorae of olive oil
> 8 for the second

For the winner of the wrestling (beardless)
> 40 amphorae of olive oil
> [8] for the second

For the winner of the boxing (beardless)
> [40 amphorae of olive] oil
> [8 for the second]

[*text fragmentary or missing*]

Column 2

For the winner of the chariot race with two foals
> 40 amphorae of olive oil
> 8 for the second

For the winner of the chariot race with two full-grown horses
> 140 amphorae of olive oil
> 40 for the second

For warriors:

For the winner of the horse race (*keles*)
> 16 amphorae of olive oil
> 4 for the second

For the winner of the chariot race with two horses
> 30 amphorae of olive oil
> 6 for the second

For the winner of the parade chariot race
> 4 amphorae of olive oil
> 1 for the second

For throwing the javelin from horseback
> 5 amphorae of olive oil
> 1 for the second

Victory prizes:

100 drachmas for the boy pyrrhic dancers and an ox

100 drachmas for the beardless pyrrhic dancers and an ox

100 drachmas for the men pyrrhic dancers and an ox

100 drachmas for the tribe winning the *euandria* contest and an ox

100 drachmas for the tribe winning the torch race and an ox

30 drachmas for the individual winning the torch-race contest and a water jar (hydria)

Prizes for the boat race:

300 drachmas for the winning tribe [and 3 oxen]

200 also for dining at state expense

200 drachmas for the second [and 2 oxen]

---

1 Estimate the number of amphorae that would be awarded for all the men's events if they were awarded twice as many as the boys. Add that to the total number required for boys and beardless youths. Assuming each amphora held 39 litres of oil and was full, how much olive oil did the *athlothetai* give to the athletes during the festival?

2 What was the standard ratio between first and second prizes?

3 What events which you might expect to see at Olympia are not recorded here?

4 Which events were more highly prized and why?

5 Compare the events for boys at Olympia in **2.4**. Which two events on this inscription were not held at Olympia at this date (*c.* 350 BC)?

Lysias (21.1) makes a defendant on a charge of accepting bribes demonstrate his good character by listing the amount he has spent on public benefactions. These three items concern the Panathenaia.

9.3 **In the archonship of Glaukippos** [I spent] 800 drachmas on pyrrhic dancers at the Great Panathenaia …

and **in the time of Diokles** [I spent] 300 drachmas on a **dithyrambic chorus** at the Little Panathenaia …

and [404–3 BC] at the Little Panathenaia I was *chorēgos* for beardless pyrrhic dancers and spent 7 **minai.**

In the archonship of Glaukippos   410–409 BC.

in the time of Diokles   409–408 BC.

dithyrambic chorus   the dithyramb was a choral song to Dionysus, god of drama.

chorēgos   the producer, responsible for all the expenses.

minai   1 mina = 100 drachmas.

In the following extract, Xenophon's description of the *anthippasia* in *The Cavalry Commander* (dating probably from the 360s BC) explains how he would recommend it to be performed (3.10–12).

9.4 When there is a display in the **hippodrome**, first it is good to order a formation to cover the width of the hippodrome with horses in line and drive out the men from the middle.

When the tribes in the *anthippasia* flee and pursue each other rapidly, with the cavalry commanders leading the **five tribes**, it is good to make both the tribal groups ride through each other. What a sight this makes: riding straight towards each other is formidable; when they have ridden the length of the hippodrome and stand facing each other again it is magnificent; and when the trumpet sounds and they charge a second time at greater speed it is a sight of beauty. Once they are in position, when the trumpet sounds again they should charge each other a third time at full speed. When they have crossed, they should all take their position in the line for the dismissal and ride up to the *boule*, as you usually do. I think these would appear more warlike and innovative.

This fragment of a marble relief (**9.5**) commemorates the victory of the tribe Leontis in the *anthippasia*. An older, bearded male rides behind two beardless young men. Is he a cavalry commander at the end of the line? Inscribed on the reverse are the words: 'Leontis was victorious'.

9.5

Fragment of a marble relief from Athens commemorating victory in the anthippasia *by the tribe Leontis; c. 400 BC.*

hippodrome   probably situated between Athens and the coast at Phaleron.

five tribes   under the democracy the Athenians were divided into ten tribes, here divided into two groups of five.

boule   see **9.1**.

In discussing physical training for the ideal state, the 'Athenian stranger' who plays the lead role in the dialogue in Plato's *Laws* gives a description of the war dance or pyrrhic dance (***pyrrichē***) (815a–b).

9.6 The war dance is different from the dance of peace and one might correctly call it pyrrhic since it both represents avoiding all blows or shots by head movements, every form of yielding, leaping high or crouching, and it represents the opposite of these, which are brought into aggressive dance forms and try to express their imitation in firing arrows, hurling javelins and delivering all sorts of blows. Among these dances, when there is a representation of good physique and spirit, the upright and vigorous form, with the limbs of the body for the most part straight, this type is accepted as right, but not the opposite.

- This passage has been described as 'nonsense' because of confusion between actual actions and their representation in dance. Does it give us any idea of the nature of pyrrhic dance?

This drawing (**9.7**) shows the Atarbos relief, found in Athens. It depicts a clothed female on the left, and two groups of four naked men in synchronized movement with shields on their left arms. This is usually thought to depict pyrrhic dancers, but the possibility that it might represent tribal competitors in the *euandria* (manly excellence) competition has been suggested.

9.7

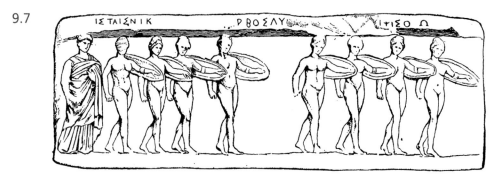

Drawing of the Atarbos relief, found near the Acropolis in Athens; fourth century BC.

1 If this relief does depict the pyrrhic dance (*pyrriche*), is it in accord with what Plato says in **9.6**?

2 What are the main differences between the Panathenaia and the Olympic Games?

10 Ancient Greece and the modern Olympics

This concluding chapter looks at some of the ways in which the modern Olympic Movement has creatively adopted and adapted ancient Greek practices and ideas.

The Olympic truce and the Olympic ideal

The *ekecheiria* or sacred truce was not confined to Olympia, but seems to have been an essential feature of festivals when visitors were expected from other states. The Greeks were often in conflict with each other and the truce, which granted free passage for those travelling to the festival, was an important safeguard. When faced with an external threat, the Greeks turned towards what united them, and since they lacked political unity, the Olympics along with the other Panhellenic games were among their most powerful symbols of national identity. They were also the best opportunity for talking to an audience from a wide range of Greek states. In the passages from Lysias and Isocrates below (**10.3** and **10.4**), both authors lay emphasis on the friendship between Greeks. These ideals have had a notable impact on the modern Olympic Movement from the beginning in the ideals promoted by Baron de Coubertin and more recently in the declaration of a modern truce by the United Nations (**10.6**). Occasional breaches of the truce are recorded in ancient times (see **10.2**), but such events seem to have been rare, although it is always unreliable to judge from silence.

The Olympic truce: *ekecheiria*

Pausanias mentions the Olympic truce both in his historical sketch of Elis and in his description of the temple of Hera in the Altis (*Description of Greece* 5.4.5 and 5.20.1–2).

10.1 Later on, **Iphitos**, a descendant of **Oxylos** and contemporary of Lykourgos who wrote the laws for the Spartans, organized the games at Olympia and re-established the festival with a fresh start and the truce which had ceased for whatever length of time. (5.4.5)

Iphitos Pausanias associates this king of Elis with the shadowy Spartan law-giver Lykourgos and the beginning of the Olympic Games in 776 BC (see p. 27).

Oxylos he acted as guide for the Heraklids and helped them conquer the Peloponnese. In return he asked to be made king of Elis.

There are other offerings here too, a couch of no great size but with decoration mostly in ivory, the discus of Iphitos and a table on which the crowns for victors are laid out. They say that it [the couch] is a toy of Hippodameia's. The discus of Iphitos has the truce which the Eleans proclaim at the time of the Olympics, though it is not written in a straight line but the letters go round the discus in a circle. The table is made of gold and ivory and is the work of **Kolotas**. (5.20.1–2)

> Philip II of Macedonia, whose expansionist policies put him in conflict with Athens, was using all diplomatic means to suggest to the Athenians that he was actually a friend. Demosthenes relates the following story from 348 BC, when Phrynon was going to the Olympic Games (*Second Hypothesis to 'On the Embassy'* 335).

10.2   An Athenian named Phrynon was on his way to Olympia, either to compete in the games or to be a spectator, when he was forcibly seized by some of Philip's soldiers in the sacred month and was robbed of all his possessions. On his return to Athens, he urged the Athenians to appoint him as an envoy so that he could go to Philip and recover what had been stolen from him. The Athenians were persuaded and appointed him and Ktesiphon. When they reached Macedonia, Philip gave them such a friendly welcome that he restored everything stolen by the soldiers and added some other gifts from his own belongings, while claiming in his defence that the soldiers had not been aware that it was the sacred month.

- Does this story tell us more about the diplomatic skills of Philip or the regard with which the sacred truce was held?

Olympic idealism

> In 388 BC the Athenian orator Lysias delivered a panegyric ('festival speech') at Olympia attacking Dionysius of Syracuse. The speech is lost apart from the opening section, which was quoted by Dionysius of Halicarnassus (Lysias, *Olympiakos* 1–3).

10.3   Gentlemen, Herakles deserves to be remembered for many fine deeds and in particular because he was the first to assemble competitors for the games on account of his good will towards Greece. Before this time city-states were unfavourably disposed towards each other. But when he brought an end to tyranny and stopped abuses of power, he created physically competitive games, an ambitious display of wealth and an exhibition of reasoning in the loveliest place in Greece so that we could gather with a unity of purpose for all these things, to

---

Kolotas   a pupil of Pheidias.

see some and listen to others. For he thought that the meeting here would be the genesis of mutual friendship among the Greeks. He it was who established these principles, but I haven't come for small talk or to dispute over words …

[*Lysias launches into his appeal for unity among the Greeks to combat the threat from Persia and Dionysius of Syracuse.*]

In the following political tract, which is in the form of a panegyric or festival speech to be delivered at Olympia, Isocrates is calling for unity among the Greeks against the threat posed by the Persian empire (*Panegyricus* 43–4). The date is 380 BC.

10.4   The founders of our festivals are rightly praised because they handed down to us the custom of making a truce with each other, laying aside current hostilities and gathering in one place. Then, by offering prayers and sacrifices together we are reminded of the ties of kinship that exist among us and we become more well-disposed towards each other for the future. We renew long-standing friendships and make new friends. It is no waste of time, either for the ordinary people or for those with particular abilities, but the gathering of the Greeks gives the latter an opportunity to display their talents and the former to watch them competing with each other. Neither group lacks enthusiasm, but each has something on which to pride themselves, one when they see the athletes making an effort for them, the other when they bear it in mind that everyone has come to watch them.

> 1   Does this extract succeed in helping to give Isocrates' audience a sense of unity?
> 2   What does this passage suggest about the truce? Can you tell whether it offered safe passage to Olympia, or a more general cessation of hostilities?

Pierre de Coubertin was the leading figure in the establishment and early history of the modern Olympic Movement. In these extracts from his voluminous writings, he discusses some of the ideals which are associated with the truce. (*Olympia*, 6 March 1929 and *The Philosophic Foundation of Modern Olympism*, 4 August 1935.)

10.5   In the eleventh century AD, one could still see at Olympia a disk into which was carved the text of the agreement reached between Lycurgus and Iphitos, king of Elis, to establish the 'sacred truce' during the games. At that time all armed conflicts and all combat among Hellenes had to cease. The territory of Olympia, declared neutral, was inviolable. (*Olympia*, 1929)

A truce must be called regarding exclusively nationalistic feelings, which must be put 'on temporary leave' so to speak.

The idea of the *truce* is another element of Olympism. It is closely related to the notion of rhythm. The Olympic Games must be held on a strictly astronomical rhythm, because they are the quadrennial celebration of human springtime, honouring the successive arrival of human generations. …

The human springtime is expressed by the *young adult male* … That is the person in whose honour the Olympic Games must be celebrated.

Personally I do not approve of women's participation in public competitions … At the Olympic Games, their role should be above all to crown the victors, as was the case in the ancient tournaments. (*Modern Olympism*, 1935)

> 1 What elements of Pierre de Coubertin's thinking seem most inappropriate now?
>
> 2 How accurate is his understanding of the ancient truce?

Eventually a modern Olympic truce requested by the International Olympic Committee (IOC) received the blessing of the United Nations.

10.6

The modern Olympic truce

Chronology

1992: The IOC launched an Appeal for the observance of the Olympic Truce and negotiated with the United Nations to facilitate athletes of the former Republic of Yugoslavia to participate in the Games of the XXIII Olympiad in Barcelona.

1993: The first resolution on the observance of the Olympic Truce was adopted by the 48th session of the UN General Assembly.

United Nations support

Since 1993, the UN General Assembly has repeatedly expressed its support for the IOC by unanimously adopting, every two years, one year before each edition of the Olympic Games, a resolution entitled 'Building a peaceful and better world through sport and the Olympic ideal'.

Through this symbolic resolution, the UN invites its member States to observe the Olympic Truce individually or collectively, and to seek, in conformity with the goals and principles of the United Nations Charter, the peaceful settling of all international conflicts through peaceful and diplomatic means, and recognizing the importance of the IOC initiatives for human well-being and international understanding.

From the official website of the Olympic Movement, www.olympic.org.

- Are there any similarities between the ancient and modern versions of the Olympic Truce?
- Are there shared ideals which lie behind both the ancient and modern truce?
- Does the involvement of the United Nations help to emphasize the differences between the modern truce and its ancient counterpart?
- Do the extracts from the speeches of Lysias and Isocrates (**10.3** and **10.4**) share the same ideals as the IOC?

The marathon

The marathon race is a modern invention, created for the 1896 Olympic revival in Athens and the only event in those games won by a Greek – Spyros or Spyridon Louis. Its length of 26 miles 385 yards (42.263 km) was adopted by the International Association of Athletics Federations in 1921, but originated with the 1908 marathon from Windsor Castle to the royal box at White City stadium in London.

There are a number of ancient sources which record long-distance runners, the most famous of whom was Philippides (or Pheidippides). His feat is recorded in Herodotus' *Histories* written some 50 years later (**10.7**), but was embellished by later versions and in particular by Lucian (second century AD) who makes Philippides run from Marathon to Athens with news of the victory and die on the spot. This dramatic story was well known in the late nineteenth century from Robert Browning's poem 'Pheidippides' published in 1879.

> In 490 BC, when the Athenians learnt that the Persians had landed their army on the plain of Marathon about 25 miles from Athens, they sent a runner to Sparta (about 150 miles) to ask for immediate assistance. The Spartathlon, a modern race held annually since 1983, follows his route. His run is described by Herodotus (*Histories* 6.105–6). See **10.15** for the Athenian response to Pan.

10.7   First [before marching out to face the Persians], while they were still in the city, the generals sent a messenger called Philippides to Sparta. This man was an Athenian and also a practised long-distance runner who, as he himself claimed in his report to the Athenians, had an encounter with Pan close to Mount Parthenion above **Tegea**. His story was that Pan shouted his name Philippides and told him to ask the Athenians why they paid him no regard although, as he was well disposed towards them, he had often been useful to them in the past and would be on other occasions in the future. … On the occasion he claimed that Pan had appeared to him, this Philippides whom the generals sent was in Sparta on the second day after leaving Athens.

Tegea   a city in Arcadia, just under 30 miles north of Sparta.

After the battle of Plataea (479 BC), the Delphic oracle told the Greeks not to sacrifice until they had cleansed the pollution caused by the Persians and rekindled their altars with pure fire from the public hearth at Delphi. Plutarch tells the story of Euchidas' run from Plataea to Delphi in *Aristides* 20.5.

10.8   Euchidas promised that he would bring the fire from the god with all possible speed and from Plataea he went to Delphi. After purifying his body with a sprinkling of lustral water, he put on a crown of laurel. He took fire from the altar and ran back to Plataea where he arrived before sunset after covering **1,000 stades** in a single day. When he had greeted his fellow citizens and had handed over the fire, he instantly collapsed and soon afterwards he breathed his last. In their admiration for him the Plataeans buried him in the sanctuary of Artemis Eucleia and inscribed this verse on his tomb: 'Euchidas ran to Pytho and returned here the same day'.

Plutarch (*Moralia* 374c) says that it was probably Eucles who took the news of the battle of Marathon to Athens.

10.9   Well, as **Heraclides Ponticus** relates, it was Thersippus of Eoeadai who brought the news of the battle at Marathon. But most historians say that it was Eucles who ran in his armour hot from the battle, burst in through the doors of the leading citizens and said just this, 'Rejoice, we have won.' And with that he expired on the spot.

Lucian's dialogue begins with a discussion of the right word to use for greeting, in the course of which he tells the story of Philippides' supposed run from Marathon (*A Slip of the Tongue in Greeting* 3).

10.10   Philippides, who was a long-distance runner, is said to have been the first to use it like this: when bringing news from Marathon of the victory, he said to the magistrates who were in session and concerned about the outcome of the battle, 'Rejoice, we have won,' and on saying this he died with his message and breathed his last with 'Rejoice.'

> 1 What does this sequence of sources tell us about the reliability of ancient writers?
> 2 What does the invention of the marathon race tell us about the relationship between the modern Olympics and ancient Greek athletics?

1,000 stades   approximately 125 miles, a slight exaggeration.

Heraclides Ponticus   fourth-century BC philosopher.

The Olympic flame

It was the custom of the Greeks to keep a fire alight in the hearth of the city, and at Olympia too a hearth was maintained, as Pausanias reports (**10.11**). However, it was not specifically linked to the festival.

The genesis of the modern 'sacred flame' can be traced from 1912 when Pierre de Coubertin, speaking in Stockholm, used the flame metaphor as a symbol of continuity: 'And now, gentlemen, see how a **great people** has, by **our arrangement**, received from your hands the Olympic flame and has undertaken to protect it and, if possible, enhance the radiance of the precious flame.'

The first occasion on which an Olympic flame was kept burning was during the Amsterdam Olympics of 1928. It was lit on top of the Marathon Tower, which was 40 metres high with a huge cauldron 3.5 metres in diameter on top. The original concept was to have a searchlight rising from the cauldron and vertical lights on each side of the tower, making a pillar of light rising into the sky. However, for some reason the architect Jan Wils submitted revised plans showing a flame in the cauldron, and this was adopted.

> In this extract from his *Description of Greece* Pausanias describes how a flame was kept burning at Olympia (5.15.9).

10.11   In the **Prytaneion** itself, as you go into the room where they have their hearth, there is an altar of Pan on the right of the entrance. The hearth, **also** made of ash, is there and on it a flame burns all day and all night too. From this hearth they take the ash, as I have already described, to the altar of Zeus.

The Olympic torch

The now familiar ritual of the Olympic torch owes a small debt to ancient Greece, where torch races were held in a variety of religious contexts. According to the official history of the Olympics and the IOC, the idea was the suggestion of Theodore Lewald, one of the three German IOC members in 1928, although most attribute the idea to Carl Diem, head of the Berlin Games organizing committee. It was proposed that the torch be lit by the rays of the sun in Olympia and carried by runners to the host city. This ritual was first performed in the 1936 games held in Berlin. While the torch race offers a symbolic link between ancient and modern Olympics which we still value, its first use was rather more sinister, since

---

great people   he is referring to Sweden.

our arrangement   that of the International Olympic Committee (IOC).

Prytaneion   the administrative building for the games. See p. 39.

also   as well as the altar of Zeus (see p. 37).

it afforded the Nazis a symbolic link with their supposed Aryan ancestors in Greece, a piece of propaganda brilliantly conveyed in the opening sequence of Leni Riefenstahl's film *Olympia*.

This fourth-century BC inscription from Athens records not only the winner of the race, but also the gymnasiarch (IG II² 3019). At Athens the ten tribes each appointed a gymnasiarch to supervise the teams for the torch race.

10.12   Akamas was victorious in the torch race at the Great Panathenaia in the **archonship of Archias**. Xenocles was the official sponsor (gymnasiarch).

In Aristophanes' *Frogs*, when Dionysus is judging a literary contest between Euripides and Aeschylus down in Hades, Aeschylus is complaining about the decline in standards since his day (lines 1087–98).

10.13   AESCHYLUS   There's no one left who can carry a torch these days because they are out of training.

DIONYSUS   No, by Zeus, not so! I was creased up with laughter at the Panathenaia when there was someone running slowly, bent over, pale, fat, left behind and really struggling. Then, at the gates, the people of the Kerameikos start hitting him in the belly, the ribs, the sides and the backside. Getting smacked with their open hands, he let rip a fart and began to run off, blowing on his torch.

> • Why do you think the runner was blowing on his torch?

Here Herodotus is describing the Persian relay system for sending messages. A fresh horse and rider take over for each leg of the journey (*Histories* 8.98.2).

10.14   The first on completing his leg hands over the orders to the second, the second to the third and from there they go to their destination, handed over from one to another like the torch race among Greeks which they hold in honour of Hephaistos.

When the runner Philippides encountered Pan near Mount Parthenion, overlooking Tegea, the god asked why the Athenians ignored him, despite his favour. Herodotus gives the Athenian response (*Histories* 6.105.3).

---

archonship of Archias   346/45 BC.

10.15 Once they had put their **affairs in order**, in the belief that it was true they established a shrine for Pan on the slopes of the Acropolis and as a consequence of this report they seek his favour with yearly sacrifices and a torch race.

> In the following passage Pausanias refers to a torch race while describing the Academy outside Athens (*Description of Greece* 1.30.2).

10.16 In the Academy is an altar of Prometheus and they run from this to the city with lighted torches. The essence of the contest is to keep the torch burning at the same time as running. If his torch goes out, the first is no longer awarded the victory, but it goes to the second instead. And if his torch is not alight either, the third is the winner. If everyone's torch has gone out, there is no one left to be awarded the victory.

1 What types of torch races in ancient Greece do we have evidence for?
2 Do they bear any resemblance to the modern torch relay?
3 What conclusions can you draw from this chapter about the way that the modern Olympics have used the ancient Olympics?
4 Does 'authenticity' matter?

---

affairs in order   probably some time later than 480 BC, after the Persians had occupied and sacked Athens.

Further reading

There is a huge quantity of scholarly literature on ancient athletics and the Olympic Games – far more than can be mentioned here. The following recommendations are selected for their availability, their accessibility and their varied approaches to the subject. Most will provide further bibliographical help for those who wish to pursue the subject in greater detail.

On the complex and obscure mythology surrounding Elis, Pisa and the founding of the Olympic Games, *The Routledge Handbook of Greek Mythology* by **Robin Hard** (Routledge, 2004) offers a very full and clear account.

Source books

Arete, **Stephen G. Miller** (University of California Press, 3rd edn. 2004) is a comprehensive collection of literary and epigraphic sources dealing with Greek sports (essentially athletics, with a chapter on ball games) from early times into the Roman period. Translations of sources are accompanied by brief introductions and dates.

Sport and Recreation in Ancient Greece, **Waldo Sweet** (Oxford University Press, 1987) has a wider range, since he includes hunting, swimming, dance, dining and much else. In addition to the translations of literary and epigraphic sources, visual evidence is supplied in black-and-white illustrations and there are more lengthy discussions of the sources with questions, and at the end of each chapter suggestions for further reading.

Reference

Sport in the Ancient World from A to Z, **Mark Golden** (Routledge, 2004) is an extremely useful dictionary of sport with informative entries, each accompanied by a list of sources.

General books

Athletics in the Ancient World, **Zahra Newby** (Bristol Classical Press, 2006) is a rapid survey in two parts covering festival culture and the world of the gymnasium. Although compact and covering athletics throughout the Greco-Roman period, it is written with both attention to detail and clarity, making it a good starting point. It also has excellent recommendations for further reading.

Ancient Greek Athletics, **Stephen G. Miller** (Yale University Press, 2004). If there is one book on Greek athletics which might be described as essential reading, this is it. Comprehensive and detailed, it acts as a supplement to *Arete* (see above) and includes a rich collection of visual evidence as well as detailed discussion.

The Ancient Olympic Games, **Judith Swaddling** (British Museum Press, new edn. 2011). Originally published in 1980, it has been expanded to cover the modern Olympics. The illustrations mostly utilize the British Museum's collection and the author's description of the site at Olympia is enhanced by excellent photographs of the Museum's model.

The Ancient Olympics, **Nigel Spivey** (Oxford University Press, 2004) is a lively guide to ancient athletics, good on the broader issues of cultural history and exploring the notions of strife, contest and love of victory before turning to violence and sport as training for warfare.

Olympia: Cult, Sport and Ancient Festival, **Ulrich Sinn** (Markus Wiener, 2000) is a lively and interesting general account of the games and the site by one of the German excavators at Olympia. It brings new perspectives for the English reader and although the translation is not always entirely clear, it is highly recommended.

The Olympic Games: The First Thousand Years, **M. I. Finley** and **H. W. Pleket** (Chatto and Windus, 1976) is a historical account with an opening chapter on ancient and modern Olympics and some sharp sociological observations, for example about professionalism in ancient sport.

A Brief History of the Olympic Games, **David D. Young** (Blackwell, 2004) is an enthusiastic and lively guide to all the basic aspects of the festival and its programme; its focus is primarily on antiquity, but ancient and modern are compared throughout.

Sport and Spectacle in the Ancient World, **Donald Kyle** (Blackwell, 2007) is an accessible overview of sports in the Greco-Roman world, full of detailed insights.

Sport and Society in Ancient Greece, **Mark Golden** (Cambridge University Press, 1998) is an influential work with a particular focus on what he calls 'a discourse of difference' or sport in the service of social distinctions.

Greek Sport and Social Status, **Mark Golden** (University of Texas Press, 2008), 'to some extent a continuation' of the previous book, consists of four papers on topics such as slavery, gladiators and modern myths.

Particularly well-illustrated accounts

The Olympic Games in Ancient Greece, edited by **Maria Koursi** (Ekdotike Athenon S.A., 2003) is the work of a number of Greek scholars, with superb colour illustrations complementing the text.

Games and Sanctuaries in Ancient Greece, **Panos Valavanis**, translated by David Hardy (Getty Publications, 2004) is a fabulously illustrated introduction to the four 'crown' games and the Panathenaia by a leading Greek scholar. After the five sites are given detailed treatment, there is a chapter on local games and the various prizes they offered for victors, and a discussion of the events themselves.

Collections of conference papers and articles

The Archaeology of the Olympics, ed. **Wendy J. Raschke** (University of Wisconsin Press, 1987) contains a number of influential articles.

Onward to the Olympics: Historical Perspectives on the Olympic Games, ed. **Gerald P. Schaus** and **Stephen R. Wenn** (Wilfrid Laurier University Press, 2007) is a collection of essays arising from a conference devoted to the ancient and modern games, including a paper by Hugh Lee which makes fresh use of evidence from vase-painting and Quintilian to conclude that athletes used a short run-up for the long jump.

Sport and Festival in the Ancient Greek World, ed. **David Phillips** and **David Pritchard** (The Classical Press of Wales, 2003) is a collection arising from a conference at Sydney in 2000 with a number of excellent papers including a discussion of a virtual reconstruction of Olympia and a very helpful introduction to the German excavations at Olympia by Helmut Kyrieleis.

Exhibition catalogues

Mind and Body: Athletic Contests in Ancient Greece at the National Archaeological Museum, Athens (Ministry of Culture, Athens, 1989–90) covers the Bronze Age, the Panathenaia and especially the four 'crown' games. This well-illustrated catalogue of 235 objects is invaluable for the descriptions and discussions of each exhibit.

Games for the Gods: the Greek Athlete and the Olympic Spirit at the Museum of Fine Arts, Boston, ed. John J. Herrmann and Christine Kondoleon (2004) is a superb collection of 162 objects, many illustrated in colour, presented in conjunction with modern images of athletes, introductory essays and a descriptive catalogue.

Specialized or more advanced studies

The Olympic Myth of Greek Amateur Athletics, **David Young** (Ares, 1985) is a fine piece of polemical scholarship which effectively demolished the idea of amateurism in Greek athletics.

Eros and Greek Athletics, **Thomas F. Scanlon** (Oxford University Press, 2002) is a detailed study of 'athletic eros' (that which 'promotes bonds' between individuals, groups and political units). Lengthy and detailed chapters deal with a range of major issues such as the growth of pederasty and its relationship to initiation.

Pindar and Bacchylides

Bacchylides: The Victory Poems, translated with an introduction and commentary by **Arthur McDevitt** (Bristol Classical Press, 2009) has very readable and reliable translations with an extensive commentary.

Pindar: Odes for Victorious Athletes, translated with an introduction by **Anne Pippin Burnett** (The Johns Hopkins University Press, 2010) has clear translations with brief introductions to each ode.

Pindar, **Anne Pippin Burnett** (Bristol Classical Press, 2008) is a good brief introduction to Pindar and his poetry.

Pindar: The Complete Odes, **Anthony Verity** (Oxford University Press, 2007) has sound, readable translations with brief but helpful notes.

The Panathenaia

The Games at Athens, **Jennifer Neils** and **Stephen V. Tracy** (American School of Classical Studies at Athens, 2003) belongs to their Agora picturebook series. It is an attractive, very brief summary of the main aspects of the greater Panathenaia with excellent illustrations throughout, and a focus on the games.

The modern Olympics

Olympics in Athens 1896: The Invention of the Modern Olympic Games, **Michael Llewellyn Smith** (Profile Books, 2004) sets out the context for the 1896 Olympics by looking at revivals before Coubertin and giving a detailed account of the preparations for the games in Athens, besides describing the actual competition.

The Official History of the Olympic Games and the IOC: Athens to Beijing, 1894–2008, **David Miller** (Mainstream Publishing, 2008) is a history of the Olympics with many details about the athletes, the IOC and the historical context of the games, with chapters on individual Olympiads.

The Complete Book of the Olympics, **David Wallechinsky** and **Jaime Loucky** (Aurum Press, 2008 edition) is a comprehensive collection of results with introductions to each sport.

War and Peace in the Ancient and Modern Olympics, **Mark Golden** (Greece and Rome, Second Series, 58, 2011, pp. 1–13) examines links between the ancient and modern Olympics critically but offers positive thoughts on the Olympic ideal of peace.

Inscriptions

Inscriptions mentioned in the text are referenced by giving their citation in the multi-volume **IG** (*Inscriptiones Graecae*) or **POxy** (Oxyrhynchus Papyri).

Authors referred to in the text but not mentioned above

Walter Burkert, *Greek Religion* (Harvard University Press, 1987).

Ludwig Drees, *Olympia* (Pall Mall Press, 1967).

E. Norman Gardiner, *Athletics in the Ancient World* (Oxford University Press, 1930).

Norman Mailer, *The Fight* (Penguin, 1991).

Glossary

Words in italics are transliterations of Greek words; those without italics are in common use in English. A mark over a vowel (e.g. *ō*) indicates that the Greek vowel is long and should be extended.

agōn   assembly, assembly at games; contest, competition; struggle

agōnothetēs   (plural *agōnothetai*) organizer, judge

agora   place of assembly, market place, a city's central square

akōn   (or *akontion*) javelin

akoniti   term used to indicate a bye, when an athlete did not have an opponent to face in the heavy events; literally, 'without dust'

Altis   the sacred area of the sanctuary at Olympia; a local variant of *alsos* (a sacred grove or precinct)

amphora   large, two-handled jar for transport and storage of liquids such as olive oil; Panathenaic amphorae full of olive oil were given as prizes at the Panathenaia

amphōtides   ear protectors sometimes worn by boxers

ankylē   thong used to spin the javelin as it was thrown

anthippasia   equestrian event at the Panathenaia in which the riders seem to have engaged in flight and pursuit and possibly charged through opposing ranks at ever-increasing speeds

apēnē   mule-cart; race for mule-carts, introduced into the programme at Olympia in 500 BC and discontinued from 444

apobatēs   (plural *apobatai*) 'one who dismounts'; at Athens, a competitor in a race for chariots with a charioteer and a rider who leapt from the chariot and ran alongside, perhaps for the last stretch of the course

archōn   magistrates in Athens; the eponymous archon gave his name to the year in which he served

aryballos   small flask which athletes used to carry olive oil

athlētēs   competitor for prizes, athlete

athlon   prize

athlos   competition for prizes

athlothetēs   (plural *athlothetai*) 'one who sets out the prizes' or an organizer of the games

Attic   Athenian; Attica is the name of the territory of the Athenian *polis* or state

aulos   wind instrument consisting of two cylindrical tubes with finger-holes; the mouthpiece held a reed, probably like that of the modern oboe

balbis stone sill at each end of the stadium which acted as the starting and finishing line for races and the line from which the discus and javelin were thrown, and perhaps the point for take-off in the jump

batēr 'thing on which one treads': the front edge of the pentathletes' dug-up area; the place from which the athletes jumped in the long jump

boulē council

Boulē Olympic Council

Bouleuterion the council chamber at Olympia

'crown' games also called 'stephanitic games', from the Greek *stephanos* (crown, wreath). The four 'crown' games formed a 'circuit' (*periodos*) made up of the Olympic, Pythian, Isthmian and Nemean Games; victors in these games were awarded crowns: of olive at Olympia, of laurel at Delphi, of pine (later dry wild celery) at Isthmia and wild celery at Nemea

diaulos double *stadion*

diskobolos discus-thrower

dolichos distance running event

ekecheiria truce, especially the truce covering the month before the games

epinīkion (plural ***epinīkia***) victory ode

euandria manly excellence (it is not certain what this means precisely)

exōmis short tunic leaving one shoulder free

gloios scrapings of oil, sweat and dirt from the athletes' bodies when using the *stlengis*

gymnasium (Greek *gymnasion*) place for naked exercise; place for practising athletics, especially running, javelin and discus

gymnikos agōn athletic competition

halma long jump

haltēres jumping weights

heavy events term used to refer to wrestling, pankration and boxing

Hellānodikai (singular ***Hellānodikās*** or ***Hellānodikēs***) officials who organized the games and acted as judges at Olympia (also at Nemea and Epidaurus)

himantes (singular ***himas***) boxing 'gloves' used in competitions, at first strips of soft leather wound around the wrist and hand, but from the fourth century BC with a stiff piece of leather across the knuckles; both types had the nickname 'ants' because of their painful bite

hippikos agōn equestrian competition

hippodrome horse and chariot-racing track

hoplite, *hoplitēs* heavy-armed infantryman; race in armour

hoplitodromos race for men in armour

hysplēx   (plural *hysplēges*) starting mechanism for the foot races and equestrian events

kalpē   race for mares, introduced into the programme at Olympia in 496 BC and discontinued from 444

kamptēr   (plural *kamptēres*) turning post for the foot races

kelēs   in Greek, a horse for riding. Modern scholars often use it to mean the race for horses

kithara   string instrument, usually translated as lyre

kōmos   revel; procession accompanying victorious athlete, song of praise at such a procession, hence the English 'encomium' (formal/elaborate praise)

kylix   drinking cup with a shallow bowl, wide rim and horizontal handles; most varieties are supported on a stem rising from a foot

kynodesmē   a string for tying back the foreskin, literally 'dog-leash' (*kuōn*, Greek for 'dog', was also slang for 'penis')

mastigophoros   literally 'whip-bearer', one of the officials often seen on vase-paintings supervising games and ready to punish anyone breaking the rules

metics   resident foreigners in Athens

metope   a plain or sculpted slab inserted between triglyphs in the frieze of the Doric order

Olympiad   this word has two distinct meanings: (1) a celebration of the festival; to calculate the date of a festival, subtract 1 (for the first), multiply by 4 and subtract from 776; thus the 26th Olympiad was held in 676 BC; (2) the four-year period between celebrations of the festival. This became useful for dating events because individual city-states used local systems (e.g. a year was named after a particular official or priest). Since the Olympic Games were held at a Panhellenic festival, this offered a uniform system which could be understood by all Greeks; thus the second-century BC historian Polybius begins at the 140th Olympiad (220–217 BC) and for 218 he uses 'the third year of the 140th Olympiad'

paidotribēs   physical education instructor (literally, 'boy polisher')

palaistra   (Latin *palaestra*) wrestling ground; place for athletic training

palē   wrestling

Panhellenic   of or for all those of Greek nationality

pankration   combat sport which combined wrestling and boxing

pannychis   all-night celebration

Pelopion   shrine for the hero Pelops at Olympia

peplos   woollen dress pinned at the shoulders

periodonīkēs   a winner at all four 'crown' games

peristyle   colonnaded courtyard

prytaneion   an important civic building, sometimes called a town hall, in which the city's hearth was located and athletes might enjoy free meals at state expense

Prytaneion   the administrative building at Olympia where celebratory banquets were held for athletes; one room housed the hearth for the sacred flame

pyrrichē   war dance performed at the Panathenaia

skamma   the area of loosened earth equivalent to the modern sand-pit, used for wrestling and long jump

stadion   Greek word for the stadium, the race track or the length of the race track; in this book the following are used: **stadium** – the venue, as in modern usage; *stadion* (plural *stadia*) – the race or the distance of the race; **stade** – the distance (of approximately 200 metres; measurements varied slightly from place to place)

stlengis   (Latin *strigil*) implement used by athletes to scrape the oil, dirt and sweat from their bodies; it was usually made of bronze and bent in the middle to form two parts shaped like a boomerang, one side forming the handle and the other shaped to form a hollow blade

stoa   a covered colonnade or portico

symposion   symposium or dinner party/drinking party

synōris   two-horse chariot race

Tabula Heroniana   eleventh-century AD text on measurement

tethrippon   four-horse chariot race

thallophoroi   men carrying branches in the Panathenaic procession

theōroi   State envoys at festivals

trireme   warship with 180 rowers and a further complement of marines and crew

Zanes   local dialect word (singular *Zān* = Zeus) for bronze statues of Zeus erected just outside the entrance to the stadium at Olympia. They were paid for with the money imposed as fines on athletes